DRAMATIC OPINIONS AND ESSAYS

DRAMATIC OPINIONS AND ESSAYS WITH AN APOLOGY BY BERNARD SHAW

CONTAINING AS WELL

A WORD ON THE DRAMATIC OPINIONS AND ESSAYS OF BERNARD SHAW BY JAMES HUNEKER

VOLUME ONE

NEW YORK: BRENTANO'S
MCMIX

PRESSWORK BY THE UNIVERSITY PRESS, CAMBRIDGE, U. S. A.

CONTENTS

Volume I

Contents

Contents

A WORD ON THE
DRAMATIC OPINIONS AND ESSAYS
OF BERNARD SHAW

BY

JAMES HUNEKER

I

THIS book is composed of selections from the dramatic criticisms of Bernard Shaw, which appeared in the London *Saturday Review,* beginning January 5th, 1895, and ending May 21st, 1898—a notable period in the history of that journal, for it inaugurated the regime of Frank Harris, and the advent of such brilliant writers as Shaw, Harris, MacColl, Runciman, Cunninghame Graham, and other distinguished spirits. Bernard Shaw did not burst like a meteor upon the British metropolis; he was known and admired in certain circles before he took to the cart and trumpet. He was a bold man in the ranks of Socialists; he wrote novels and plays; he criticized music and pictures and, as he confesses, he lived through it all; indeed, he waxed strong therefrom. But he admits that the theatre nearly killed him. For over three years he sat in the seat of the critical mighty and filled his eyes and ears with bad, mad, and mediocre plays. His famous hob-nailed Alpine shoes worn for the purpose of tramping London picture galleries, failed him in the theatre. His soul grew soggy, his bones softened; and after an accident he threw over his self-imposed task with a gasp of relief and the stalls knew him no more. He now produces plays instead of rowing in the galleys with the critical

Introduction

II

By this time the world is aquainted with the Shaw opinions, the Shaw plays, novels, prefaces and the Shavian philosophy. If not, then it is no fault of the illustrious G. B. S. He has toiled for publicity. He acknowledges the fact. And there is no denying that such muscularity in behalf of one's personality must have proved mortifying to a man of Shaw's retiring nature; he remarks somewhere that he is "congenitally shy." Yet when popularity came he fought against it. He metaphorically twiddled the fingers of scorn in the face of a credulous and eager public. Like Richard Wagner Bernard Shaw insulted the English world only to capture, in the end, its suffrage, its sympathy, its admiration. Little wonder, then, there are moments when he doubts himself, his mission, even his originality. Success during one's lifetime is not always the reward of genius.

If you wish the entire solution of that puzzle which once kept London up late o'nights trying to solve it, read with care the judgment passed by Mr. Shaw's physician upon the eyes of his distinguished patient. This eminent authority on optics found the Shaw vision normal. Therefore like the world at large? Not at all—I quote from memory—replied, in effect, the medical man. Normal eyesight is possessed by about ten per cent. of humanity. The remainder, presumably, being abnormal. By a swift transposition of vision to intellectual judgment Mr. Shaw claimed the gift of seeing things differently and better— Ah! the canny Irishman.

Let us succumb to this assertion, for upon it depends the validity of my argument—and also explains Shaw to the universe at large and to Shaw in particular. The

Introduction

Shaw eye and brain being perfectly normal, it is safe, therefore, to assume that the Shaw verdicts upon life are equally so. Ibsen swears the minority is always right; but here is a minority with a vengeance; it is a more aristocratic a court of supremacy than M. Huysmans' "dozen superior persons scattered throughout the universe." However, let us agree to accept the Shavian self-valuation. The world is in the wrong as a consequence of this logic; wrong in its material living, wrong in its spiritual beliefs; wrong in its intellectual assents. From Shakespeare to the musical glasses we have been, all of us, on the wrong track about the drama; our religious faiths are modified ancestor worship; our social life a sham; our glories—civic and military, poetic and practical, artistic and mechanical, have been a huge mistake. But this wholesale accusation of error, this brief of Shaw *vs.* the Cosmos, has a suspiciously familiar ring. We have heard it before. Other men's voices from Koheleth to Jonathan Swift's, from Diogenes to Schopenhauer's, have been lifted up against life as lived on our unimportant planet. True, cries our beloved Bernard, I do not claim originality. The other fellows said it before I did; they, too, had normal vision—and you can't assure fools that they are fools too often!

Have we our clue to Shaw? Yes: for he is that rare bird, a perfectly honest man. He means what he says and he is never more in earnest than when he is most whimsical. He laughs at love and London shrieks at his exquisite humor. But he is not making fun. He finds in our art and literature that the sexual passion plays far too important a rôle. We are "oversexed," he cries, especially in the theatre. The slimy sentimentalities of the popular play are too much for his nerves. He is a

Introduction

Puritan in the last analysis and the degradation of dramatic art attendant upon sensuality moves him to strong utterances. "I have, I think, always been a Puritan in my attitude towards Art. I am as fond of fine music and handsome buildings as Milton was, or Cromwell, or Bunyan; but if I found that they were becoming the instruments of systematic idolatry of sensuousness, I would hold it good statesmanship to blow every cathedral in the world to pieces with dynamite, organ and all, without the least heed to the screams of the art critics and cultured voluptuaries." He would light the fuse himself, just as he would go to the stake for a principle. He is at once the slayer and the slain; Calvin and Servetus.

Brave are his very Tolstoian words. Nor does he claim priority in those attacks upon Shakespeare which he so happily terms, Bardolatry. You may notice after reading his critical animadversions upon this sacred topic that he is not so often attacking Shakespeare as the ultra-Shakespeareans; that he is by no means so sharp in his criticisms of the bard as were Ben Jonson, Dr. Johnson, Voltaire, and Taine,—(did not Mr. George Moore invoke destruction when he dared to harness the names of Balzac and Shakespeare?)—that his assaults are really a plea for a more sane critical attitude toward Shakespeare; and, finally, that the entire public discussion—which assumed alarming aspects during the spring of 1905 in London—has illuminated the fact that Bernard Shaw is by no means to be despised as a student of the divine William. Besides, a critic may look at a king, and this critic has let in much light on his own peculiar psychology by these very criticisms. And it may be added that Shakespeare's reputation has not suffered violence.

More inexplicable is Shaw's dislike of the Elizabethans.

Introduction

His lips curl with scorn when their names are mentioned.
He forgives Shakespeare many extravagances; Marlowe,
Ford, Massinger, Beaumont and Fletcher, Middleton,
Dekker, none. Their rhetoric is insane and hideous; they
are a crew of insufferable bunglers and dullards; the
Renaissance was an orgie; Marlowe might, if he had
lived to-day, have been a tolerable imitation of Kipling;
all these plays are full of murder, lust, obscenity, cruelty;
no ray of noble feeling, no touch of faith, beauty, nor even
common kindliness is to be discovered in them, says
critic Shaw. Shades of Charles Lamb! What will Swin-
burne say!

Touching again on Shakespeare it will not be amiss to
calmly face some of the Shavian blasphemies. An ounce
of sincerity is worth a ton of hypocrisy. The *optique* of
the theatre always magnifies, often falsifies. Great reputations should have their centennial critical bath—they
would look all the brighter after it. And there are whole
continents steeped in artistic—rather, in inartistic—hypocrisy. Witness the Parsifal craze; witness the eye-ball
ecstasy when the name of Bach is mentioned—whereas
most people loathe a Bach fugue as they loathe a Beethoven string quartette. But criticism makes cowards
of us all. Ready-made admiration is ever dangerous;
luckily Shaw, a Nietzschean before he ever heard of
Nietzsche, was not taken in by the verdicts of yesterday.
He carried his transvaluing scales in his pocket, and his
alpenstock could be, if necessary, transformed into a critical measuring yardstick. He loved Wagner's music and
knew it so well that he was the first English critic who
called attention to the fact that the composer, instead of
being rhapsodic and formless, was, perhaps, a victim to
the widespread Teutonic passion for Chinese formalism
and systematism.

Introduction

He finds Shakespeare's work full of moral platitudes, jingo claptrap, tavern pleasantries, bombast and drivel; while the bard's incapacity for following up the scraps of philosophy he stole so aptly, is noteworthy; his poetic speech, feeling for nature and the knack of character drawing, fun and heart wisdom, for which he was ready like a true son of the theatre, to prostitute to any subject, occasion and any theatrical employment—these are some Shakespearean attributes. He thinks Bunyan the truer man—which is quite aside from the argument—and he believes that we are outgrowing Shakespeare, who will become with Byron a "household pet." And most incontinently, he concludes by asserting that when he, Shaw, began to write dramatic criticism Shakespeare was a divinity; now he is become a fellow creature. He will never forgive him for the sensuality of "Antony and Cleopatra" or for the cruel treatment accorded Julius Caesar's magnificent personality. (But what would Shakespeare have said to Bernard Shaw's Julius Cæsar?) In short, Mr. Shaw finds that Shakespeare's wisdom is Montaigne's, his history Plutarch's, his plots Bandello's and several others. Yet he is a Shakespeare worshipper —though he cannot endure the accepted spelling of the great name; and declares that the ear should be the true clue to him:—"In a deaf nation these plays would have died long ago." He berates Garrick, Colley Cibber, Irving, Augustin Daly and all the "vaudeville adapters" of the Shakespeare plays for their horrible taste, their vulgar excisions, and their substitution of scenic claptrap for the real Shakespeare. He wishes his Shakespeare naked and undefiled by stupid commentators and barbarian stage-managers.

Of latter-day playwrights Shaw has written, learnedly

and most piquantly. His Ibsen partisanship needs no vindication at this hour. The star of the great dead Norwegian has risen, no longer a baleful portent, but a beneficial orb in whose light we see ourselves—well, normally; as normally as Shaw sees us? For the modern English dramatists he has always exhibited a firm dislike until they achieved something that extorted his praise. He was among the first to attack Pinero's "The Second Mrs. Tanqueray" as an artificial bit of stage technique. He speedily exposed the inherent structural weakness and lack of logic in "The Notorious Mrs. Ebbsmith"; but he found sufficient words of admiration for "The Benefit of the Doubt," by all odds the best, because truest, of the Pinero dramas.

Henry Arthur Jones is rated highly by Mr. Shaw. This writer has "creative imagination, curious observation, inventive humor, sympathy and sincerity." He admired "Michael and his Lost Angel," as did a few discerning critics in New York—and he has never ceased wondering why this fine play was withdrawn in London before it had a fair chance.

The reader will find scattered throughout these pages many treasures of wit and observation. And, oh! the wicked, the clever things that have dropped from the nib of the Shaw pen. "Who is Hall Caine?" Of Shaw's own criticisms: "Those who think the things I say severe, or even malicious, should just see the things I do *not* say." "Boiled Heroine." "On the stage we get the geniuses and the *hysteriques;* but the intermediate talents are drawn back from a profession in which brains and self-respect have no chance against emotional facility and neurotic sexuality." "The stock actor is a stage calamity." "Falstaff is human but disgusting." (St. Bernard is not

Introduction

a lover of flesh, nor a consumer of sack.) "Mary Anderson was no actress—she lacked the actress temperament." "G. B. S. is a philosopher—his material, humanity." "Rostand is pasteboard." "Sardoodledom"—which is capital. "A Puritan is a fanatical idealist to whom all stimulations of the sense of beauty are abhorred; a philistine is a prosaic person who has no ideals." "I have a technical objection to making sexual infatuation a tragic theme. Experience proves that it is only effective in the comic spirit."

Mr. Shaw, let us solemnly call your attention to "Hedda Gabler"; not to mention "Romeo and Juliet"! Duse *vs.* Bernhardt is an excellent study of the old and the new artists—old and new in an artistic sense. Of dramatic criticism again: "The actor will get money and applause from the contemporary mob; but posterity will only see him through the spectacles of the elect; if he displeases them (i. e., the dramatic critics) his credit will be interred with his bones." Which is a curious paraphrase of Hamlet's remarks about the players. "Marie Corelli's works are cheap victories of a profuse imagination over an apparently commonplace and carelessly cultivated mind." "Thackeray is an author I cannot abide." "For my part I do not indorse all Ibsen's views; I even prefer my own plays to his in some respects." "Pinero is no interpreter of character, but simply an adroit describer of people as the ordinary man sees and judges them." "A character actor is one who can not act and therefore makes an elaborate study of disguises and stage tricks by which acting can be grotesquely simulated. Pinero is simply character acting in the domain of authorship." Many pinchbeck histrionic reputations in England and America would be shattered by this dictum if the public but realized it. "Oscar Wilde is an arch-artist; he is colossally lazy." And hitting off the critical condescension with which Wilde's pieces were once received by many critics in England, Shaw cooly remarks: "I am the only person in London who can not sit down and write an Oscar Wilde play at will." "Mr. Barrie makes a pretty character as a milliner makes a bonnet, by matching materials; he has no eye for human character, only a keen sense for human qualities."

III

But enough. Here is a plethora of riches. Remember, too, that when Shaw wrote the criticisms in this volume he was virginal to fame. It is his best work, the very pith of the man. It contains his most buoyant prose, the quintessence of Shaw. His valedictory is incomparable. He found that after taking laughing gas he had many sub-conscious selves. He describes them; perhaps he realizes now that they often come to the surface in his writings without being invoked by gas. After nominating that gentle mid-Victorian, Max Beerbohm, as his successor, he concludes: "I'm off duty forever and I am going to sleep." He has been, however, desperately awake since then, and with him kept us all awake. His physician was clairvoyant. The normality of Shaw has made his reputation in a world of abnormal beings! He should be grateful to his vision. Bernard Shaw is an *I*.

THE AUTHOR'S APOLOGY

IN justice to many well-known public persons who are handled rather recklessly in the following pages, I beg my readers not to mistake my journalistic utterances for final estimates of their worth and achievements as dramatic artists and authors. It is not so much that the utterances are unjust; for I have never claimed for myself the divine attribute of justice. But some of them are not even reasonably fair: I must therefore warn the reader that what he is about to study is not a series of judgments aiming at impartiality, but a siege laid to the theatre of the XIXth Century by an author who had to cut his own way into it at the point of the pen, and throw some of its defenders into the moat.

Pray do not conclude from this that the things hereinafter written were not true, or not the deepest and best things I know how to say. Only, they must be construed in the light of the fact that all through I was accusing my opponents of failure because they were not doing what I wanted, whereas they were often succeeding very brilliantly in doing what they themselves wanted. I postulated as desirable a certain kind of play in which I was destined ten years later to make my mark as a playwright (as I very well foreknew in the depth of my own unconsciousness); and I brought everybody, authors, actors, managers, to the one test: were they coming my way or staying in the old grooves?

Sometimes I made allowances for the difference in aim, especially in the case of personal friends. But as

as eternal and sacred as any professed religion in the world. And so, consciously or unconsciously, I was forgiven when many of my colleagues, less severe because less in earnest on the subject, gave deadly offence.

Nevertheless, though much tempted by publishers, I allowed these essays to sleep in the files of the *Saturday Review* for eight years, and should have left them there still if the decision had rested with me, knowing well that though many strokes may be struck at public performers quite justifiably and beneficially on an ephemeral page with the object of heading off those momentary rushes in the wrong direction which occur in the drama and in acting no less than in politics and fashion, some of them should not be repeated in permanent literary form until the period and the persons pass out of the struggle for existence into history. But my control over my writings goes no further than my copyright. Being powerless to prevent the publication of these articles in America, I have been forced (not, of course, *very* unwillingly) to make the best of the situation by inviting my own American publishers to anticipate the inevitable, so that the publication shall be at least in friendly hands. As the pressure of other affairs made it impossible for me to undertake the work of editing and selection it was placed, at my own suggestion, in the hands of Mr. James Huneker, who has done it better than I should have done. To forbid an extension of the circulation to British territory would be useless: the smugglers would take care of that; so the volumes must run their course with my sincere prayer for pardon to those survivors of the conflict who may have received a scratch or two from my pen.

I have to thank the proprietors of the *Saturday Review* for their consent to the circulation of this reprint in the

The Author's Apology

British Empire, and to express my regret that my articles must reappear without the brilliant setting at first provided for them by the pens of my colleagues on the staff of that journal.

BERNARD SHAW.

Ayot St. Lawrence, 1906.

SLAVES OF THE RING

Slaves of the Ring: a new and original play in three acts. By Sydney Grundy. Garrick Theatre, 29 December, 1894.

O
F ALL wonderful scenes that the modern theatre knows, commend me to that in the first act of Wagner's "Tristan," where Tristan and Isolde drink the death draught. There is nothing else for them to do; since Tristan, loving Isolde and being beloved by her, is nevertheless bringing her across the sea to be the bride of his friend, King Mark. Believing themselves delivered by death from all bonds and duties and other terrestrial fates, they enter into an elysium of love in perfect happiness and freedom, and remain there until their brief eternity is cut short by the shouts of the sailors and the letting go of the anchor, and they find themselves still on earth, with all secrets told and barriers cast down between them, and King Mark waiting to receive his bride. The poison had been exchanged by a friendly hand for a love potion.

At what period Mr. Sydney Grundy came under the spell of this situation, and resolved that he, too, would have a "new and original" turn at it, I do not know. It may be, since these dramatic imaginings are really the common heritage of the human imagination, and belong to no individual genius, however grandly he may have shaped them into a masterpiece of his art, that Mr. Grundy may have found the situation in the air, and not at Bayreuth. Howbeit he conceived it somehow, and proceeded to make out of it the play entitled "Slaves of the Ring," which differs from Wagner's "Tristan" in this very essential respect, that whereas "Tristan" is the greatest work of its kind of the century, "Slaves of the Ring" is not sufficiently typical or classical to deserve being cited even as the worst. It is not a work of art at all: it is a mere contrivance for filling a theatre bill, and not, I am bound to say, a very apt contrivance even at that.

Here was the problem as it presented itself to Mr. Grundy. Wanted, a married lady declaring her love for a man other than her husband under the impression that she and he are both dead, and consequently released from all moral obligations (this, observe, is the indispensable condition which appears to lie at the back of the popular conception of Paradise in all countries). The lady's conviction that she has passed the gates of death preserves her innocence as an English heroine. But what about the gentleman? Wagner made the gentleman believe himself dead also, and so preserved his innocence. But the English stage gentleman is as frail as the English stage lady is pure: therefore Mr. Grundy's Tristan, though perfectly alive and well aware of it, takes the deluded lady to his bosom. Hereupon Mr. Grundy owes it to his character as a master of drama that Tristan's wife should overhear these proceedings; and he owes it to his reputation as a master af stage technique that she should announce her presence by turning up a lamp, which the other lady has previously had turned down for that express purpose (as every experienced playgoer in the house plainly foresees) on the somewhat emaciated pretext that she prefers to sit in the dark. But it is of course possible that this also is a reminiscence of Tristan and Isolde's love of night and death. At all events, Miss Rorke turns up the lamp with the expertness due to long practice; and then, the dramatic possibilities of the theme being exhausted, the parties get off the stage as best they can.

Here you have the whole play. Once this scene was invented, nothing remained for the author to do except to prepare for it in a first act, and to use up its backwash in a third. And concerning that first act, I can only say that my utter lack of any sort of relish for Mr. Grundy's school of theatrical art must be my excuse if I fail, without some appearance of malice, adequately to convey my sense of the mathematic lifelessness and intricacy of his preliminaries. I am not alluding to the inevitable opening explanations on the subject of "the old Earl" and "the late Countess," which Mrs. Boucicault industriously offers to Miss Kate Phillips, who replies with much *aplomb,* "I see your point." Even if I could follow such explanations, I could not remember them. Often as I have sat them out, I have never listened to them, and I never will; though I am far from objecting to a device which gives me leisure to look at the scenery and dresses, and helps to attune the ear of the pit to the conversational pitch of the house. But I do expect the author to get through the task of introducing the persons of the drama to the audience in a lucid and easily memorable way, and not to leave me at the end of half-an-hour feeling like a boy on his first day at a new school, or a stranger at an At-Home in a new set. Mr. Grundy somehow managed to plunge me into the densest confusion as to who was who, a confusion which almost touched aberration when I saw a double leading lady

3

walk on to the stage, both of her in full wedding dress.
Like the dying Mousquetaire in the Ingoldsby Legends,
when his friends tried to cure him of seeing a ghost by
dressing up a nurse exactly like it, I exclaimed:

> "Mon Dieu! V'la deux!
> By the Pope, *there are two!*"

The spectacular effect alone of so much white silk was
sufficiently unhinging. But when the two brides proceeded solemnly to marry one another with a wedding
ring, I really did feel for a moment a horrible misgiving
that I had at last broken through that "thin partition"
which divides great wits from madness. It was only afterwards, when we came to the "Tristan" scene, for which
all this was mere preparation, that I realized how Mr.
Grundy's imagination, excited solely by that one situation, and unhappily not fertilized by it sufficiently to
bring its figures to life as created characters, was inert
during this first act; so that in elaborating a tissue of
artificialities to lead us to accept a situation which we
would willingly have taken for granted without any
explanations at all, he was unable to visualize the stage,
even with two brides on it in full fig. Well was it for
Mr. Grundy that that act was under the wing of Mr.
Hare at the Garrick Theatre. Even as it was, there were
moments when even the firmest faith that something must
be coming presently showed signs of breaking down.

The third act was better. There were no explanations,
because, the murder being out, there was nothing more
to explain. Unfortunately, though the plot was over,
it was too late to begin the play. Further, the scene
was in a conservatory, lit with so many lamps that Miss
Rorke could not have made any particular difference by

4

turning down one of them; so she jumped through a palm-tree instead, and cried, "Aha! I've caught you at last," just as the other lady, though now convalescent and in her right mind, was relapsing into her dream with Tristan. In spite of this and a few other claptraps, there was a certain force at work in this act, a force which finally revealed itself as a burning conviction in Mr. Grundy that our law and custom of making marriage indissoluble and irrevocable, except by the disgrace of either party, is a cruel social evil. Under the stimulus of this, the only definite "view" anywhere discoverable in his works, he does manage to get some driving weight of indignant discontent into the end of the play, though even in the very heat of it he remains so captivated by worn-out French stage conventions that he makes one of his characters strike the supposed lover of his wife across the face with a white glove. Whereat it is really impossible to do anything but laugh and fish out one's hat to go. Being safely at home, well-disposed to Mr. Grundy, and desirous above all things to slip gently over the staring fact that the play might be a better one, let me note gratefully that there is no villain, no hero, a quadrille of lovers instead of a pair, and that Mr. Grundy's imagination, stretched and tortured as it is on the Procrustean framework of "the well-made play," yet bursts fitfully into activity—though not, alas! into rebellion—with angry vigor.

As to the acting, it is, on the whole, much worse than the play. Miss Kate Rorke, comely, ladylike and self-possessed, turns her emotion on and off by her well-established method with a business-like promptitude that makes the operation as certain as the turning up and down of the lamp. I feel sure that Miss Rorke would regard what I call acting as mere hysteria; and indeed I should be loth to recommend it to her, as she is no doubt quite as popular, and perhaps a good deal happier without it. Miss Calhoun, equally experienced, also obliged with whatever was wanted at the right moment. Her outcries in the first act, and again in the last, were discordant and unconvincing; and she should have made the Tristan scene at least six times as effective. Mr. Brandon Thomas, as a broken-hearted personage charged with the duty of accompanying the play by an explanatory lecture in the manner of Dumas *fils,* was in a deplorable situation throughout. It happens that the plot devised by Mr. Grundy to bring off his one scene has all the potentialities of a capital comedy plot. Mr. Brandon Thomas divined this, and knew in his soul (as I read him) that if only he might be allowed the smallest twinkle of humor, he could make the play go like wild-fire. Under these circumstances his enforced gravity had a baffled quality which was the more ludicrous because it looked as if he were killing the play, whereas the play was really killing him. Mr. Gilbert Hare had a more important part than he would have been cast for in any other theatre; but as he played it with great care and thoroughness to the very best of his ability, it would be churlish to grudge him his advantage. Mr. Bourchier had nothing to act, though, fundamentally, this observation is perhaps hardly more true of him than of the rest. Some comic relief gave an opportunity to Mr. Hare and Miss Kate Phillips. Mr. Hare, to be quite frank, had a very cheap job; but he got the last inch of effect out of it. He, also, was provided with a patent broken heart, though he happily kept it to himself until a moment before his final exit. Miss Phillips was hampered in the first two

6

acts by that sort of comic part which is almost as much a nuisance as a relief; but she played a little scene with Mr. Hare in the last act very cleverly, and was, it seemed to me, the only lady in the cast whose artistic sensitiveness had survived the case-hardening of professional routine. The stage-mounting and coloring were solidly and expensively Philistine, the dresses in the last act, and the style of domestic decoration in the first, epitomizing the whole history of plutocracy in England during the expiring century.

TWO NEW PLAYS

Guy Domville: a play in three acts. By Henry James. St. James's Theatre, 5 January, 1895.
An Ideal Husband: a new and original play of modern life. By Oscar Wilde. Haymarket Theatre, 3 January, 1895.

THE truth about Mr. James's play is no worse than that it is out of fashion. Any dramatically disposed young gentleman who, cultivating sentiment on a little alcohol, and gaining an insight to the mysteries of the eternal feminine by a couple of squalid intrigues, meanwhile keeps well aloof from art and philosophy, and thus preserves his innocence of the higher life of the senses and of the intellect, can patch up a play to-morrow which will pass as real drama with the gentlemen who deny that distinction to the work of Mr. Henry James. No doubt, if the literary world were as completely dominated by the admirers of Mr. Rider Haggard as the

7

dramatic world is by their first cousins, we should be told that Mr. James cannot write a novel. That is not criticism; it is a mere begging of the question. There is no reason why life as we find it in Mr. James's novels— life, that is, in which passion is subordinate to intellect and to fastidious artistic taste—should not be represented on the stage. If it is real to Mr. James, it must be real to others; and why should not these others have their drama instead of being banished from the theatre (to the theatre's great loss) by the monotony and vulgarity of drama in which passion is everything, intellect nothing, and art only brought in by the incidental outrages upon it. As it happens, I am not myself in Mr. James's camp: in all the life that has energy enough to be interesting to me, subjective volition, passion, will, make intellect the merest tool. But there is in the centre of that cyclone a certain calm spot where cultivated ladies and gentlemen live on independent incomes or by pleasant artistic occupations. It is there that Mr. James's art touches life, selecting whatever is graceful, exquisite, or dignified in its serenity. It is not life as imagined by the pit or gallery, or even by the stalls: it is, let us say, the ideal of the balcony; but that is no reason why the pit and gallery should excommunicate it on the ground that it has no blood and entrails in it, and have its sentence formulated for it by the fiercely ambitious and wilful professional man in the stalls. The whole case against its adequacy really rests on its violation of the cardinal stage convention that love is the most irresistible of all the passions. Since most people go to the theatre to escape from reality, this convention is naturally dear to a world in which love, all powerful in the secret, unreal, day-dreaming life of the imagination, is in the real active life the abject slave of every trifling habit, prejudice, and cowardice, easily stifled by shyness, class feeling, and pecuniary prudence, or diverted from what is theatrically assumed to be its hurricane course by such obstacles as a thick ankle, a cockney accent, or an unfashionable hat. In the face of this, is it good sense to accuse Mr. Henry James of a want of grip of the realities of life because he gives us a hero who sacrifices his love to a strong and noble vocation for the Church? And yet when some unmannerly playgoer, untouched by either love or religion, chooses to send a derisive howl from the gallery at such a situation, we are to sorrowfully admit, if you please, that Mr. James is no dramatist, on the general ground that "the drama's laws the drama's patrons give." Pray which of its patrons?—the cultivated majority who, like myself and all the ablest of my colleagues, applauded Mr. James on Saturday, or the handful of rowdies who brawled at him? It is the business of the dramatic critic to educate these dunces, not to echo them.

Admitting, then, that Mr. James's dramatic authorship is valid, and that his plays are *du théâtre* when the right people are in the theatre, what are the qualities and faults of "Guy Domville"? First among the qualities, a rare charm of speech. Line after line comes with such a delicate turn and fall that I unhesitatingly challenge any of our popular dramatists to write a scene in verse with half the beauty of Mr. James's prose. I am not now speaking of the verbal fitness, which is a matter of careful workmanship merely. I am speaking of the delicate inflexions of feeling conveyed by the cadences of the line, inflexions and cadences which, after so long a course of the ordinary theatrical splashes and daubs of passion and emphasis, are as grateful to my ear as the

am the only person in London who cannot sit down and write an Oscar Wilde play at will. The fact that his plays, though apparently lucrative, remain unique under these circumstances, says much for the self-denial of our scribes. In a certain sense Mr. Wilde is to me our only thorough playwright. He plays with everything: with wit, with philosophy, with drama, with actors and audience, with the whole theatre. Such a feat scandalizes the Englishman, who can no more play with wit and philosophy than he can with a football or a cricket bat. He works at both, and has the consolation, if he cannot make people laugh, of being the best cricketer and footballer in the world. Now it is the mark of the artist that he will not work. Just as people with social ambitions will practise the meanest economies in order to live expensively, so the artist will starve his way through incredible toil and discouragement sooner than go and earn a week's honest wages. Mr. Wilde, an arch-artist, is so colossally lazy that he trifles even with the work by which an artist escapes work. He distils the very quintessence, and gets as product plays which are so unapproachably playful that they are the delight of every playgoer with twopenn'orth of brains. The English critic, always protesting that the drama should not be didactic, and yet always complaining if the dramatist does not find sermons in stones and good in everything, will be conscious of a subtle and pervading levity in "An Ideal Husband." All the literary dignity of the play, all the imperturbable good sense and good manners with which Mr. Wilde makes his wit pleasant to his comparatively stupid audience, cannot quite overcome the fact that Ireland is of all countries the most foreign to England, and that to the Irishman (and Mr. Wilde is almost as acutely

Irish an Irishman as the Iron Duke of Wellington) there is nothing in the world quite so exquisitely comic as an Englishman's seriousness. It becomes tragic, perhaps, when the Englishman acts on it; but that occurs too seldom to be taken into account, a fact which intensifies the humor of the situation, the total result being the Englishman utterly unconscious of his real self, Mr. Wilde keenly observant of it and playing on the self-unconsciousness with irresistible humor, and finally, of course, the Englishman annoyed with himself for being amused at his own expense, and for being unable to convict Mr. Wilde of what seems an obvious misunderstanding of human nature. He is shocked, too, at the danger to the foundations of society when seriousness is publicly laughed at. And to complete the oddity of the situation, Mr. Wilde, touching what he himself reverences, is absolutely the most sentimental dramatist of the day.

It is useless to describe a play which has no thesis: which is, in the purest integrity, a play and nothing less. The six worst epigrams are mere alms handed with a kind smile to the average suburban playgoer; the three best remain secrets between Mr. Wilde and a few choice spirits. The modern note is struck in Sir Robert Chiltern's assertion of the individuality and courage of his wrongdoing as against the mechanical idealism of his stupidly good wife, and in his bitter criticism of a love that is only the reward of merit. It is from the philosophy on which this scene is based that the most pregnant epigrams in the play have been condensed. Indeed, this is the only philosophy that ever has produced epigrams. In contriving the stage expedients by which the action of the piece is kept going, Mr. Wilde has been once or twice a little too careless of stage illusion: for

and epergnes laden with grapes, regaled guests who walked off and on through illusory wainscoting simulated by the precarious perspective of the wings. The scene-painter built the rooms; the costumier made the dresses; the armor was made apparently by dipping the legs of the knights in a solution of salt of spangles and precipitating the metal on their calves by some electro-process; the leader of the band made the music; and the author wrote the verse and invented the law, the morals, the religion, the art, the jurisprudence, and whatever else might be needed in the abstract department of the play. Since then we have seen great changes. Real walls, ceilings, and doors are made by real carpenters; real tailors and dressmakers clothe the performers; real armorers harness them; and real musicians write the music and have it performed with full orchestral honors at the Crystal Palace and the Philharmonic. All that remains is to get a real poet to write the verse, a real philosopher to do the morals, a real divine to put in the religion, a real lawyer to adjust the law, and a real painter to design the pictorial effects. This is too much to achieve at one blow; but Mr. Irving made a brave step towards it when he resolved to get rid of the author and put in his place his dear old friend Comyns Carr as an encyclopædic gentleman well up to date in most of these matters. And Mr. Comyns Carr, of course, was at once able to tell him that there was an immense mass of artistic and poetic tradition, accumulated by generations of poets and painters, lying at hand all ready for exploitation by any experienced dealer with ingenuity and literary faculty enough to focus it in a stage entertainment. Such a man would have to know, for instance, that educated people have ceased to believe that architecture means "ruins by moonlight" (style, ecclesiastical Gothic) ; that the once fashionable admiration of the Renaissance and "the old masters" of the sixteenth and seventeenth centuries has been swept away by the growth of a genuine sense of the naïve dignity and charm of thirteenth-century work, and a passionate affection for the exquisite beauty of fifteenth-century work, so that nowadays ten acres of Carracci, Giulio, Romano, Guido, Domenichino, and Pietro di Cortona will not buy an inch of Botticelli, or Lippi, or John Bellini—no, not even with a few yards of Raphael thrown in; and that the whole rhetorical school in English literature, from Shakespeare to Byron, appears to us in our present mood only another side of the terrible *degringolade* from Michael Angelo to Canova and Thorwaldsen, all of whose works would not now tempt us to part with a single fragment by Donatello, or even a pretty foundling baby by Della Robbia. And yet this, which is the real art culture of England to-day, is only dimly known to our dramatic authors as a momentary bygone craze out of which a couple of successful pieces, "Patience" and "The Colonel," made some money in their day. Mr. Comyns Carr knows better. He knows that Burne-Jones has made himself the greatest among English decorative painters by picking up the tradition of his art where Lippi left it, and utterly ignoring "their Raphaels, Correggios, and stuff." He knows that William Morris has made himself the greatest living master of the English language, both in prose and verse, by picking up the tradition of the literary art where Chaucer left it, and that Morris and Burne-Jones, close friends and co-operators in many a masterpiece, form the highest aristocracy of English art to-day. And he knows exactly how far their culture has spread and penetrated, and

how much simply noble beauty of Romanesque architecture, what touching loveliness and delicate splendor
of fifteenth-century Italian dresses and armor, what blue
from the hills round Florence and what sunset gloom
deepening into splendid black shadow from the horizons
of Giorgione will be recognized with delight on the stage
if they be well counterfeited there; also what stories we
long to have as the subject of these deeply desired pictures. Foremost among such stories stands that of King
Arthur, Lancelot, and Guinevere; and what Mr. Comyns
Carr has done is to contrive a play in which we have
our heart's wish, and see these figures come to life, and
move through halls and colonnades that might have been
raised by the master-builders of San Zeno or San Am-
brogio, out into the eternal beauty of the woodland spring,
acting their legend just as we know it, in just such
vestures and against just such backgrounds of blue hill
and fiery sunset. No mere dramatic author could have
wrought this miracle. Mr. Comyns Carr has done it
with ease, by simply knowing whom to send for. His
long business experience as a man of art and letters, and
the contact with artists and poets which it has involved,
have equipped him completely for the work. In Mr.
Irving's theatre, with Burne-Jones to design for him,
Harker and Hawes Craven to paint for him, and Malory
and Tennyson and many another on his bookshelves, he
has put out his hand cleverly on a ready-made success,
and tasted the joy of victory without the terror of battle.

But how am I to praise this deed when my own art,
the art of literature, is left shabby and ashamed amid the
triumph of the arts of the painter and the actor? I
sometimes wonder where Mr. Irving will go to when he
dies—whether he will dare to claim, as a master artist,

to walk where he may any day meet Shakespeare whom he has mutilated, Goethe whom he has travestied, and the nameless creator of the hero-king out of whose mouth he has uttered jobbing verses. For in poetry Mr. Comyns Carr is frankly a jobber and nothing else. There is one scene in the play in which Mr. Irving rises to the height of his art, and impersonates, with the noblest feeling, and the most sensitive refinement of execution, the King Arthur of all our imaginations in the moment when he learns that his wife loves his friend instead of himself. And all the time, whilst the voice, the gesture, the emotion expressed are those of the hero-king, the talk is the talk of an angry and jealous costermonger, exalted by the abject submission of the other parties to a transport of magnanimity in refraining from reviling his wife and punching her lover's head. I do not suppose that Mr. Irving said to Mr. Comyns Carr in so many words, "Write what trash you like: I'll play the real King Arthur over the head of your stuff"; but that was what it came to. And the end of it was that Mr. Comyns Carr was too much for Mr. Irving. When King Arthur, having broken down in an attempt to hit Lancelot with his sword, Guinevere groveling on the floor with her head within an inch of his toes, and stood plainly conveying to the numerous bystanders that this was the proper position for a female who had forgotten herself so far as to prefer another man to him, one's gorge rose at the Tappertitian vulgarity and infamy of the thing; and it was a relief when the scene ended with a fine old Richard the Third effect of Arthur leading his mail-clad knights off to battle. That vision of a fine figure of a woman, torn with sobs and remorse, stretched at the feet of a nobly superior and deeply wronged lord of creation, is no doubt still as popular with the men whose sentimental vanity it flatters as it was in the days of the "Idylls of the King." But since then we have been learning that a woman is something more than a piece of sweetstuff to fatten a man's emotions; and our amateur King Arthurs are beginning to realize, with shocked surprise, that the more generous the race grows, the stronger becomes its disposition to bring them to their senses with a stinging dose of wholesome ridicule. Mr. Comyns Carr miscalculated the spirit of the age on this point; and the result was that he dragged Mr. Irving down from the height of the loftiest passage in his acting to the abyss of the lowest depth of the dialogue.

Whilst not sparing my protest against this unpardonable scene, I can hardly blame Mr. Comyns Carr for the touch of human frailty which made him reserve to himself the honor of providing the "book of the words" for Burne-Jones's picture-opera. No doubt, since Mr. Carr is no more a poet than I am, the consistent course would have been to call in Mr. William Morris to provide the verse. Perhaps, if Mr. Irving, in his black harness, with his visor down and Excalibur ready to hand and well in view, were to present himself at the Kelmscott Press fortified with a propitiatory appeal from the great painter, the poet might, without absolutely swearing, listen to a proposal that he should condescend to touch up those little rhymed acrostics in which Merlin utters his prophecies, leaving the blank verse padding to Mr. Comyns Carr. For the blank verse is at all events accurately metrical, a fact which distinguishes the author sharply from most modern dramatists. The ideas are second-hand, and are dovetailed into a coherent structure instead of developing into one another by any life of their own; but they are sometimes very well chosen; and Mr. Carr is often guided to his choice of them by the strength and sincerity of their effect on his own feelings. At such moments, if he does not create, he reflects so well, and sometimes reflects such fine rays too, that one gladly admits that there are men whose originality might have been worse than his receptivity. There are excellent moments in the love scenes: indeed, Lancelot's confession of his love to Guinevere all but earns for the author the poet's privilege of having his chain tested by its strongest link.

The only great bit of acting in the piece is that passage of Mr. Irving's to which I have already alluded—a masterly fulfilment of the promise of one or two quiet but eloquent touches in his scene with Guinevere in the second act. Popularly speaking, Mr. Forbes Robertson as Lancelot is the hero of the piece. He has a beautiful costume, mostly of plate-armor of Burne-Jonesian design; and he wears it beautifully, like a fifteenth-century St. George, the spiritual, interesting face completing a rarely attractive living picture. He was more than applauded on his entrance: he was positively adored. His voice is an organ with only one stop on it: to the musician it suggests a clarionet in A, played only in the chalumeau register; but then the chalumeau, sympathetically sounded, has a richly melancholy and noble effect. The one tune he had to play throughout suited it perfectly: its subdued passion, both in love and devotion, affected the house deeply; and the crowning moment of the drama for most of those present was his clasping of Guinevere's waist as he knelt at her feet when she intoxicated him by answering his confession with her own. As to Miss Ellen Terry, it was the old story, a born actress of real women's parts condemned to figure as a mere artist's model in costume plays which, from the woman's point of view, are foolish flatteries written by gentlemen for gentlemen. It is pathetic to see Miss Terry snatching at some fleeting touch of nature in her part, and playing it not only to perfection, but often with a parting caress that brings it beyond that for an instant as she relinquishes it, very loth, and passes on to the next length of arid sham-feminine twaddle in blank verse, which she pumps out in little rhythmic strokes in a desperate and all too obvious effort to make music of it. I should prove myself void of the true critic's passion if I could pass with polite commonplaces over what seems to me a heartless waste of an exquisite talent. What a theatre for a woman of genius to be attached to! Obsolete tomfooleries like "Robert Macaire," schoolgirl charades like "Nance Oldfield," blank verse by Wills, Comyns Carr, and Calmour, with intervals of hashed Shakespeare; and all the time a stream of splendid women's parts pouring from the Ibsen volcano and minor craters, and being snapped up by the rising generation. Strange, under these circumstances, that it is Mr. Irving and not Miss Terry who feels the want of a municipal theatre. He has certainly done his best to make every one else feel it.

The rest of the acting is the merest stock company routine, there being only three real parts in the play. Sir Arthur Sullivan (who, in the playbill, drops his knighthood whilst Burne-Jones parades his baronetcy) sweetens the sentiment of the scenes here and there by penn'orths of orchestral sugarstick, for which the dramatic critics, in their soft-eared innocence, praise him above Wagner. The overture and the vocal pieces are pretty specimens of his best late work. Some awkwardness in the construction of the play towards the end has led the stage manager into a couple of absurdities. For instance, when the body of Elaine is done with, it should be taken off the stage and not put in the corner like a portmanteau at a railway station. I do not know what is supposed to happen in the last act—whether Guinevere is alive or a ghost when she comes in at Arthur's death (I understood she was being burnt behind the scenes), or what becomes of Lancelot and Mordred, or who on earth the two gentlemen are who come in successively to interview the dying Arthur, or why the funeral barge should leave Mr. Irving lying on the stage and bear off to bliss an impostor with a strikingly different nose. In fact, I understand nothing that happened after the sudden blossoming out of Arthur into Lohengrin, Guinevere into Elsa, Mordred into Telramund, and Morgan le Fay into Ortruda in the combat scene, in which, by the way, Mr. Comyns Carr kills the wrong man, probably from having read Wagner carelessly. But I certainly think something might be done to relieve the shock of the whole court suddenly bolting and leaving the mortally wounded king floundering on the floor without a soul to look after him. These trifles are mere specks of dust on a splendid picture; but they could easily be brushed off.

POOR SHAKESPEARE!

All's Well that Ends Well. Performance by the Irving Dramatic Club at St. George's Hall, 22 and 24 January, 1895.

WHAT a pity it is that the people who love the sound of Shakespeare so seldom go on the stage! The ear is the sure clue to him: only a musician can understand the play of feeling which is the real rarity in his early plays. In a deaf nation these plays would have died long ago. The moral attitude in them is conventional and secondhand: the borrowed ideas, however finely expressed, have not the overpowering human interest of those original criticisms of life which supply the rhetorical element in his later works. Even the individualization which produces that old-established British specialty, the Shakespearian "delineation of character," owes all its magic to the turn of the line, which lets you into the secret of its utterer's mood and temperament, not by its commonplace meaning, but by some subtle exaltation, or stultification, or slyness, or delicacy, or hesitancy, or what not in the sound of it. In short, it is the score and not the libretto that keeps the work alive and fresh; and this is why only musical critics should be allowed to meddle with Shakespeare—especially early Shakespeare. Unhappily, though the nation still retains its ears, the players and playgoers of this generation are for the most part deaf as adders. Their appreciation of Shakespeare is sheer hypocrisy, the proof being that where an early play of his is revived, they take the utmost pains to suppress as much of it as possible, and disguise the rest past recognition, relying for success on extraordinary scenic attractions; on very popular performers, including, if possible, a famously beautiful actress in the leading part; and above all, on Shakespeare's reputation and the consequent submission of the British public to be mercilessly bored by each of his plays once in their lives, for the sake of being able to say they have seen it. And not a soul has the hardihood to yawn in the face of the imposture. The manager is praised; the bard is praised; the beautiful actress is praised; and the free list comes early and comes often, not without a distinct sense of conferring a handsome compliment on the acting manager. And it certainly is hard to face such a disappointment without being paid for it. For the more enchanting the play is at home by the fireside in winter, or out on the heather of a summer evening—the more the manager, in his efforts to realize this enchantment by reckless expenditure on incidental music, colored lights, dances, dresses, and elaborate rearrangements and dislocations of the play—the more, in fact, he departs from the old platform with its curtains and its placards inscribed "A street in Mantua," and so forth, the more hopelessly and vulgarly does he miss his mark. Such crown jewels of dramatic poetry as "Twelfth Night" and "A Midsummer Night's Dream," fade into shabby colored glass in his purse; and sincere people who do not know what the matter is, begin to babble insufferably about plays that are meant for the study and not for the stage.

Yet once in a blue moon or so there wanders on to the stage some happy fair whose eyes are lode-stars and whose tongue's sweet air's more tunable than lark to shepherd's ear. And the moment she strikes up the true Shakespearian music, and feels her way to her part al-

formance of it during his lifetime). It certainly explains why Phelps, the only modern actor-manager tempted by it, was attracted by the part of Parolles, a capital study of the adventurous yarn-spinning society-struck coward, who also crops up again in modern fiction as the hero of Charles Lever's underrated novel, "A Day's Ride: a Life's Romance." When I saw "All's Well" announced for performance by the Irving Dramatic Club, I was highly interested, especially as the performers were free, for once, to play Shakespeare for Shakespeare's sake. Alas! at this amateur performance, at which there need have been none of the miserable commercialization compulsory at the regular theatres, I suffered all the vulgarity and absurdity of that commercialism without its efficiency. We all know the stock objection of the Brixton Family Shakespeare to "All's Well"—that the heroine is a lady doctor, and that no lady of any delicacy could possibly adopt a profession which involves the possibility of her having to attend cases such as that of the king in this play, who suffers from a fistula. How any sensible and humane person can have ever read this sort of thing without a deep sense of its insult to every charitable woman's humanity and every sick man's suffering is, fortunately, getting harder to understand nowadays than it once was. Nevertheless "All's Well" was minced with strict deference to it for the members of the Irving Dramatic Club. The rule for expurgation was to omit everything that the most pestiferously prurient person could find improper. For example, when the non-commissioned officer, with quite becoming earnestness and force, says to the disgraced Parolles: "If you could find out a country where but women were that had received so much shame, you might begin an impudent nation," the speech was suppressed as if it were on all fours with the obsolete Elizabethan badinage which is and should be cut out as a matter of course. And to save Helena from anything so shocking as a reference to her virginity, she was robbed of that rapturous outburst beginning

"There shall your master have a thousand loves—
A mother and a mistress and a friend," etc.

But perhaps this was sacrificed in deference to the opinion of the editor of those pretty and handy little books called the Temple Shakespeare, who compares the passage to "the nonsense of some foolish conceited player" —a criticism which only a commentator could hope to live down.

The play was, of course, pulled to pieces in order that some bad scenery, totally unconnected with Florence or Rousillon, might destroy all the illusion which the simple stage directions in the book create, and which they would equally have created had they been printed on a placard and hung up on a curtain. The passage of the Florentine army beneath the walls of the city was managed in the manner of the end of the first act of Robertson's "Ours," the widow and the girls looking out of their sitting-room window, whilst a few of the band gave a precarious selection from the orchestral parts of Berlioz's version of the Rackoczy March. The dresses were the usual fancy ball odds and ends, Helena especially distinguishing herself by playing the first scene partly in the costume of Hamlet and partly in that of a waitress in an Aerated Bread shop, set off by a monstrous auburn wig which could by no stretch of imagination be taken for her own hair. Briefly, the whole play was vivisected, and the fragments mutilated, for

AN OLD NEW PLAY AND A NEW OLD ONE

The Importance of Being Earnest: a trivial comedy for serious people. By Oscar Wilde. St. James's Theatre, 14 February, 1895.

? A play in ? acts. By ?. Opera Comique, 16 February, 1895.

The Second Mrs. Tanqueray: a play in four acts. By Arthur W. Pinero. London: W. Heinemann. 1895.

I T IS somewhat surprising to find Mr. Oscar Wilde, who does not usually model himself on Mr. Henry Arthur Jones, giving his latest play a five-chambered title like "The Case of Rebellious Susan." So I suggest with some confidence that "The Importance of Being Earnest" dates from a period long anterior to Susan. However it may have been retouched immediately before its production, it must certainly have been written before "Lady Windermere's Fan." I do not suppose it to be Mr. Wilde's first play: he is too susceptible to fine art to have begun otherwise than with a strenuous imitation of a great dramatic poem, Greek or Shakespearian; but it was perhaps the first which he designed for practical commercial use at the West End theatres. The evidence of this is abundant. The play has a plot—a gross anachronism; there is a scene between the two girls in the second act quite in the literary style of Mr. Gilbert, and almost inhuman enough to have been conceived by him; the humor is adulterated by stock mechanical fun to an extent that absolutely scandalizes one in a play with such an author's name to it; and the punning title and

several of the more farcical passages recall the epoch of
the late H. J. Byron. The whole has been varnished, and
here and there veneered, by the author of "A Woman of
no Importance"; but the general effect is that of a farcical comedy dating from the seventies, unplayed during
that period because it was too clever and too decent, and
brought up to date as far as possible by Mr. Wilde in
his now completely formed style. Such is the impression
left by the play on me. But I find other critics, equally
entitled to respect, declaring that "The Importance of Being Earnest" is a strained effort of Mr. Wilde's at ultra-
modernity, and that it could never have been written but
for the opening up of entirely new paths in drama last
year by "Arms and the Man." At which I confess to a
chuckle.

I cannot say that I greatly cared for "The Importance
of Being Earnest." It amused me, of course; but unless
comedy touches me as well as amuses me, it leaves me
with a sense of having wasted my evening. I go to
the theatre to be moved to laughter, not to be tickled or
bustled into it; and that is why, though I laugh as much
as anybody at a farcical comedy, I am out of spirits before the end of the second act, and out of temper before
the end of the third, my miserable mechanical laughter
intensifying these symptoms at every outburst. If the
public ever becomes intelligent enough to know when
it is really enjoying itself and when it is not, there will
be an end of farcical comedy. Now in "The Importance
of Being Earnest" there is a good deal of this rib-tickling:
for instance, the lies, the deceptions, the cross-purposes,
the sham mourning, the christening of the two grown-up
men, the muffin eating, and so forth. These could only
have been raised from the farcical plane by making them

occur to characters who had, like Don Quixote, convinced us of their reality and obtained some hold on our sympathy. But that unfortunate moment of Gilbertism breaks our belief in the humanity of the play. Thus we are thrown back on the force of daintiness of its wit, brought home by an exquisitely grave, natural, and unconscious execution on the part of the actors. Alas! the latter is not forthcoming. Mr. Kinsey Peile as a man-servant, and Miss Irene Vanburgh as Gwendolen Fairfax, alone escaped from a devastating consciousness of Mr. Wilde's reputation, which more or less preoccupied all the rest, except perhaps Miss Millard, with whom all comedy is a preoccupation, since she is essentially a sentimental actress. In such passages as the Gilbertian quarrel with Gwendolen, her charm rebuked the scene instead of enhancing it. The older ladies were, if they will excuse my saying so, quite maddening. The violence of their affectation, the insufferable low comedy soars and swoops of the voice, the rigid shivers of elbow, shoulder, and neck, which are supposed on the stage to characterize the behavior of ladies after the age of forty, played havoc with the piece. In Miss Rose Leclerq a good deal of this sort of thing is only the mannerism of a genuine if somewhat impossible style; but Miss Leclerq was absent through indisposition on the night of my visit, so that I had not her style to console me. Mr. Aynesworth's easy-going "Our Boys" style of play suited his part rather happily; and Mr. Alexander's graver and more refined manner made the right contrast with it. But Mr. Alexander, after playing with very nearly if not quite perfect conviction in the first two acts, suddenly lost confidence in the third, and began to spur up for a rattling finish. From the moment that began, the play was done with. The speech in which Worthing forgives his supposed mother, and the business of searching the army lists, which should have been conducted with subdued earnestness, was bustled through to the destruction of all verisimilitude and consequently all interest. That is the worst of having anyone who is not an inveterate and hardened comedian in a leading comedy part. His faith, patience, and relish begin to give out after a time; and he finally commits the unpardonable sin against the author of giving the signal that the play is over ten minutes before the fall of the curtain, instead of speaking the last line as if the whole evening were still before the audience. Mr. Alexander does not throw himself genuinely into comedy: he condescends to amuse himself with it; and in the end he finds that he cannot condescend enough. On the whole I must decline to accept "The Importance of Being Earnest" as a day less than ten years old; and I am altogether unable to perceive any uncommon excellence in its presentation.

I am in a somewhat foolish position concerning a play at the Opera Comique, whither I was bidden this day week. For some reason I was not supplied with a programme; so that I never learnt the name of the play. I believe I recognized some of the members of the company—generally a very difficult thing to do in a country where, with a few talented exceptions, every actor is just like every other actor—but they have now faded from my memory. At the end of the second act the play had advanced about as far as an ordinary dramatist would have brought it five minutes after the first rising of the curtain; or, say, as far as Ibsen would have brought it ten years before that event. Taking advantage of the second interval to stroll out into the Strand for a little exercise, I unfortunately forgot all about my business, and actually reached home before it occurred to me that I had not seen the end of the play. Under these circumstances it would ill become me to dogmatize on the merits of the work or its performance. I can only offer the management my apologies.

I am indebted to Mr. Heinemann for a copy of "The Second Mrs. Tanqueray," which he has just published in a five-shilling volume, with an excellent photographic portrait of the author by Mr. Hollyer. Those who did not see the play at the St. James's Theatre can now examine the literary basis of the work that so immoderately fascinated playgoing London in 1893. But they must not expect the play to be as imposing in the library as it was on the stage. Its merit there was relative to the culture of the playgoing public. Paula Tanqueray is an astonishingly well-drawn figure as stage figures go nowadays, even allowing for the fact that there is no cheaper subject for the character draughtsman than the ill-tempered sensual woman seen from the point of view of the conventional man. But off the stage her distinction vanishes. The novels of Anthony Trollope, Charles Lever, Bulwer Lytton, Charles Reade, and many other novelists, whom nobody praised thirty years ago in the terms in which Mr. Pinero is praised now, are full of feats of character drawing in no way inferior—to say the least—to Mr. Pinero's. The theatre was not ready for that class of work then: it is now; and accordingly Mr. Pinero, who in literature is a humble and somewhat belated follower of the novelists of the middle of the nineteenth century, and who has never written a line from which it could be guessed that he is a contemporary of Ibsen, Tolstoi, Meredith, or Sarah Grand, finds himself at the dawn of the twentieth hailed as a man of new ideas, of daring originality, of supreme literary distinction, and even—which is perhaps oddest—of consummate stage craft. Stage craft, after all, is very narrowly limited by the physical conditions of stage representation; but when one turns over the pages of "The Second Mrs. Tanqueray," and notes the naïve machinery of the exposition in the first act, in which two whole actors are wasted on sham parts, and the hero, at his own dinner party, is compelled to get up and go ignominiously into the next room "to write some letters" when something has to be said behind his back; when one follows Cayley Drummle, the confidant to whom both Paula and her husband explain themselves for the benefit of the audience; when one counts the number of doors which Mr. Pinero needs to get his characters on and off the stage, and how they have finally to be supplemented by the inevitable "French windows" (two of them); and when the activity of the postman is taken into consideration, it is impossible to avoid the conclusion that what most of our critics mean by mastery of stage craft is recklessness in the substitution of dead machinery and lay figures for vital action and real characters. I do not deny that an author may be driven by his own limitations to ingenuities which Shakespeare had no occasion to cultivate, just as a painter without hands or feet learns to surpass Michael Angelo in the art of drawing with the brush held in the mouth; but I regard such ingenuity as an extremity to be deplored, not as an art to be admired. In "The Second Mrs. Tanqueray" I find little except a scaffold for the situation of a step-daughter and a step-mother finding themselves in the positions respectively of affianced wife and discarded mistress to the same man. Obviously, the only necessary conditions of this situation are that the persons concerned shall be respectable enough to be shocked by it, and that the step-mother shall be an improper person. Mr. Pinero has not got above this minimum. He is, of course, sufficiently skilled in fiction to give Ellean, Mrs. Cortelyon, Ardale, Tanqueray, and Cayley Drummle a passable air of being human beings. He has even touched up Cayley into a Thackerayan flaneur in order to secure toleration of his intrusiveness. But who will pretend that any of these figures are more than the barest accessories to the main situation? To compare them with the characters in Robertson's "Caste" would be almost as ridiculous as to compare "Caste" with "A Doll's House." The two vulgar characters produce the requisite jar—a pitilessly disagreeable jar—and that is all. Still, all the seven seem good as far as they go; and that very little way may suggest that Mr. Pinero might have done good creative work if he had carried them further. Unfortunately for this surmise, he has carried Paula further; and with what result? The moment the point is reached at which the comparatively common gift of "an eye for character" has to be supplemented by the higher dramatic gift of sympathy with character—of the power of seeing the world from the point of view of others instead of merely describing or judging them from one's own point of view in terms of the conventional systems of morals, Mr. Pinero breaks down. I remember that when I saw the play acted I sat up very attentively when Tanqueray said to Paula, "I know what you were at Ellean's age. You hadn't a thought that wasn't a wholesome one; you hadn't an impulse that didn't tend towards good; you never harbored a notion you couldn't have gossiped about to a parcel of children. And this was a very few years back, etc., etc." On the reply to that fatuous but not unnatural speech depended the whole question of Mr. Pinero's rank as a dramatist. One can imagine how, in a play by a master-hand, Paula's reply would have opened Tanqueray's foolish eyes to the fact that a woman of that sort is already the same at three as she is at thirty-three, and that however she may have found by experience that her nature is in conflict with the ideals of differently constituted people, she remains perfectly valid to herself, and despises herself, if she sincerely does so at all, for the hypocrisy that the world forces on her instead of for being what she is. What reply does Mr. Pinero put into her mouth? Here it is, with the stage directions: "A few—years ago! (*She walks slowly towards the door, then suddenly drops upon the ottoman in a paroxysm of weeping.*) O God! A few years ago!" That is to say, she makes her reply from the Tanqueray-Ellean-Pinero point of view, and thus betrays the fact that she is a work of prejudiced observation instead of comprehension, and that the other characters only owe their faint humanity to the fact that they are projections of Mr. Pinero's own personal amiabilities and beliefs and conventions. Mr. Pinero, then, is no interpreter of character, but simply an adroit describer of people as the ordinary man sees and judges them. Add to this a clear head, a love of the stage, and a fair talent for fiction, all highly cultivated by hard and honorable work as a writer of effective stage plays for the modern commercial theatre; and you have him on his real level. On that level he is entitled to all the praise "The Second Mrs. Tanqueray" has won him; and I very heartily regret that the glamor which Mrs.

Patrick Campbell cast round the play has forced me to
examine pretensions which Mr. Pinero himself never put
forward rather than to acknowledge the merits with
which his work is so concisely packed.

MR. PINERO'S NEW PLAY

The Notorious Mrs. Ebbsmith: an original play in
four acts. By A. W. Pinero. Garrick Theatre, 13
March, 1895.

MR. PINERO's new play is an attempt to reproduce
that peculiar stage effect of intellectual drama,
of social problem, of subtle psychological study
of character, in short, of a great play, with which he was
so successful in "The Profligate" and "The Second Mrs.
Tanqueray." In the two earlier plays, it will be remembered, he was careful to support this stage effect with a
substantial basis of ordinary dramatic material, consisting of a well worked-up and well worn situation which
would have secured the success of a conventional Adelphi
piece. In this way he conquered the public by the exquisite flattery of giving them plays that they really liked,
whilst persuading them that such appreciation was only
possible from persons of great culture and intellectual
acuteness. The vogue of "The Second Mrs. Tanqueray"
was due to the fact that the commonplace playgoer, as
he admired Mrs. Patrick Campbell, and was moved for
the twentieth time by the conventional wicked woman
with a past, consumed with remorse at the recollection

of her innocent girlhood, and unable to look her pure
step-daughter (from a convent) in the face, believed that
he was one of the select few for whom "the literary
drama" exists, and thus combined the delights of an
evening at a play which would not have puzzled Madame
Celeste with a sense of being immensely in the modern
movement. Mr. Pinero, in effect, invented a new sort
of play by taking the ordinary article and giving it an
air of novel, profound, and original thought. This he
was able to do because he was an inveterate "character
actor" (a technical term denoting a clever stage performer who cannot act, and therefore makes an elaborate
study of the disguises and stage tricks by which acting
can be grotesquely simulated) as well as a competent
dramatist on customary lines. His performance as a
thinker and social philosopher is simply character acting
in the domain of authorship, and can impose only on
those who are taken in by character acting on the stage.
It is only the make-up of an actor who does not understand his part, but who knows—because he shares—the
popular notion of its externals. As such, it can never
be the governing factor in his success, which must always
depend on the commonplace but real substratum of ordinary drama in his works. Thus his power to provide
Mrs. Tanqueray with equally popular successors depends
on his freedom from the illusion he has himself created
as to his real strength lying in his acuteness as a critic
of life. Given a good play, the stage effect of philosophy
will pass with those who are no better philosophers than
he; but when the play is bad, the air of philosophy can
only add to its insufferableness. In the case of "The
Notorious Mrs. Ebbsmith," the play is bad. But one of
its defects: to wit, the unreality of the chief female char-

patient who falls in love with her. He is married to a shrew; and he proposes to spend the rest of his life with his nurse, preaching the horrors of marriage. Off the stage it is not customary for a man and woman to assume that they cannot co-operate in bringing about social reform without living together as man and wife: on the stage, this is considered inevitable. Mrs. Ebbsmith rebels against the stage so far as to propose that they shall prove their disinterestedness by making the partnership a friendly business one only. She then finds out that he does not really care a rap about her ideas, and that his attachment to her is simply sexual. Here we start with a dramatic theme capable of interesting development. Mr. Pinero, unable to develop it, lets it slip through his fingers after one feeble clutch at it, and proceeds to degrade his drama below the ordinary level by making the woman declare that her discovery of the nature of the man's feelings puts within her reach "the only one hour in a woman's life," in pursuance of which detestable view she puts on an indecent dress and utterly abandons herself to him. A clergyman appears at this crisis, and offers her a Bible. She promptly pitches it into the stove; and a thrill of horror runs through the audience as they see, in imagination, the whole Christian Church tottering before their eyes. Suddenly, with a wild scream, she plunges her hand into the glowing stove and pulls out the Bible again. The Church is saved; and the curtain descends amid thunders of applause. In that applause I hope I need not say I did not join. A less sensible and less courageous stage effect I have never witnessed. If Mr. Pinero had created for us a woman whose childhood had been made miserable by the gloomy terrorism which vulgar, fanatical parents extract from the Bible, then he

might fitly have given some of the public a very wholesome lesson by making the woman thrust the Bible into
the stove and leave it there. Many of the most devoted
clergymen of the Church of England would, I can assure
him, have publicly thanked him for such a lesson. But
to introduce a woman as to whom we are carefully assured that she was educated as a secularist, and whose
one misfortune—her unhappy marriage—can hardly by
any stretch of casuistry be laid to the charge of St. Paul's
teaching; to make this woman senselessly say that all
her misfortunes are due to the Bible; to make her throw
it into the stove, and then injure herself horribly in pulling it out again: this, I submit, is a piece of claptrap so
gross that it absolves me from all obligation to treat Mr.
Pinero's art as anything higher than the barest art of
theatrical sensation. As in the "The Profligate," as in
"The Second Mrs. Tanqueray," he has had no idea beyond
that of doing something daring and bringing down the
house by running away from the consequences.

I must confess that I have no criticism for all this stuff.
Mr. Pinero is quite right to try his hand at the higher
drama; only he will never succeed on his present method
of trusting to his imagination, which seems to me to have
been fed originally on the novels and American humor
of forty years ago, and of late to have been entirely
starved. I strongly recommend him to air his ideas a
little in Hyde Park or "the Iron Hall, St. Luke's," before
he writes his next play. I shall be happy to take the
chair for him.

I should, by the way, like to know the truth about the
great stage effect at the end of the second act, where
Mrs. Patrick Campbell enters with her plain and very
becoming dress changed for a horrifying confection ap-

THE INDEPENDENT THEATRE
REPENTS

A Man's Love: a play in three acts, from the Dutch of J. C. de Vos; and *Salvê,* a Dramatic Fragment, in one act, by Mrs. Oscar Beringer. The Independent Theatre (Opéra Comique), 15 March, 1895.

THE Independent Theatre is becoming wretchedly respectable. Nobody now clamors for the prosecution of Mr. Grein under Lord Campbell's Act, or denounces myself and the other frequenters of the performances as neurotic, cretinous degenerates. This is not as it should be. In my barbarous youth, when one of the pleasures of theatre-going was the fierce struggle at the pit-door, I learnt a lesson which I have never forgotten: namely, that the secret of getting in was to wedge myself into the worst of the crust. When ribs and breastbone were on the verge of collapse, and the stout lady in front, after passionately calling on her escort to take her out of it if he considered himself a man, had resigned herself to death, my hopes of a place in the front row ran high. If the pressure slackened I knew I was being extruded into the side eddies where the feeble and half-hearted were throwing away their chance of a good seat for such paltry indulgences as freedom to breathe and a fully expanded skeleton. The progressive man goes through life on the same principle, instinctively making for the focus of struggle and resisting the tendency to edge him out into the place of ease. When the Independent Theatre was started, its supporters all made for it, I presume—certainly I did—because it was being heavily squeezed.

There was one crowded moment when, after the first performance of "Ghosts," the atmosphere of London was black with vituperation, with threats, with clamor for suppression and extinction, with everything that makes life worth living in modern society. I have myself stood before the independent footlights in obedience to my vocation (literally) as dramatic author, drinking in the rapture of such a hooting from the outraged conventional first-nighter as even Mr. Henry James might have envied. But now that glory has departed to the regular theatres. My poor little audacity of a heroine who lost her temper and shook her housemaid has been eclipsed by heroines who throw the Bible into the fire. Mr. Grein, no longer a revolutionist, is modestly bidding for the position left vacant by the death of German Reed, and will shortly be consecrated by public opinion as the manager of the one theatre in London that is not a real wicked Pinerotic theatre, and is, consequently, the only theatre in London that it is not wrong for good people to go to. His latest playbill is conclusive on this point. It begins with "A Man's Love," from the Dutch of J. C. de Vos, and ends with "Salvê," by Mrs. Oscar Beringer. The first would be contemptuously rejected by Mr. Hare as a snivelling, pietistic insult to the spirit of the age; and the second might without the least incongruity be played as a curtain-raiser before "Green Bushes" or "The Wreck Ashore."

The defence to this grave disparagement will probably be that, in "A Man's Love," the hero makes advances to his undeceased wife's sister, and that "Salvê" ends unhappily. I cannot allow the excuse. Any man, on the stage or off it, may make love to his sister-in-law without rousing the faintest sense of unexpectedness in the spectator. And when, as in Mr. de Vos's play, the young lady tells him he ought to be ashamed of himself, and leaves the house without making her sister miserable by telling her why, the situation becomes positively triter than if he had not made love to her at all. There is only one Independent Theatre drama to be got out of such a theme; and that is the drama of the discovery by the man that he has married the wrong sister, and that the most earnest desire on the part of all concerned to do their duty does not avail against that solid fact. Such a drama occurred in the life of one of the greatest English writers of the nineteenth century, one who was never accused by his worst enemies of being a loose liver. But Mr. de Vos has not written that drama, or even pretended to write it. As to the unhappy ending of "Salvê," unhappy endings are not a new development in the theatre, but a reversion to an older stage phase. I take it that the recently defunct happy ending, which is merely a means of sending the audience away in good humor, was brought in by the disappearance of the farce. Formerly you had "The Gamester" to begin with; and then, when Beverley had expired yelling from the effects of swallowing some powerful mineral irritant, there was a screaming farce to finish with. When it suddenly occurred to the managers that for twenty-five years or so no experienced playgoer had ever been known to wait for the farce, it was dropped; and nothing was left in the bill except the play of the evening and a curtain-raiser to keep the gallery amused whilst waiting for the plutocracy to finish their dinners and get down to their reserved seats. Still the idea of sending away the audience in a cheerful temper survived, and led to the incorporation of that function of the farce into the end of the play. Hence the happy ending. But in course of time this produced the same effect as the farce. The people got up and made for the doors the moment they saw it coming; and managers were reduced to the abject expedient of publishing in the programme a request to the audience not to rise until the fall of the curtain. When even this appeal *ad misericordiam* failed, there was nothing for it but to abolish the happy ending, and venture on the wild innovation of ringing down the curtain the moment the play was really over. This brought back the old tragic ending of the farce days, which was of course immediately hailed, as the custom is whenever some particularly ghastly antiquity is trotted out, as the newest feature of the new drama.

So much then for the novelty of Mrs. Beringer's idea of ending her little play by making the mother slay her long-lost cheeyild, and go mad then and there like Lucia de Lammermoor. Indeed, if Mrs. Theodore Wright had struck up "Spargi d'amaro pianto," with flute obbligato and variations, my old Italian operatic training would have saved me from the least feeling of surprise, though the younger generation would certainly have thought us both mad. The variations would have been quite in keeping with the bags of gold poured out on the table, and with the spectacle of a mother taking up the bread-knife and transfixing her healthy young son full in the public view. Is it possible that Mrs. Beringer has not yet realized that these mock butcheries belong to the babyhood of the drama? She may depend on it there is a solid reason for Hedda Gabler shooting herself behind the scenes instead of stabbing herself before them. In that, Ibsen shakes hands with the Greek dramatic poets just as clearly as Mrs. Beringer, with her gory breadknife, shakes hands with the most infantile melodramatists of

51

the Donizettian epoch. "Salvê" is not at all a bad piece of work of its naïve kind: indeed, except for a few unactable little bits here and there, it would merit high praise at the Pavilion or Marylebone theatres; but what, in the name of all that's Independent, has it to do with the aims of Mr. Grein's society?

To find any sort of justification for the performance I must turn to the acting—for let me say that I should consider Mr. Grein quite in order in giving a performance of Robertson's "Caste," followed by "Box and Cox," if he could handle them so as to suggest fresh developments in stage art. Unfortunately, the management made an incomprehensible mistake in casting "A Man's Love." It had at its disposal Miss Winifred Fraser and Miss Mary Keegan; and the two women's parts in the play were well suited to their strongly contrasted personalities. Accordingly, it put Miss Keegan into the part which suited Miss Fraser, and Miss Fraser into the part which suited Miss Keegan. The two ladies did what they could under the circumstances; but their predicament was hopeless from the outset. The resultant awkwardness made the worst of the very clumsy devices by which the action of the play is maintained—impossible soliloquies, incidents off the stage described by people on it as they stare at them through the wings, and the like: all, by the way, reasons why the Independent Theatre should not have produced the work unless these crudities were atoned for by boldness or novelty in some other direction.

The two ladies being practically out of the question, the burden of the play fell upon Mr. Herbert Flemming, whose work presented a striking contrast to the sort of thing we are accustomed to from our popular "leading men." We all know the faultlessly dressed, funereally wooden, carefully phrased walking negation who is so careful not to do anything that could help or hinder our imaginations in mending him into a hero. His great secret is to keep quiet, look serious, and, above all, not act. To this day you see Mr. Lewis Waller and Mr. George Alexander struggling, even in the freedom of management, with the habits of the days when they were expected to supply this particular style of article, and to live under the unwritten law: "Be a nonenity, or you will get cast for villains," a fate which has actually overtaken Mr. Waring because his efforts to suppress himself stopped short of absolute inanity. Only for certain attractive individual peculiarities which have enabled Mr. Forbes Robertson to place himself above this law occasionally as a personal privilege, our stage heroes would be as little distinguishable from one another as bricks in a wall. Under these circumstances, I was quite staggered to find Mr. Flemming, though neither a comic actor nor a "character actor," acting—positively acting—in a sentimental leading part. He was all initiative, life, expression, with the unhesitating certainty of execution which stamps an actor as perfectly safe for every effect within his range. This amounted to a combination of the proficiency and positive power (as distinguished from negative discretion) of the old stock actor, with the spontaneity, sensitiveness, and touch with the cultivated non-professional world which the latest developments of the drama demand. Mr. Flemming first made his mark here by his performances in certain Ibsen parts, and by his playing of the hero in Voss's "Alexandra," Stuttgart's pet tragedy. Yet when he appeared recently in such an absurd melodrama as "Robbery Under Arms," he was as equal to the occasion as the veteran Mr.

Clarance Holt; and his return without effort to the new style in "A Man's Love" is interesting as a sign that the new drama is at last beginning to bring in its harvest of technically efficient actors, instead of being, as it was at first, thrown into hands which were, with one or two brilliant exceptions, comparatively unskilled. The occasion was not a favorable one for Mr. Flemming—quite the contrary. He was not on his mettle; he was in the unmistakable attitude of an experienced actor towards a play which he knows to be beyond saving; the extent to which he fell back on his mere stage habits showed that he had refused to waste much time in useless study of a dramatically worthless character, and was simply using his professional skill to get through his part without damage to his reputation; and he was sometimes taken out of the character by his very free recourse to that frankly feminine style of play which is up to a certain point the secret, and beyond it the mere stage trick, of modern acting, and which is enormously effective in a man who, like Mr. Flemming, is virile enough to be feminine without risk of effeminacy. None the less this half-studied performance in a third-rate play at a depressing matinée (I was not present at the first performance) was striking enough to demand, at the present moment, all the attention I have given to it.

Mrs. Theodore Wright, as the mother in "Salvê," had no difficulty in touching and harrowing the audience to the necessary degree. Her acting, also, has the imaginative quality which the reviving drama requires. She made a mistake or two over Mrs. Beringer's unactable bits, trying to worry some acting into them instead of letting them quietly slip by; but that was a fault on the right side; and one felt sorry for her sake when the breadknife

reduced the little play to absurdity, and half spoiled the
admirable effect of her playing in the scenes just before
and after her journey of intercession. Happily, the audience did not mind the breadknife at all, and made her
an ovation.

L'OEUVRE

Théâtre de l'Œuvre de Paris. Performances at the
Opera Comique, London, of Ibsen's *Rosmersholm*
and *Master Builder,* and of Maeterlinck's *L'Intruse*
and *Pelléas et Mélisande.* 25-30 March, 1895.

M Lugné-Poë and his dramatic company called
"L'Œuvre" came to us with the reputation of
having made Ibsen cry by their performance of
one of his works. There was not much in that: I have
seen performances by English players which would have
driven him to suicide. But when the first act of "Rosmersholm" had hardly begun on Monday night, when I
recognized, with something like excitement, the true atmosphere of this most enthralling of all Ibsen's works
rising like an enchanted mist for the first time on an
English stage. There were drawbacks, of course. The
shabbiness of the scenery did not trouble me; but the
library of Pastor Rosmer got on my nerves a little. What
on earth did he want, for instance, with "Sell's World's
Press"? That he should have provided himself with a
volume of my own dramatic works I thought right and
natural enough, though when he took that particular volume down and opened it, I began to speculate rather

55

uneasily on the chances of his presently becoming so absorbed as to forget all about his part. I was surprised, too, when it appeared that the Conservative paper which attacked the Pastor for his conversion to Radicalism was none other than our own *Globe;* and the thrill which passed through the house when Rebecca West contemptuously tore it across and flung it down, far exceeded that which Mrs. Ebbsmith sends nightly through the Garrick audiences. Then I was heavily taken aback by Mortensgard. He, in his determination to be modern and original, had entrusted the making-up of his face to an ultra-Impressionist painter who had recklessly abused his opportunity. Kroll, too, had a frankly incredible wig, and a costume of which every detail was a mistake. We know Kroll perfectly well in this country: he is one out of many instances of that essential and consequently universal knowledge of mankind which enables Ibsen to make his pictures of social and political life in outlandish little Norwegian parishes instantly recognizable in London and Chicago (where Mr. Beerbohm Tree, by the way, has just made a remarkable sensation with "An Enemy of the People"). For saying this I may be asked whether I am aware that many of our critical authorities have pointed out how absurdly irrelevant the petty parochial squabblings which stand for public life in Ibsen's prose comedies are to the complex greatness of public affairs in our huge cities. I reply that I am. And if I am further pressed to declare straightforwardly whether I mean to disparage these authorities, I reply, pointedly, that I do. I affirm that such criticisms are written by men who know as much of political life as I know of navigation. Any person who has helped to "nurse" an English constituency, local or parliamentary, and organized the election from the inside, or served for a year on a vestry, or attempted to set on foot a movement for broadening the religious and social views of an English village, will not only vouch for it that "The League of Youth," "An Enemy of the People," and "Rosmersholm," are as true to English as they can possibly be to Norwegian society, but will probably offer to supply from his own acquaintances originals for all the public characters in these plays.

I took exception, then, to Kroll, because I know Kroll by sight perfectly well (was he not for a long time chairman of the London School Board?) ; and I am certain he would die sooner than pay a visit to the rector in a coat and trousers which would make a superannuated coffee-stall keeper feel apologetic, and with his haircutting and shampooing considerably more than three months overdue.

I take a further exception which goes a good deal deeper than this. Mdlle. Marthe Mellot, the clever actress who appeared as Rebecca West, Pelléas, and Kaia, played Rebecca in the manner of Sarah Bernhardt, the least appropriate of all manners for the part. Rebecca's passion is the cold passion of the North—that essentially human passion which embodies itself in objective purposes and interests, and in attachments which again embody themselves in objective purposes and interests on behalf of others—that fruitful, contained, governed, instinctively utilized passion which makes nations and individuals great, as distinguished from the explosive, hysterical, wasteful passion which makes nothing but a scene. Now in the third and fourth acts of "Rosmersholm," Mdlle. Mellot, who had played excellently in the first and second, suddenly let the part slip through her fingers by turning to the wrong sort of passion. Take, for example, the

is nothing but costly and highly organized routine, deliberately used, like the ceremonial of a court, to make second-rate human material presentable. In the Théâtre de l'Œuvre there is not merely the ordinary theatrical intention, but a vigilant artistic conscience in the diction, the stage action, and the stage picture, producing a true poetic atmosphere, and triumphing easily over shabby appointments and ridiculous incidents. Of course, this is so much the worse for the Théâtre de l'Œuvre from the point of view of the critics who represent the Philistinism against which all genuinely artistic enterprises are crusades. It is a stinging criticism on our theatre that ten years of constant playgoing in London seem to reduce all but the strongest men to a condition in which any attempt to secure in stage-work the higher qualities of artistic execution—qualities which have been familiar for thousands of years to all art students—appears an aberration absurd enough to justify reputable newspapers in publishing as criticism stuff which is mere street-boy guying. I am not here quarreling with dispraise of the Théâtre de l'Œuvre and M. Maeterlinck. I set the highest value on a strong Opposition both in art and politics; and if Herr Max Nordau were made critic of the *Standard* (for instance) I should rejoice exceedingly. But when I find players speaking with such skill and delicacy that they can deliver M. Maeterlinck's fragile word-music throughout five acts without one harsh or strained note, and with remarkable subtlety and conviction of expression; and when I see these artists, simply because their wigs are not up to Mr. Clarkson's English standard, and the curtain accidentally goes up at the wrong time, denounced as "amateurs" by gentlemen who go into obedient raptures when M. Mounet Sully plasters his cheeks with white and his lips with vermilion, and positively howls his lines at them for a whole evening with a meaningless and discordant violence which would secure his dismissal from M. Lugné-Poë's company at the end of the first act, then—Well, what then? Shall I violate the sacredness of professional etiquette, and confess to a foreigner that the distinction some of our critics make between the amateur and the expert is really a distinction between a rich enterprise and a poor one, and has nothing in the world to do with the distinction made by the trained senses of the critic who recognizes art directly through his eyes and ears, and not by its business associations? Never! Besides, it would not be fair: no man, be he ever so accomplished a critic, can effectively look at or listen to plays that he does not really want to see or hear.

The interest taken in the performances culminated at that of "The Master Builder" on Wednesday. At first it seemed as if M. Lugné-Poë's elaborate and completely realized study of a self-made man breaking up, was going to carry all before it, a hope raised to the highest by the delightful boldness and youthfulness of Mdlle. Suzanne Despres in the earlier scenes of Hilda. Unfortunately, Madame Gay as Mrs. Solness was quite impossible: Miss Florence St. John as Lady Macbeth would have been better suited. And in the second act, where Solness, the dominator and mesmerizer of Kaia, becomes himself dominated and mesmerized by the impulsive, irresponsible, abounding youth and force of Hilda, Mdlle. Despres lost ground, and actually began to play Kaia—Kaia prettily mutinous, perhaps, but still Kaia. The last act, with a subjugated Hilda, and a Mrs. Solness, who was visibly struggling with a natural propensity to cheerful common

AT THE THEATRES

Vanity Fair: a caricature. By G. W. Godfrey. Court Theatre, 27 April, 1895.

The Passport. By B. C. Stephenson and W. Yardley. Terry's Theatre, 25 April, 1895.

A Human Sport: a drama in one act. By Austin Fryers. Globe Theatre, 1 May, 1895.

ON THE whole, I am inclined to congratulate Mr. Godfrey on Mrs. John Wood, rather than Mrs. John Wood on Mr. Godfrey, in the matter of "Vanity Fair." Mrs. John Wood is herself a character; and by providing her with some new dialogue Mr. Godfrey has given himself an air of creation; but I doubt if the other parts can be said to bear him out on this point. When I saw the piece, on the third night, Mr. Arthur Cecil was still so unequal to the mere taskwork of remembering long strings of sentences which were about as characteristic and human as the instructions on the back of a telegram form, that he had to be spoon-fed by the prompter all the evening. Mr. Anson as Bill Feltoe, the blackmailer, had a part which was certainly memorable in the sense that he could preserve the continuity of his ideas; but it did not go beyond that. The play, as a drama, is nothing. As an entertainment "written round" Mrs. John Wood, it is a success. But it also pretends to be "Vanity Fair," a picture of society. Mr. Godfrey guards himself by calling it a caricature; but he none the less presents it as a morality, a satire, a sermon! And here he appeals to the love of the public for edification. Dickens' group of cronies at the Maypole

Inn, with their cry of "Go on improvin' of us, Johnnie," exactly typifies the playgoing public in England. When an English playgoer is not by temperament, if not by actual practice, nine-tenths a chapel-goer, he is generally ten-tenths a blackguard; and so, if you cannot produce a genuine drama, and conquer him legitimately in that way, you must either be licentious at the cost of your respectability, or else moral and idealistic. Mr. Godfrey, running short for the moment, of character and drama, of course chose the respectable alternative, and resorted to idealism. He moralizes on fine lady spectators at murder trials, on matrimonial scandals and high life, on Christianity conquering Africa with a maxim gun, and on the prevarications of the Treasury Bench. As further evidence of the corruption of society, he instances the interest taken by it in eminent explorers, in Buffalo Bill, and in foreign violinists, the inference being, as I understand it, that to invite Mr. Stanley to dine, or Herr Joachim to play a partita by Bach, is a proceeding as fraught with degenerate heartlessness as to show your "horror" of a crime by rushing down to the court to gloat over the trial, or to give a gentleman who pays your wife's bills the right to call you to account for being seen in her company. Mr. Godfrey's explanation of all this depravity is simple. It is the work of the New Woman and of the Problem Play.

You are now in a position to appreciate the scene at the beginning of the third act, where Mr. Arthur Cecil, as the gently cynical Thackerayan observer of "Vanity Fair" receives, with the assistance of the prompter, the wondering questions of Miss Nancy Noel as to whether the relations between young men and young women ever really were as they are represented in the novels of Sir

Walter Scott. To which I regret to say, Mr. Cecil does not hesitate to reply in the affirmative, without mentioning that no change that has taken place in this century has been more obviously a change for the better than the changes in the relations between men and women. "Good night, little girl," he adds with unction, after a brief reference to his guide, philosopher, and friend in the prompter's box. "Trust to the teachings of your own pure heart. God bless you!"

Mr. Godfrey must excuse me; but that sort of social philosophy is not good enough for me. It does not matter, perhaps, because I am far from attributing to the claptrap play the devastating social influence he apparently attaches to the problem play (which I am getting rather anxious to see, by the way). But I must at least declare my belief that Mr. Godfrey will never succeed as a critic of society, by merely jumbling together all the splenetic commonplaces that sound effective to him, and tacking on an Adelphi moral. In order to make a stage drawing-room a microcosm of Vanity Fair, you may, I grant, mix your sets to any extent you please; but you need not therefore produce an impression that the sort of man that never reads a serious book or ventures above burlesque and farcical comedy at the theatre, has been led into his habit of not paying his bills, and of winking at his wife's relations with useful acquaintances, by "The Heavenly Twins" and Ibsen's plays. I do not say that Mr. Godfrey has produced such impressions intentionally: my quarrel with him is, that he has begun to criticize life without first arranging his ideas. The result is, that it is impossible for the most credulous person to believe in Mrs. Brabazon-Tegg's Grosvenor Square reception even to the extent of recognizing it as a caricature. It is not that the real thing is more respectable, or that the most extravagant bits (the scene with the sham millionaire, for instance) are the least lifelike; quite the contrary. But a drawing-room is not like Margate Sands for all that; however loose the selection of guests, there is enough logic in it to keep the music, bad though it may be, in one predominant key. It requires a very nice knowledge of what is reasonable to be safely outrageous in society of any grade; and this knowledge is as essential to the dramatist depicting society on the stage, as to the diner out who wishes to be allowed the privilege of unconventionality. In putting the drawing-room on the stage, Mr. Godfrey's master is obviously Mr. Oscar Wilde. Now Mr. Wilde has written scenes in which there is hardly a speech which could conceivably be addressed by one real person at a real at-home to another; but the deflection from common-sense is so subtle that it is evidently produced as a tuner tunes a piano; that is, he first tunes a fifth perfectly, and then flattens it a shade. If he could not tune the perfect fifth he could not produce the practicable one. This condition is imposed on the sociological humorist also. For instance, Don Quixote's irresistibly laughable address to the galley slaves, like the rest of his nonsense, is so close to the verge of good sense that thickwitted people, and even some clever ones, take the Don for a man of exceptionally sound understanding. None the less he is a hopeless lunatic, the sound understanding which he skirts so funnily being that of Cervantes. Mr. Godfrey fails to produce the same effect because he tries to say the absurd thing without precisely knowing the sensible thing, with the result that, though he makes epigrams most industriously, he never tickles the audience except by strokes of pure fun, such as Mrs. Brabazon-Tegg's "Don't disturb my maid: she's upstairs doing my hair." There are passages which are effective because they give voice to grievances or allude to abuses upon which the audience feels, or feels obliged to pretend to feel, highly indignant; but this is not art or drama; the effect would be the same if the point were made on a political platform: indeed, it would be better there. For example, in Mrs. Brabazon-Tegg's dream of her trial for bigamy, she is made to complain of the practice of eminent counsel accepting retainers in more cases than they can possibly attend to. The complaint would be more effective at an ordinary public meeting, because the trial represented on the stage, is precisely the sort of one from which no counsel would dream of absenting himself. Such effect, then, as Mrs. Brabazon-Tegg's speech from the dock actually does produce is due, not to the author's knowledge of his subject, but to the extraordinary spontaneity and conviction with which Mrs. John Wood delivers herself.

There is one point on which I am unable to say whether Mr. Godfrey was satirical or sincere. When Mrs. Brabazon-Tegg's conscience is awakened she does what most rich people do under similar circumstances: that is to say, the most mischievous thing possible. She begins to scatter hundred pound checks in conscience-money to various charities. Whether Mr. Godfrey approves of this proceeding I do not know; but he at any rate conquered my respect by remorselessly making his woman of fashion presently reduce all the checks to five pounds and re-plunge into fashionable life not a whit the better for her hard experience. This seems to in-

Dramatic Opinions and Essays

dicate that Mr. Godfrey has that courage of his profession in which most of our dramatists are shamelessly wanting. For its sake he may very well be forgiven his random satire, and even—on condition that he undertakes not to do it again—the insufferable conversations of Mr. Arthur Cecil and Miss Granville.

"The Passport," at Terry's, is an amusing piece, with thirteen parts, of which no less than eight are very well acted. I was not surprised at this, except in the case of Miss Gertrude Kingston, who, when I last saw her, was a clever lady with a certain virtuosity in the art of dress, and made of metal hard enough to take a fine edge, but still not then a skilled actress, though the critics had instinctively recognized her as a person to whom it was best to be civil, perhaps because she so suggested that terrible person, the lady who has walked straight from her drawing-room on to the stage. Most of that is gone now, except what was worth keeping in it. Miss Kingston's utterance and movements are acquiring a definite artistic character; and the circulation of feeling, which is more important to the stage artist than the circulation of the blood, seems to be establishing itself in spite of the refractory nature of the conducting medium; whilst her cleverness is still conspicuous, and her dresses make me feel more keenly than ever that I have left one corner of critical journalism unconquered; to wit, the fashion article. In short, Miss Kingston confronted me in "The Passport" as a rising actress, holding my interest from her entrance to her final exit, and indeed determining the success of the play, which, without her, might have broken down badly in the second and third acts, hampered as they are with the stuff about Bob, Algy, and Violet which is neither sensible, amusing, nor credible. The main thread of the story is presented by a very powerful combination of artists: Mr. Yorke Stephens, Mr. Maltby, Mr. Giddens, Mr. Mackay, Miss Gertrude Kingston, Miss Cicely Richards, and Miss Fanny Coleman. Their parts are all funny; and some of them are individual and interesting, notably the exasperating but fascinating young widow with the impossible memory, and the perfectly normal respectable maid, an excellent character, played admirably by Miss Cicely Richards. Mr. Yorke Stephens is a little under-parted: after the first act, which he carries off with all the debonair grace and smartness of style which distinguish him, he takes the part a little too easily. Even a widower could not be so completely unembarrassed on his wedding-day; and however obvious it may be that the misunderstandings created by the widow can be explained away, still, whilst they last, they need the assistance of a little alarm on the part of the bridegroom. As to the play, it is not a mere farcical imbroglio in which neither the figures who work the puzzle nor the places in which they work it have any real individuality: the scenes and circumstances, both in the frontier railway station and in the London house, are fully imagined and realized. The value and, alas! the rarity of this is shown by the comparative freshness and interest of the action, and the genial indulgence with which the audience accepts the complications of the last two acts, which are, it must be confessed, anything but ingenious, not to mention the silly episode of Algy, Violet, and Bob as aforesaid.

The one act piece, "A Human Sport" (in the evolutionary sense), by Mr. Austin Fryers, produced at the Globe Theatre at a matinèe in aid of the Actors' Benevolent Fund on Wednesday last, is hardly a drama at all;

it is rather the exhibition of an incident which does not
develop in any way. An ironmaster (I think it was an
ironmaster) has some operation spoiled by a workman
getting drunk at the critical moment. In order to prevent
this occurring again, he resolves to take a step which,
simple and obvious as it is, has not, as far as I am aware,
ever been thought of before; namely, to take the man
into partnership so as to increase his self-respect. With
this view he invites him to tea. The drunkard recognizes
in his master's wife and mother-in-law his own deserted
daughter and wife. Finding that respectability will involve a reunion with his family, he pretends to get drunk
again, and is promptly kicked out as incorrigible. This
unconventional and rather amusing notion has been ruined
by Mr. Austin Fryers' inveterate sentimentality. The
"human sport," instead of behaving sportively, plunges
into the stalest maudlin pathos over his long-lost
daughter. If Mr. Austin Fryers will cut out the daughter
and make the sport get really drunk in order to escape
from respectability and his wife, the play will do very
well. Or if he will write a temptation scene round the
decanter of brandy, and make the wife rush in and
struggle with her husband for the glass until the contest
is decided in her favor by the sound of their daughter's
voice singing a hymn in the next room, the whole ending
with the partnership and domestic bliss, that will be
equally satisfactory. But I implore Mr. Austin Fryers
not to mix his *genres*. Let us have the new ideas in the
new style, or the old tricks in the old style; but the new
ideas combined with the old tricks in no style at all cannot be borne. Mr. James Welch, as the sport, pulled the
play through by a piece of acting impressive enough to
keep the audience believing, up to the last moment, that

something really interesting was imminent. If only for Mr. Welch's sake, Mr. Austin Fryers, who is by no means deficient in ability, should extirpate that daughter, and build up the part into something worthy of the actor's rare talent.

TWO BAD PLAYS

The Girl I Left Behind Me: a drama in four acts. By Franklin Fyles and David Belasco. Adelphi Theatre, 13 April, 1895.

Delia Harding. By Victorien Sardou. Adapted by J. Comyns Carr. Comedy Theatre, 17 April, 1895.

LAST Saturday was made memorable to me by my first visit to the Adelphi Theatre. My frequent allusions to Adelphi melodrama were all founded on a knowledge so perfect that there was no need to verify it experimentally; and now that the experiment has been imposed on me in the course of my professional duty, it has confirmed my deductions to the minutest particular.

Should any one rush to the conclusion hereupon that my attitude towards the Adelphi Theatre is that of a superior person, he will be quite right. It is precisely because I am able to visit all theatres as a superior person that I am entrusted with my present critical function. As a superior person, then, I hold Adelphi melodrama in high consideration. A really good Adelphi melodrama is of first-rate literary importance, because it only needs elaboration to become a masterpiece. Molière's "Festin de Pierre" and Mozart's "Don Juan" are elaborations of

"Punch and Judy," just as "Hamlet," "Faust," and "Peer Gynt" are elaborations of popular stories. Unfortunately, a really good Adelphi melodrama is very hard to get. It should be a simple and sincere drama of action and feeling, kept well within that vast tract of passion and motive which is common to the philosopher and the laborer, relieved by plenty of fun, and depending for variety of human character, not on the high comedy idiosyncrasies which individualize people in spite of the closest similarity of age, sex, and circumstances, but on broad contrasts between types of youth and age, sympathy and selfishness, the masculine and the feminine, the serious and the frivolous, the sublime and the ridiculous, and so on. The whole character of the piece must be allegorical, idealistic, full of generalizations and moral lessons; and it must represent conduct as producing swiftly and certainly on the individual the results which in actual life it only produces on the race in the course of many centuries. All of which, obviously, requires for its accomplishment rather greater heads and surer hands than we commonly find in the service of the playhouse.

The latest Adelphi melodrama, "The Girl I Left Behind Me," is a very bad one. The only stroke in it that comes home is at the close of the second act, where the heroine sends her soldier lover, who has been accused of cowardice, off on a dangerous duty, and tells him that she loves him. The authors, I need hardly say, did not invent this situation, nor did they freshen it or add anything to it; but they at least brought it off without bungling it, and so saved the piece from the hostility of that sceptical spirit which is now growing among first-night audiences in a very marked degree. This is an inevitable reaction against the artificialities, insincerities, and im-

daughters; but still there is no good reason why they should not have moments of efficiency when nothing but routine business is in hand. Private Jones, who is cordially received by his officer when he describes, with an air of conscious merit, how he has just run away on being actually fired at by the enemy, and who calmly quits his post as sentry (at a stockade which may be surprised at any moment) to sit down beside his sleeping lady love, and is supported in that proceeding by the general against a not unnatural remonstrance from his lieutenant—Private Jones is certainly consistent; but what he is consistent with is not himself—for as an individual human being he has no credible existence—but the trained incapacity of the Adelphi audience to understand true military valor. Instead of being, as he should be in a popular melodrama, a typically good soldier, he is a mere folly of the ignorant civil imagination. There is also a medical man, an army surgeon, who makes love to a girl of sixteen by way of comic relief. He relaxed the tension of the third act very happily by a slight but astonishingly effective alteration of a single syllable in the author's text. In the agony of the siege, when all hope was gone, he sat down with heroic calmness to write two documents: one a prescription which there was no apparent means of getting compounded, and the other a farewell—I did not quite catch to whom—probably to his mother. The last touching words of this communication were prefaced by the author with the sentence, "I will add a postcript." The doctor, however, adroitly substituted, "I will add a post-card," and sent the audience, just at the moment when their feelings could bear no further harrowing, into shrieks of refreshing laughter.

The third act, by the way, is an adaptation of the Relief

of Lucknow, which, as a dramatic situation, is so strong and familiar that it is hardly possible to spoil it, though the authors have done their best. The main difficulty is the foreknowledge of the hopelessly sophisticated audience that Mr. Terriss will rush in at the last moment, sword in hand, and rescue everybody. The authors' business was to carry us on from incident to incident so convincingly and interestingly as to preoccupy us with the illusion of the situation sufficiently to put Mr. Terriss out of our heads. Messrs. Fyles and Belasco have not been equal to this. They have lamely staved off Mr. Terriss for the necessary time by a flabbily commonplace treatment of the question of killing the women to save them from the Indians, and by bringing in the Indian chief's daughter to die in the stockade at the instant when the sound of her voice would have won quarter for the garrison. This is ill contrived, and only passes because the explanation is deferred until the last act, which is so transcendently imbecile that an absurdity more or less does not matter. As to the heroine, who had to kneel in the middle of the stage and rave her way through the burial service whilst her father, the general, hopped about, pulling horrible faces, and trying to make up his mind to shoot her, she was so completely out of the question from any rational human point of view, that I think the effort to impersonate her temporarily unhinged Miss Millward's reason; for when the rescue came. and she had to wave the American flag instead of expressing her feelings naturally, she all but impaled the general on it in a frightful manner. Miss Millward and Mr. Terriss and the rest of the company must bear with my irreverent way of describing the performance. I quite appreciate their skill, which is perhaps more indispensable for non-the applause on first nights, the receptions and exit demonstrations, are silly enough: the rule ought to be silence whilst the curtain is up and as much noise as you please when it is down. But that is a matter of taste and custom rather than of police. Where the police ought to come in without mercy is in the case of offensive and disorderly remarks or exclamations shouted at the stage during the performance. One or two well chosen examples pursued to the police court would settle the matter for the next ten years.

The acting of "Delia Harding" calls for no special notice. Mr. Mackintosh, who appeared as Stanley French, was warmly received. His acting was not lacking in force; but his gesture and facial expression were grotesque and carricatured, though there was nothing in the part to give occasion for such extravagant handling.

SPANISH TRAGEDY AND ENGLISH FARCE

Mariana and *The Son of Don Juan.* By José Echegaray. Translated from the Spanish by James Graham. Two volumes of the Cameo Series. London: Fisher Unwin. 1895.

T HERE is somewhere in Froissart a record of a hardy knight who discovered, as most men do in their middle age, that "to rob and pill is a good life." When Mr. Fisher Unwin sent me "The Son of Don Juan" I began at the end, as my custom is (otherwise I seldom reach the end at all), and found the following:

"LAZARUS (*Speaking like a child, and with the face of an idiot*):
'Mother—the sun—the sun; give me the sun. For God's sake —for God's sake—for God's sake, mother, give me the sun.'"

To a person familiar with Ibsen's "Ghosts," this was sufficient to establish a warm interest in an author who, like Froissart's knight, takes his goods so boldly where he finds them. I had never heard of José Echegaray before; but I soon learnt, from Mr. Graham's sketch of his life, that he is a celebrated Spanish dramatist, and that it will be decorous for me in future to pretend to know all about him. To tell the truth, I wish I had some other authority than Mr. Graham to consult; for though I have no excuse for questioning the entire trustworthiness of the little memoir he has prefixed to "The Son of Don Juan," I can hardly bring myself to believe more than half of it. No doubt Echegaray is a greater physicist

than Newton, and a greater mathematician than De
Morgan and Professor Karl Pearson rolled into one.
Perhaps he really did walk out of a drawing-room ignorant of a word of German, and presently return a master
of that intractable tongue, and intimate with the secrets
of Hegel and all the other philosophers of the Fatherland. And why should there be any difficulty in believing in that discussion on fencing, which again made him
leave the room, only to come back so consummate a
swordsman that no professional in Madrid could as much
as keep hold of his foil when confronted with him? And
yet, somehow, I don't believe it. It is all the fault of that
unfortunate musical criticism which I practised so long
and assiduously. A musical critic gets supplied gratuitously with biographies of distinguished artists, compiled
by musical agents or other experts in fiction, and circulated to the press and to persons with whom the artist
desires to do business. These biographies seldom appear
among the books of reference in first-rate libraries. They
all contain at least two anecdotes, one to illustrate the
miraculous powers of their hero's brain, and another to
exhibit his courage and dexterity in personal combat.
Mind, I do not say these anecdotes are untrue; I simply
confess apologetically that I never find myself able to
believe them. When I receive from an agent or from a
bookseller a life of Sarasate, or Mr. Edison, or any other
celebrated person, I try to believe as much of it as I can;
and the breakdown of my faith must not be taken as a
breakdown of the celebrated person's credit. Besides,
after all, Mr. Graham's memoir of Echegaray may not
mean anything so very staggering. There is something
momentous at first sight in the statement that "the first
three years of the dramatist's life were passed in the

capital of Spain"; but now I come to think of it, the first three years of my life (and more) were passed in the capital of Ireland, which was a much harder trial. Again, the attention he gave to "the infinitesimal calculus, theoretical and applied mechanics, hydrostatics, curve tracing, descriptive geometry and its applications, solid geometry, and so on into the dimmest heights of the science," might have happened to many a university don. I remember once buying a book entitled "How to Live on Sixpence a Day," a point on which at that time circumstances compelled me to be pressingly curious. I carried out its instructions faithfully for a whole afternoon; and if ever I have an official biography issued, I shall certainly have it stated therein, in illustration of my fortitude and self-denial, that I lived for some time on sixpence a day. On the whole, I am willing to take Mr. Graham's word for it that Echegaray is, apart from his capacity as a dramatic poet, an exceptionally able man, who, after a distinguished university career, turned from the academic to the political life; attained Cabinet rank, with its Spanish inconveniences of proscription and flight at the next revolution; and in 1874, being then forty-two years of age, and in exile in Paris, took to writing plays, and found himself famous in that line by the time his political difficulties had settled themselves.

As a dramatist, I find Echegaray extremely readable. Mr. Graham has translated two of the most famous of his plays into a language of his own, consisting of words taken from the English dictionary, and placed, for the most part, in an intelligible grammatical relation to one another. I say for the most part; for here and there a sentence baffles me. For example: "The hall is approached by two or three saloons, whether in front of it, whether in converging lines, but in such fashion that they are partly visible." This is a hard saying, which I humbly pass on to the stage manager in the hope that he may be able to make more out of it than I can. Happily, the dialogue is pellucid as to its meaning, even where it is least vernacular. If Mrs. Patrick Campbell, for instance, plays Mariana (and she might do worse: it would be a far wiser choice than Juliet), I shall, if she uses Mr. Graham's translation, listen with interest to the effect on the audience of such a speech as "The sickness of the journey has not left me. I suspect that I am going to have a very violent megrim." I fear it is useless to pretend to accept Mr. Graham's work as a translation after this: it is clearly only a crib, though in some of the burning passages it rises to considerable force and eloquence. In such passages the full meaning can be gathered from the words alone; for most nations express themselves alike when they are red-hot; but in passages of comedy the word is often nothing, and the manner and idiom everything, in proof whereof I will undertake to recast any scene from, say, "The School for Scandal," in such a manner that without the least alteration of its meaning it will become duller than an average sample of the evidence in a Blue-book. Therefore, as I do not know a word of Spanish, I can only guess at the qualities which have eluded Mr. Graham's crib.

Echegaray is apparently of the school of Schiller, Victor Hugo, and Verdi—picturesque, tragic to the death, showing us the beautiful and the heroic struggling either with blind destiny or with an implacable idealism which makes vengeance and jealousy points of honor. "Mariana" is a lineal descendant of "Ruy Blas" or "Don Carlos." In "The Son of Don Juan," the modern scientific culture comes in, and replaces the "villain" of the older school, the Sallustio or Ruy Gomez, by destiny in the shape of hereditary disease. In spite of the line "Give me the sun, mother," for which Echegaray acknowledges his indebtedness to Ibsen, his treatment of the "Ghosts" theme is perfectly original: there is not in it a shadow of the peculiar moral attitude of Ibsen. Echegaray remorselessly fixes all the responsibility on Don Juan (Alving), who is as resolutely vicious as Shelley's Count Cenci. Ibsen, on the contrary, after representing Mrs. Alving as having for years imputed her late husband's vices to his own wilful dissoluteness, brings home to her the conviction that it was really she herself and her fellow Puritans who, by stamping men and women of Alving's temperament into the gutter, and imposing shame and disease on them as their natural heritage, had made the ruin into which Alving fell. Accordingly, we have those terrible scenes in which she desperately tries to reverse towards the son the conduct that was fatal to the father, plying Oswald with champagne and conniving at his intrigue with his own half-sister. There is not the slightest trace of this inculpation of respectability and virtue in "The Son of Don Juan." Indeed, had Echegaray adapted Ibsen's moral to the conditions of domestic life and public opinion in Spain, the process would have destroyed all that superficial resemblance to "Ghosts" which has led some critics hastily to describe Echegaray's play as a wholesale plagiarism. The fact that the doctor who is only mentioned in "Ghosts" actually appears on the stage in the "The Son of Don Juan" is a point, not of resemblance, but of difference; whilst the fact that Mrs. Alving and Manders have no counterparts in the Spanish play, and that the dissipated father, who does not appear in "Ghosts" at all, is practically Echegaray's hero, will make it plain to any one who has really comprehended "Ghosts" that the story has been taken on to new ground nationally, and back to old ground morally. Echegaray has also created a new set of characters. Paca, the woman of Tarifa; the poor little consumptive Carmen, betrothed to Lazarus (Oswald); Timoteo and Nemesio, the shattered old boon companions of Don Juan; Dolores, the wife of Don Juan, who is not even twentieth cousin to Mrs. Alving: all these are original creations. Echegaray makes his puppets dance ruthlessly. He writes like a strong man to whom these people are all "poor devils" whom he pities and even pets, but does not respect. This again contrasts strongly with the Norwegian feeling. Ibsen never presents his play to you as a romance for your entertainment: he says, in effect, "Here is yourself and myself, our society, our civilization. The evil and good, the horror and the hope of it, are woven out of your life and mine." There is no more of that sort of conscience about Echegaray's plays than there is about "Hernani," or, for the matter of that, "The Babes in the Wood." The woman who looks at Hedda Gabler or Mrs. Alving may be looking at herself in a mirror; but the woman who looks at Mariana is looking at another woman, a perfectly distinct and somewhat stagy personality. Consequently the howl of rage and dread that follows each stroke of Ibsen's scalpel will not rise when one of our actresses pounces on Mariana: we shall only whimper a little because our childish curiosity is not indulged in the last scene to the extent of letting us see whether Daniel kills Pablo and then himself, or whether Pablo kills Daniel. This last scene, or epilogue, as it is called, is magnificently dramatic; so much so that if some adapter will change the name of the piece from "Mariana" to "Daniel," and transfer all the lady's best speeches to the gentleman, some of our actor-managers will probably produce it as soon as they realize its existence—say in twenty years or so. Unless, indeed, the actress-manageress arrives in the meantime and snaps it up.

I can best convey a notion of the style and dramatic method of Echegaray by a couple of quotations. In both of the plays just translated, a narrative by the principal character makes an indelible impression on the imagination, and comes into action with great effect at the Climax of the tragedy. Both narratives are characteristically modern in their tragi-comedy. Here is Mariana's:

"Listen. I was eight years old. It must have been two or three o'clock in the morning. I was sleeping in my crib; and I dreamt that I was giving a great many kisses to my doll, because it had called me 'mamma.' The doll soon began to kiss me in return, but so fiercely that it caused me pain; and the doll became very large; and it was my mother. She was holding me in her arms; and I—I was not sleeping now: it was no dream: I was awake. Behind my mother there was a man standing. It was Alvarado, who was saying, 'Come.' My mother said, 'No: not without her.' And he said, 'Devil take it, then, *with* her.' The rest was like another dream—a nightmare—anything that whirls you away and will not let you breathe. My mother dressed me as people dress lunatics or dolls, pulling me about, shaking me, nearly beating me. And Alvarado was all the time hurrying her with whispers of 'Quick, quick, make haste.' I have never gone through anything like it: trivial—ludicrous as it was, it was horrible. She could not get the little socks rightly on me; she could not manage to button my boots;

my drawers were put on the wrong way, the petticoats left with the opening at the side, my dress half loose, though I kept saying, 'It wants to be fastened: it should be fastened.' And all the time Alvarado was saying, 'Quick, quick: make haste, make haste.' I was wound up in a cloak of my mother's; and a hat ribbon was tied round my head so that it nearly choked me. Then my mother snatched me up in her arms; and we got into a carriage and went very fast. Then I heard a kiss; and I thought, 'My God, who was that for, who was that for: nobody has kissed me.' Ah, my own mother, my own mother!"

At the end of the play, Daniel, Mariana's lover, in persuading her to elope, picks up her cloak, and by trying to wrap her in it and carry her out to the carriage, reminds her of this passage in her childhood, and of Alvarado, whose son Daniel is. She calls in her husband, who kills her; and the two men disappear to fight it out to the death in the garden as the curtain falls.

Don Juan's narrative is an instance of the same dramatic device.

"It was a grand night—a grand supper. There were eight of us—each with a partner. Everybody was drunk—even the Guadalquiver. Aniceta went out on the balcony and began to cry out, 'Stupid, insipid, waterish river: drink wine for once,' and threw a bottle of Manzanilla into it. Well, I was lying asleep along the floor, upon the carpet, close to a divan. And on the divan there had fallen, by one of the usual accidents, the Tarifena—Paca the Tarifena. She was asleep; and in her tossings to and fro her hair had become loose—a huge mass; and it fell over me in silky waves—a great quantity, enfolding me as in a splendid black mantle of perfumed lace.

The dawn arrived—a delightful morning, the balcony open, the East with splendid curtains of mist and with little red clouds; the sky blue and stainless; a light more vivid kindling into flame the distant horizon. Slowly the crimson globe ascended. I opened my eyes wide; and I saw the sun, I saw it from between the interlaced tresses of the Tarifena. It inundated me with light; and I stretched forth my hand instinctively to grasp it. Something of a new kind of love—a new desire—agitated me; great brightness, much azure, very broad spheres, vague yet burning aspirations for something very beautiful. For a minute I understood that there is something higher than the pleasures of the senses: for a minute I felt myself another being. I wafted a kiss to the sun, and angrily pulled aside the girl's hair. One lock clung about my lips: it touched my palate and gave me nausea. I flung away the tress; I awoke the Tarifena; and vice dawned through the remains of the orgie, like the sun through the vapors of the night, its mists, and its fire-colored clouds."

I need only add that Don Juan is on the stage at the end of the play when the heir to his debauchery says, "Give me the sun, mother." On the whole, though I am afraid some of our critics will be as nauseated as Don Juan was by that stray lock of the Tarifena's hair, I suspect the Spaniards will compel us to admit that they have produced a genius of a stamp that crosses frontiers, and that we shall yet see some of his work on our own stage.

companiment improvised by himself on an old harp-
sichord, and, above all—for here his glee attained its
climax—inadvertently pulling a large assortment of
stolen handkerchiefs out of his pocket whilst explaining
matters to the police officer, and clinching his account
by throwing one into his hat, which, having no crown,
allowed it to fall through to the floor. This alternation
of the grotesque, the impish, the farcical, with the serious
and exalted, is characteristic of the nineteenth century.
Goethe anticipated it in his Faust and Mephistopheles,
obviously two sides of the same character; and it was
in the foolish travesty of "Faust" perpetrated by Wills
that Mr. Irving found a part in which he could be melodramatic actor, mocker, and buffoon all in one evening.
Since then he has had a trying time of it. Becket on top
of Wolsey was enough to provoke a graver man to go
Fantee; and Lear followed Becket. But when King Arthur capped Lear, all of us who knew Mr. Irving's constitution felt that a terrific reaction must be imminent.
It has come in the shape of Don Quixote, in which he
makes his own dignity ridiculous to his heart's content.
He rides a slim white horse, made up as Rozinante with
painted hollows just as a face is made up; he has a set
of imitation geese waggling on springs to mistake for
swans; he tumbles about the stage with his legs in the
air; and he has a single combat, on refreshingly inde-
corous provocation, with a pump. And he is perfectly
happy. I am the last person in the world to object; for
I, too, have something of that aboriginal need for an
occasional carnival in me. When he came before the
curtain at the end, he informed us, with transparent good
faith, that the little play practically covered the whole of
Cervantes' novel, a statement which we listened to with

respectful stupefaction. I get into trouble often enough by my ignorance of authors whom every literate person is expected to have at his fingers' ends; but I believe Mr. Irving can beat me hollow in that respect. If I have not read Don Quixote all through, I have at least looked at the pictures; and I am prepared to swear that Mr. Irving never got beyond the second chapter.

Any one who consults recent visitors to the Lyceum, or who seeks for information in the Press as to the merits of Mr. Conan Doyle's "Story of Waterloo," will in nineteen cases out of twenty learn that the piece is a trifle raised into importance by the marvelous acting of Mr. Irving as Corporal Gregory Brewster. As a matter of fact, the entire effect is contrived by the author, and is due to him alone. There is absolutely no acting in it—none whatever. There is a make-up in it, and a little cheap and simple mimicry which Mr. Irving does indifferently because he is neither apt nor observant as a mimic of doddering old men, and because his finely cultivated voice and diction again and again rebel against the indignity of the Corporal's squeakings and mumblings and vulgarities of pronunciation. But all the rest is an illusion produced by the machinery of "a good acting play," by which is always meant a play that requires from the performers no qualifications beyond a plausible appearance and a little experience and address in stage business. I had better make this clear by explaining the process of doing without acting as exemplified by "A Story of Waterloo," in which Mr. Conan Doyle has carried the art of constructing an "acting" play to such an extreme that I almost suspect him of satirically revenging himself, as a literary man, on a profession which has such a dread of "literary plays." (A "literary play," I should

of the oil of youth. We feel that we could watch him sitting down for ever. Hark! a band in the street without. Soldiers pass: the old warhorse snorts feebly, but complains that bands don't play so loud as they used to. The band being duly exploited for all it is worth, the Bible comes into play. What he likes in it are the campaigns of Joshua and the battle of Armageddon, which the poor dear old thing can hardly pronounce, though he had it from "our clergyman." How sweet of the clergyman to humor him! Blessings on his kindly face and on his silver hair! Mr. Fuller Mellish comes back with the breech-loading carbine. The old man handles it; calls it a firelock; and goes crazily through his manual with it. Finally, he unlocks the breech, and as the barrel drops, believes that he has broken the weapon in two. Matters being explained, he expresses his unalterable conviction that England will have to fall back on Brown Bess when the moment for action arrives again. He takes out his pipe. It falls and is broken. He whimpers, and is petted and consoled by a present of the sergeant's beautiful pipe with "a hamber mouthpiece." Mr. Fuller Mellish, becoming again superfluous, is again got rid of. Enter a haughty gentleman. It is the Colonel of the Royal Scots Guards, the corporal's old regiment. According to the well-known custom of colonels, he has called on the old pensioner to give him a five-pound note. The old man, as if electrically shocked, staggers up and desperately tries to stand for a moment at "attention" and salute his officer. He collapses, almost slain by the effort, into his chair, mumbling pathetically that he "were a'most gone that time, Colonel." "A masterstroke! who but a great actor could have executed this heart-searching movement?" The veteran returns to the fireside: once more he depicts with convincing art the state of an old man's joints. The Colonel goes; Mr. Fuller Mellish comes; the old man dozes. Suddenly he springs up. "The Guards want powder; and, by God, the Guards shall have it." With these words he falls back in his chair. Mr. Fuller Mellish, lest there should be any mistake about it (it is never safe to trust the intelligence of the British public), delicately informs Miss Hughes that her granduncle is dead. The curtain falls amid thunders of applause.

Every old actor into whose hands this article falls will understand perfectly from my description how the whole thing is done, and will wish that he could get such Press notices for a little hobbling and piping, and a few bits of mechanical business with a pipe, a carbine, and two chairs. The whole performance does not involve one gesture, one line, one thought outside the commonest routine of automatic stage illusion. What, I wonder, must Mr. Irving, who of course knows this better than any one else, feel when he finds this pitiful little handful of hackneyed stage tricks received exactly as if it were a crowning instance of his most difficult and finest art? No doubt he expected and intended that the public, on being touched and pleased by machinery, should imagine that they were being touched and pleased by acting. But the critics! What can he think of the analytic powers of those of us who, when an organized and successful attack is made on our emotions, are unable to discriminate between the execution done by the actor's art and that done by Mr. Conan Doyle's ingenious exploitation of the ready-made pathos of old age, the ignorant and maudlin sentiment attaching to the army and "the Dook," and the vulgar conception of the battle of

Waterloo as a stand-up street fight between an Englishman and a Frenchman, a conception infinitely less respectable than that which led Byron to exclaim, when he heard of Napoleon's defeat, "I'm damned sorry"?

The first item in the Lyceum triple bill is Mr. Pinero's "Bygones," in which Mr. Sydney Valentine, as Professor Mazzoni, acts with notable skill and judgment. Mr. Pinero used to play the part himself; but he was bitten then, like every one else at that time, with the notion that "character acting," especially in parts that admitted of a foreign accent, was the perfection of stage art; and his Mazzoni was accordingly worse than anyone could believe without having seen it. Matters were made worse by the detestable and irredeemable scene in which the old man proposes marriage to the girl. Mazzoni might excusably offer her, as a means of escape from her humiliating predicament, the position of his wife, and his friendly affection and fatherly care until he left her a widow; and he might make this offer being secretly in love with her, and so preserve the pathos of his subsequent disappointment. But to propose a serious love match to her as he does seems to me abominable: the scene makes my flesh creep: it always did. Mr. Valentine could not reconcile me to it; nor should I have thanked him if he had; but he softened it as far as it could be softened; and his final leavetaking, with its effect of sparing us the exhibition of a grief which he nevertheless made us feel keenly behind that last sincere and kindly smile, was a fine stroke of art. He here, as elsewhere in the play, showed himself able to do with a few light and sure touches what most of our actors vainly struggle with by publicly wallowing in self-pity for minutes at a stretch.

I hope I have not conveyed an impression that the

triple bill makes a bad evening's entertainment. Though it is my steady purpose to do what I can to drive such sketches as "A Story of Waterloo," with their ready-made feeling and prearranged effects, away to the music-hall, which is their proper place now that we no longer have a "Gallery of Illustration," I enjoy them, and am entirely in favor of their multiplication so long as it is understood that they are not the business of fine actors and first-class theatres. And, abortive as "Don Quixote" is, there are moments in it when Wills vanishes, and we have Cervantes as the author and Mr. Irving as the actor—no cheap combination. Apart from the merits of the three plays, I suggest that it is a mistake—easily avoidable by a manager with Mr. Irving's resources at his disposal— to cast Miss Annie Hughes and Mr. Webster for parts in two different pieces. I half expected to see Miss Hughes again in the third play; but Mr. Irving drew the line there, and entrusted the leading young lady's part in "Don Quixote" to Miss de Silva. In "Bygones," Miss Ailsa Craig succeeds in giving a touch of interest to the part of the ill-conditioned servant who works the plot. Miss Hughes grows younger and prettier, and acts better, continually; only her voice still slyly contradicts her efforts to be pathetic, which are in all other respects credible and graceful enough.

THE TWO LATEST COMEDIES

The Home Secretary: an original modern play. By
R. C. Carton. Criterion Theatre, 7 May, 1895.

*The Triumph of the Philistines, and how Mr. Jorgan
preserved the morals of Market Pewbury under very
trying circumstances:* an original comedy in three
acts. By Henry Arthur Jones. St. James's Theatre,
11 May, 1895.

I MUST not stop to make an exordium before dealing
with Mr. Carton's play, for, to tell the truth, I am
forgetting it so rapidly that in another half-hour it
may all have escaped me. I must in fairness add that I
did not see it very well, because, though there are only
two pillars in the Criterion theatre that you cannot see
round, and consequently only two stalls from which the
stage is not visible, I was placed in one of those two stalls.
That is the worst of having a reputation as a critic of
acting. They place you behind an obstacle which prevents you from seeing more than one person at a time,
calculating that since you will always keep your eye on
the actor-manager, your attention will be concentrated on
him by the impossibility of your seeing any one else. This
time, however, Mr. Wyndham had nothing particular to
show me. There was no character for him to create,
and consequently nothing for him to do that was more
than the merest routine for an actor of his accomplishment. Though supposed to be a Home Secretary, he
presented us with exactly the sort of Cabinet Minister
who never goes to the Home Office. I fancy he has
formed his political style on the Foreign Office, or the
Colonial Office, perhaps even on the Duchy of Lancaster,

and is under the erroneous impression that the same sort of thing would do for the comparatively popular Home Office. But at all events, Mr. Wyndham knows more about Home Secretaries than Mr. Carton: in fact, he could not possibly know less. Mr. Carton has a second-hand imagination and a staggering indifference to verisimilitude. Inspired by Miss Neilson's appearance in the play of "An Ideal Husband" as the beautiful wife who is too truthful to approve of all the official utterances of the Cabinet Minister whom she has rashly married, he shoots Miss Neilson on to the stage in that relation to Mr. Wyndham, with nothing better to account for her domestic unhappiness than the articles in the Opposition papers. Imagine Mrs. Asquith's domestic peace being shattered by an article in the *St. James's Gazette!* The rest of the play is of less recent origin; but one need go no further back than "The House in the Marsh," or "Captain Swift," in tracing the descent of Dangerfield, the Anarchist. Anything more wantonly nonsensical than the way in which Mr. Carton rearranges the facts of English society and politics so as to represent Dangerfield as being engaged in a deadly duel of the Pompey and Cæsar kind with the Home Secretary, would be hard to cite. As to all the stuff about mighty secret brotherhoods, and abysses of revolution opening at the feet of society, I invite Mr. Carton to manufacture his plays in future out of some less mischievous kind of absurdity.

Apart from this serious bearing of the play on life, it is amusing enough to hear Mr. Lewis Waller at a West-end theatre spouting the stalest commonplaces of the Socialist platforms with the full approval of the audience. No fashionable dramatist's library will henceforth be complete without a copy of Mr. Hyndman's "England for

All." Mr. Brookfield contributes one of those little imitations of social types of which he is fond. They are amusing; and they fulfil two indispensable conditions: to wit, they impress the public as being all different from one another, thereby creating a high estimate of Mr. Brookfield's skill and versatility; and they are all exactly alike, so that the public has only one taste to acquire for them. Miss Julia Neilson plays very much better than in "An Ideal Husband." In that comedy she made the worst of a good part: in this, she made the best of an indifferent one, though it was hard on her to have to sit down and examine her mind and conscience very slowly just when the audience had finally made up their minds that Mr. Carton had fashioned her perfectly hollow. In fact, the less interesting both the Home Secretary and his wife became, the more slowly Mr. Wyndham and Miss Neilson had to play, in order to make the final scene at least mechanically impressive. The effect was a little trying. The comedy scenes, which are laughable enough, were child's play to Miss Mary Moore, Miss Maud Millet, Mr. de Lange, and Mr. Alfred Bishop; and Mr. Lewis Waller would hardly thank me for compliments on a performance so easily within his powers as the impersonation of Captain Swift Dangerfield. Mr. Sidney Brough's part enabled him to show that rare quality of his of being at the same time a very "useful" actor and a very attractive one. On the whole, "The Home Secretary" is a well acted, well staged, occasionally entertaining, and hopelessly slovenly play.

Mr. Henry Arthur Jones's comedy with the nineteen-word title, affords material for the social essayist rather than the dramatic critic, being avowedly an object-lesson in British lower middle-class hypocrisy. And the attack is not the usual sham attack of the stage moralist: it is courageous, uncompromising, made with sharp weapons, and left without the slightest attempt to run away at the end. When Mr. Jones appeared before the curtain several persons howled piteously, like dogs who had been purposely run over. Every play which is a criticism of contemporary life, must, if it is an honest play, involve a certain struggle with the public. Accordingly, Mr. Jones was not so unanimously applauded when the curtain fell on poor Mr. Jorgan's very mixed "triumph" as Mr. Pinero was after Mrs. Ebbsmith pulled the Bible out of the fire. But his courage was respected; and there, I think, he had the advantage of Mr. Pinero.

There is a sense in which Mr. Jones's plays are far more faulty than those of most of his competitors, exactly as a row of men is more faulty than a row of lampposts turned out by a first-rate firm. His qualities are creative imagination, curious observation, inventive humor, originality, sympathy, and sincerity; and the risks of trusting to these are, like the rewards, very great. It is safer and cheaper to depend on the taste, judgment, instinct for fashion and knowledge of the stage and the public, by which plays can be constructed out of ready-made materials, and guaranteed to pass an evening safely and smoothly, instead of, like the real live work of Mr. Jones, rousing all sorts of protests and jarring all sorts of prejudices, besides disgusting the professorial critics and amateurs by its impenitent informality. And then, Mr. Jones, following in the footsteps of Dickens, plays every sort of extravagant and fanciful trick with his characters, inventing insane names for them, making them express themselves in the most impossible way, and sometimes exasperating dull and literal people beyond all bounds. Thus, in "The Triumph of the Philistines," we have such a freak as Thomas Blagg, the butcher's boy, clearly of the family of Trabb's boy, of immortal memory; and with him are a Pumblechookian band of local tradesmen, who are not humanity simple and direct, but humanity made fun of. Still, if the details are outrageous, the general effect is mostly right; for Mr. Jones knows his Market Pewbury well enough to joke with it. On the subject of Art I find him less convincing. His identification of it with the sort of Epicurean philosophy which is always at daggers drawn with Puritanism is roughly true to life—sufficiently so, at all events, for dramatic purposes. But his identification of Puritanism with Philistinism seems to me to be a fundamental confusion. A Philistine is a prosaic person whose artistic consciousness is unawakened and who has no ideals. A Puritan is no doubt often at the same disadvantage as the Philistine in respect of his insensibility to Art; but he is a fanatical idealist, to whom all stimulations of the sense of beauty are abhorrent; because he is only conscious of them in so far as they appeal to his sex instinct, which he regards as his great enemy. However, it is not this point that Mr. Jones has missed; for his Mr. Jorgan, though called a Philistine, corresponds exactly to a Puritan. Even when Sir Valentine Fellowes, a thorough Philistine, is put in opposition to the Philistines and in sympathy with Willie Hesslewood the painter, he remains nevertheless as lifelike a Philistine as Mr. Jorgan is a Puritan; so that one is tempted to ask whether it matters what the twain are called, since the author's method of working upon life instead of upon theories of society and canons of art seems sure to save him from anything worse than a confusion of names. But thought has its empire after all; and when Mr. Jones claims the sympathy of the audience for the Philistine as against the Puritan, the Puritan snatches the sympathy from him; for the idealist, being the higher if more dangerous animal, always does beat the Philistine. A picture of Bacchante is exhibited on the stage, with its back to the audience, an arrangement which gives it away from the beginning as not fit to be seen. Mr. Jorgan the Puritan, having no artistic sense, denounces the artist as a mere pandar, and the picture as an artifice to make men more sensual. Sir Valentine's defense is in effect "Why not? Life would not be worth living unless people are allowed to sow a few wild oats, as I do occasionally; and if you interfere with my pleasures I'll spend my income on the Continent instead of in your shops." Mr. Jones's instinct for character led him rightly to make Sir Valentine take that line. But what chance is there of the audience taking his side? They must feel, as I feel, that the Puritan's attitude is more respectable than the Philistine's. If Art were really a matter of Bacchante pictures painted by amorous young artists from rapscallionly little models, to be defended only by easy-going men of pleasure and cynical old society ladies who regard men as incurable voluptuaries, then surely we should all say Amen to Mr. Skewett's "Burn it, I say. Burn it; and have done with the iniquity." The fact is, Mr. Jones, revelling in his characters and scenes and dialogues, and keen on the scent of the narrowness and hyprocisy of Market Pewbury, has not got up his case thoroughly; and the result is that the plan of action which he has invented, with its studio machinery and its substitution of a picture for a question of conduct, does not strike one as being quite the right plan; whilst Market Pewbury is left, after all, with the best of the argument.

The acting is hardly as good as the play. Mr. Alexander's comedy is too smart: Sir Valentine is never really distressed or at a loss, as he certainly ought to be at the end of the second act. Mr. Waring, as Jorgan, is admirable in action; but before he gets to work, it is plain that the part does not naturally fit him. Mr. Esmond's Willie Hesslewood is perhaps the most entirely successful of all the impersonations involved, except Miss Juliette Nesville's immense, irresistible Sally Lebrune. Mr. Jones has carried out the idea of this character to a hair's breadth; and the disadvantage at which the young woman's entire and perfect worthlessness puts all the more respectable characters is of the essence of comedy. Lady Monckton's work is less interesting to the audience than technically important to the play; and only the expert can be expected to appreciate how very well she does it. Miss Elliott Page was quite ladylike and natural as Alma Suleny; but I am afraid the only thanks she got for not overdressing herself and forcing the significance of every sentence was a sense that she was underacting. She certainly added nothing to her part, an omission which would be rather serious in some plays, since nothing plus nothing equals nothing; but it did not matter with Mr. Jones as the author. The half-dozen little sallies of character-acting which filled up the stage with the Puritans of Market Pewbury were, of course, easily and amusingly done; but they were too funny and too intentional to be convincing, and the total effect was only made creditable by the acting of Mr. Waring.

A NEW LADY MACBETH AND A NEW MRS. EBBSMITH

25 May, 1895.

LAST Saturday evening found me lurking, an uninvited guest, in an obscure corner of the Garrick Theatre, giving Mrs. Ebbsmith another trial in the person of Miss Olga Nethersole. This time I carefully regulated the dose, coming late for the preliminary explanations, and hurrying home at the end of the second act, when Mrs. Ebbsmith had put her fine dress on, and was beginning to work up towards the stove. I cannot say I enjoyed myself very much; for the play bored me more than ever; but I perceived better than I did before that the fault was not altogether Mr. Pinero's. The interest of the first act depends on Mrs. Thorpe really affecting and interesting her audience in her scene with Agnes. Miss Ellis Jeffreys fails to do this. I do not blame her, just as I should not blame Mr. Charles Hawtrey if he were cast for the ghost in Hamlet and played it somewhat disappointingly. On the contrary, I congratulate her on her hopeless incapacity to persuade us that she is the victim of an unhappy marriage, or that she lives in a dreary country rectory where she walks about like a ghost about her dead child's room in the intervals of housekeeping for her parson brother. She has obviously not a scrap of anything of the kind in her whole disposition; and that Mr. Pinero should have cast her for such business in a part on which his whole first act and a good deal of the rest of the play depends, suggests that his experience of the impossibility of getting all his characters fitted in a metropolis which has more theatres than companies is making him reckless. The impression left is that the scene between Agnes and Mrs. Thorpe is tedious and colorless, and that between Agnes and the Duke biting and full of character. But really one scene is as good as the other; only Mr. Hare's Duke of St. Olpherts is a consummate piece of acting, whilst Miss Jeffreys' Mrs. Thorpe is at best a graceful evasion of an impossible task. This was less noticeable before, because Mrs. Patrick Campbell counted for so much in both scenes that the second factor in them mattered less. With Miss Nethersole, who failed to touch the character of Agnes at any point as far as I witnessed her performance, it mattered a great deal. I have no doubt that Miss Nethersole pulled the Bible out of the stove, and played all the "emotional" scenes as well as Mrs. Campbell or any one else could play them; but certainly in the first two acts, where Mrs. Ebbsmith, not yet reduced to a mere phase of hysteria, is a self-possessed individual character, Miss Nethersole gave us nothing but the stage fashion of the day in a very accentuated and conscious manner. Mrs. Campbell's extraordinary power of doing anything surely and swiftly with her hands whilst she is acting, preoccupation seeming an embarrassment unknown to her, is a personal peculiarity which cannot reasonably be demanded from her competitors. But Miss Nethersole seems to set a positive value on such preoccupation. When she pretends to darn a stocking she brings it down to the footlights, and poses in profile with the stockinged hand raised above the level of her head. She touches nothing without first poising her hand above it like a bird about to alight, or a pianist's fingers descending on a chord. She cannot even take up the box containing the rich dress to bundle it off into the next room, without disposing her hands round it with an unmistakable reference to the conventional laws of grace. The effect in these first two acts, throughout which Mrs. Ebbsmith is supposed to be setting Lucas Cleeve's teeth on edge at every turn by her businesslike ways, plain dress, and impatience of the effects that charm the voluptuary, may be imagined. The change of dress, with which Mrs. Campbell achieved such a very startling effect, produced hardly any with Miss Nethersole, and would have produced none but for the dialogue; for Mrs. Ebbsmith had been so obviously concerned all through with the effect of her attitudes, that one quite expected that she would not neglect herself when it came to dressing for dinner. The "Trafalgar Squaring" of the Duke, a complete success on Mr. Hare's part, was a complete failure on Miss Nethersole's. Mrs. Campbell caught the right platform tone of political invective and contemptuous social criticism to perfection: Miss Nethersole made the speech an emotional outburst, flying out at the Duke exactly as, in a melodrama, she would have flown out at the villain who had betrayed her. My inference is that Miss Nethersole has force and emotion without sense of character. With force and emotion, and an interesting and plastic person, one can play "the heroine" under a hundred different names with entire success. But the individualized heroine is another matter; and that is where Mrs. Patrick Campbell comes in.

It is usual to describe Mr. Hare as an actor who does not do himself justice on first nights because he is nervous. His Duke of St. Olpherts is certainly not an instance of this. It is still capital; but compared to his superb performance on the first night, it is minced in diction and almost off-hand in deportment. I have come

admirer of the Elizabethan school. When Mr. Henry Arthur Jones, whose collected essays on the English drama I am now engaged in reading, says: "Surely the crowning glory of our nation is our Shakespeare; and remember he was one of the great school," I almost burst with the intensity of my repudiation of the second clause in that utterance. What Shakespeare got from his "school" was the insane and hideous rhetoric which is all that he has in common with Jonson, Webster, and the whole crew of insufferable bunglers and dullards whose work stands out as vile even at the beginning of the seventeenth century, when every art was corrupted to the marrow by the orgie called the Renaissance, which was nothing but the vulgar exploitation in the artistic professions of the territory won by the Protestant movement. The leaders of that great self-assertion of the growing spirit of man were dead long before the Elizabethan literary rabble became conscious that "ideas" were in fashion, and that any author who could gather a cheap stock of them from murder, lust and obscenity, and formulate them in rhetorical blank verse, might make the stage pestiferous with plays that have no ray of noble feeling, no touch of faith, beauty, or even common kindness in them from beginning to end. I really cannot keep my temper over the Elizabethan dramatists and the Renaissance; nor would I if I could. The generation which admired them equally admired the pictures of Guido, Giulio Romano, Domenichino, and the Carracci; and I trust it is not nowadays necessary to offer any further samples of its folly. A masterpiece by Carracci— say the smirking Susanna in the National Gallery—would not fetch seven pounds ten at Christie's to-day; but our literary men, always fifty years behind their time because they never look at anything nor listen to anything, but go on working up what they learnt in their boyhood when they read books instead of writing them, still serve up Charles Lamb's hobby, and please themselves by observing that Cyril Tourneur could turn out pretty pairs of lines and string them monotonously together, or that Greene had a genuine groatsworth of popular wit, or that Marlowe, who was perhaps good enough to make it possible to believe that if he had been born thirty years ago he might now have been a tolerable imitator of Mr. Rudyard Kipling, dealt in a single special quality of "mighty line." On the strength of these discoveries, they keep up the tradition that these men were slightly inferior Shakespeares. Beaumont and Fletcher are, indeed, sometimes cited as hardly inferior; but I will not go into that. I could not do justice to it in moderate language.

As to this performance of "Macbeth" at St. George's Hall, of course it was, from the ordinary professional standpoint, a very bad one. I say this because I well know what happens to a critic when he incautiously praises an amateur. He gets by the next post a letter in the following terms: "Dear Sir,—I am perhaps transgressing the bounds of etiquette in writing privately to you; but I thought you might like to know that your kind notice of my performance as Guildenstern has encouraged me to take a step which I have long been meditating. I have resigned my position as Governor of the Bank of England with a view to adopting the stage as a profession, and trust that the result may justify your too favorable opinion of my humble powers." Therefore I desire it to be distinctly understood that I do not recommend any member of the "Macbeth" cast to go on the stage. The three witches, Miss Florence Bourne, Miss Longvil, and

Miss Munro, were as good as any three witches I ever saw; but the impersonation of witches, as a profession, is almost as precarious as the provision of smoked glasses for looking at eclipses through. Macduff was bad: I am not sure that with his natural advantages he could very easily have been worse; but still, if he feels himself driven to some artistic career by a radical aversion to earning an honest livelihood, and is prepared for a hard apprenticeship of twenty years in mastering the art of the stage —for that period still holds as good as when Talma prescribed it—he can become an actor if he likes. As to Lady Macbeth, she, too, was bad; but it is clear to me that unless she at once resolutely marries some rich gentleman who disapproves of the theatre on principle, she will not be able to keep herself off the stage. She is as handsome as Miss Neilson; and she can hold an audience whilst she is doing everything wrongly. The murder scene was not very good, because Macbeth belonged to the school of the Irish fiddler who, when Ole Bull asked him whether he played by ear or from notes, replied that he played "by main strength"; and you cannot get the brooding horror of the dagger scene by that method. Besides, Miss Lillah McCarthy—that is the lady's name as given in my programme—is happily too young to conceive ambition and murder, or the temptation of a husband with a sickly conscience, as realities: they are to her delicious excitements of the imagination, with a beautiful, splendid terror about them, to be conveyed by strenuous pose, and flashing eye, and indomitable bearing. She went at them bravely in this spirit; and they came off more or less happily as her instinct and courage helped her, or her skill failed her. The banquet scene and the sleep-walking scene, which are the easiest passages in the part technically to a lady with the requisite pluck and personal fascination, were quite successful; and if the earlier scenes were immature, unskilful, and entirely artificial and rhetorical in their conception, still, they were very nearly thrilling. In short, I should like to see Miss Lillah McCarthy play again. I venture on the responsibility of saying that her Lady Macbeth was a highly promising performance, and that some years of hard work would make her a valuable recruit to the London stage. And with that very rash remark I will leave "Macbeth," with a fervent wish that Mr. Pinero, Mr. Grundy, and Monsieur Sardou could be persuaded to learn from it how to write a play without wasting the first hour of the performance in tediously explaining its "construction." They really are mistaken in supposing that Scribe was cleverer than Shakespeare.

SARDOODLEDOM

Fedora (Herman Merivale's English version). By Victorien Sardou. Haymarket Theatre, 25 May, 1895.
Gismonda. By Victorien Sardou. Daly's Theatre, 27 May, 1895.

U P TO this day week I had preserved my innocence as a playgoer sufficiently never to have seen "Fedora." Of course I was not altogether new to it, since I had seen Diplomacy Dora, and Theodora, and La Toscadora, and other machine dolls from the same firm. And yet the thing took me aback. To see that curtain go up again and again only to disclose a bewildering profusion of everything that has no business in a play, was an experience for which nothing could quite prepare me. The postal arrangements, the telegraphic arrangements, the police arrangements, the names and addresses, the hours and seasons, the tables of consanguinity, the railway and shipping time-tables, the arrivals and departures, the whole welter of Bradshaw and Baedeker, Court Guide and Post Office Directory, whirling round one incredible little stage murder and finally vanishing in a gulp of impossible stage poison, made up an entertainment too Bedlamite for any man with settled wits to preconceive. Even the murder was arranged, in pure wantonness, flatly contrary to common sense. The hero is suspected by the heroine of having been a. Nihilist at a period when matters were so bad in Russia that refugees who made no secret of their sympathy with the Terrorists were sympathetically welcomed by the strictest Constitutionalists in every other country in Europe. He completely regains her sympathy by proving to her that he is no Nihilist at all, but a common assassin who has deliberately murdered a man out of jealousy. Surely, if dramatists are bent on the fundamentally impossible task of inventing pardonable assassinations, they should recognize that the man who, for no reward or satisfaction to his direct personal instincts, but at the risk of his own life, kills for the sake of an idea, believing that he is striking in the cause of the general weal, is at any rate more respectable than the dehumanized creature who stabs or shoots to slake a passion which he has in common with a stag. I strongly object to heroic criminals, whether political or personal; but if the stage cannot yet get on without its illustrated police news, let us at least shun the most repulsive motives for the stage crimes we are expected to condone. This Loris Ipanoff is a vulgar scoundrel as far as he is credibly human at all; and Fedora, who has at first the excuse of being the avenger of blood, sinks to his level when, on learning that her husband preferred another woman to her, she gloats over his murder, and is disappointed because Loris did not kill his wife on the spot, too. Why need plays be so brutally, callously, barbarously immoral as this? I wish Sir Henry Irving would give us at least a matinée of "The Lady from the Sea" to show the playgoing public how a humane gentleman acts when he finds he has had the misfortune to lose the affection of his wife. Miss Terry as Ellida would be quite as worthy of the Lyceum Theatre as Nance Oldfield as Miss Terry.

It is greatly to Mrs. Patrick Campbell's credit that, bad as the play was, her acting was worse. It was a masterpiece of failure. Not, pray observe, that Mrs. Campbell herself did not succeed. The moment she was seen, our reason collapsed and our judgment fled. Every time the curtain fell there was a delirious roar. If the play was not tragic, our infatuation was. I solemnly warn all and sundry that no common man's opinion of the artistic merits of that performance was worth a farthing after the first flash of the heroine's eyes. It was not Fedora; but it was Circe; and I, as sworn critic, must make the best attempt I can to be Ulysses.

It cannot, I think, be disputed now that Mrs. Campbell's force, which is intense enough, has only one mode, and that one the vituperative. This was proved at one stroke in the first act, when Fedora goes to her husband's bedside and discovers him dead. Mrs. Campbell uttered a shriek, as any actress would; but it was a shriek that suggested nothing of grief, or mortally wounded tenderness, or even horror. What it did suggest very strongly was that Fedora had surprised the secret which Loris reveals to her in the third act. In short, it was a scream of rage. Again, in the second act, when Loris admitted the killing of Vladimir, her cry of "Murderer, assassin," might have been any abusive term hurled at a man, appropriately or not, under an impulse of violent anger. Last week I politely attributed to Mrs. Campbell's sense of character her catching, as Mrs. Ebbsmith, what Miss Nethersole misses: namely, the tone of invective in "Trafalgar Squaring" the Duke of St. Olpherts. But it now appears that her emotion declines to take any other form than that of invective. When she is not abusing somebody, she sits visibly concentrating her forces to restrain the vituperative pressure which is struggling to expand in reckless aggression, the general effect being that of a magnificent woman with a magnificent temper, which she holds in or lets loose with exciting uncertainty. This of course means that Mrs. Campbell is not yet mistress of her art, though she has a rare equipment for it. Even her diction is technically defective. In order to secure refinement of tone, she articulates with the tip of her tongue against her front teeth as much as possible. This enters for what it is worth and no more into the method of every fine speaker; but it should not suggest the snobbish Irishman who uses it as a cheap recipe for speaking genteel English; and once or twice Mrs. Campbell came dangerously near to producing this mincing effect. For instance, "One absorbing thought which meeks a sleeve of me," is clearly not the excess of a genuine refinement of diction, like Sir Henry Irving's pure vowel method, which would lead him to say "One ap-sorbing thot which mèks a slèv of me" (the p in absorbing being a German b, and the italic letters pronounced as in the French *fidèle*). I am only moderately pedantic in this matter, and do not object at all to Mrs. Campbell's saying "Forgimme" for "Forgive me," or the traditional and ugly "Be't so" for the correct and pretty "Be it so"; but I protest against "hatrid" and "disseived," which are pure inaccuracies produced by that Irish recipe. I make no apology for going into these details; for stage usage is one of our few standards of diction; and it is rather alarming to hear the extent to which our younger actresses are left to pick up the stage trick of speech without in the least understanding the phonetic part of it.

The death scene begins like a feeble drawing-room plagiarism of the murder of Nancy by Bill Sykes, and ends with the Gilbertian absurdity of the woman, as she realizes with disgust that her husband actually proposes to commit the vulgarity of strangling her, rising with a dignity which paralyzes him, and saying, "Oh, if you are determined to behave in that way, I will poison myself like a lady; and you, I hope, will look on quietly like a gentleman," or words to that effect. Here Mrs. Campbell did for a moment produce the effect which Sardou has so tediously and laboriously lath-and-plastered up, and produce it in a way which showed unmistakably that she is quite capable of the modern equivalents of the whole Bernhardtian range of sensational effects—effects so enormously popular and lucrative that, though their production is hardly more of a fine art than lion-taming, few women who are able for them can resist the temptation to devote their lives to them. At every other point, Mrs. Campbell threw Sardou out of the window and substituted her own personal magnetism for the stale mechanical tragedy of Fedora. It was irrelevant; but it was effective.

Sardou's latest edition of the Kiralfian entertainment which Madame Bernhardt has for years past dragged from sea to sea in her Armada of transports, is called "Gismonda," and is surpassingly dreary, although it is happily relieved four times by very long waits between the acts. The scene being laid in the Middle Ages, there are no newspapers, letters, or telegrams; but this is far from being an advantage, as the characters tell each other the news all through except when a child is dropped into a tiger's cage as a cue for Madame Bernhardt's popular scream; or when the inevitable stale, puerile love scene is turned on to show off that "voix celeste" stop which Madame Bernhardt, like a sentimental New England villager with an American organ, keeps always pulled out; or when, in a paroxysm of the basest sensationalism, we are treated to the spectacle of Gismonda chopping a man to death with a hatchet as a preliminary to appearing as a mediæval saint with a palm in her hand at the head of a religious procession. What does it matter whether such an entertainment is called Gismonda, or Theodora, or Venice, or Constantinople, or The Orient, or Captain Boyton's water show? Personally, I prefer the water show, because the sixty-foot header interested me, which Madame Bernhardt has long ceased to do; and the sensation of shooting the chute thrilled me, which "Gismonda" does not. As a pageant the affair may pass very well with people who, never having been touched by the peculiar spiritual beauty of the art of the Middle Ages, compare the scene-painter's titivated imitations with the Lord Mayor's Show and the architecture of Regent Street with the originals; but it is no more to be compared to the pageantry of "King Arthur" at the Lyceum than the clever but thoroughly shoppy stage business of Madame Bernhardt is to be compared to the acting of Miss Ellen Terry. I confess I regard with a certain jealousy the extent to which this ex-artist, having deliberately exercised her unquestioned right to step down from the national theatre in which she became famous to posture in a traveling show, is still permitted the privileges and courtesies proper to her former rank. It is open to all actresses to say either, "Give me a dignified living wage and let me work at my art," or "Give me as much money and applause as can possibly be got out of me, and let my art go hang." Only, when the choice is made, it is the business of the critic to see that the chooser of the lower level does not take precedence of the devoted artist who takes the higher one. Madame Bernhardt has elected to go round the world pretending to kill people with hatchets and hairpins, and making, I presume, heaps of money. I wish her every success; but I shall certainly not treat her as a dramatic artist of the first rank unless she pays me well for it. As a self-respecting critic I decline to be bought for nothing.

It seems a strange thing to me that we should still be so little awake to the fact that in these plays which depend wholly on poignant intensity of expression for the simple emotions the sceptre has passed to the operatic artist. What surprises me is not that this exhibition of Madame Bernhardt's should be flagrantly vulgar and commercial, or that it should be hackneyed and old-fashioned, but that we should dream of going to see it now that we have seen Calve as Carmen and La Navarraise. In the front ranks of art there is a place for the methods of Duse, and for the drama in which emotion exists only to make thought live and move us, but none for Sarah Bernhardt and the claptraps which Sardou contrives for her. To me, at least, the whole affair seems antiquated and ridiculous, except when I regard it as a high modern development of the circus and the waxworks. I have seen it, just as I have seen, in my time, Madame Celeste in "Green Bushes" and "The Red Woman." Though I always preferred Buckstone to Sardou as a tragic dramatist, and still do, I used to think Madame Bernhardt a greater actress than Celeste. But I almost believe now that this must have been a delusion of the departed days when Madame Bernhardt was so slim that when she went for a trip in a captive balloon, it was said that her stepping into the car had the same effect as throwing out ballast. At all events, I am quite sure that if I had to choose between seeing Miami and Gismonda again, I should vote eagerly for Miami, who was at least amusing.

To revert for a moment to Fedora, I hope Mrs. Campbell will note that Sarah Bernhardt's career cannot be repeated now—that her art is out of date and her dramas dead. The proof is that Mrs. Campbell cannot act Fedora, although to any actress over forty-five Fedora is more natural than Mrs. Tanqueray. By the way, I have forgotten to say that Mrs. Bancroft is in the cast, and is as amusing and skilful as ever. Mr. Tree, confronted with the impossible Loris Ipanoff, was forced to take the part seriously, and, with the help of a Polish make-up, try to pull it through by a creditably awkward attempt at conventional melodramatic acting. Besides, Mrs. Campbell ruined his clothes. Wherever her beautiful white arms touched him they left their mark. She knelt at his feet and made a perfect zebra of his left leg with bars across it. Then she flung her arms convulsively right round

him; and the next time he turned his back to the footlights there was little to choose between his coatback and
his shirtfront. Before the act was over a gallon of benzine
would hardly have set him right again. Mr. Tree had
his revenge at the end of the play, when, in falling on
Fedora's body, he managed to transfer a large black patch
to her cheek, which was strikingly in evidence when she
bowed her acknowledgment of the frantic applause with
which the evening ended; but he was still so unhinged
by the futility of Loris and the ill-treatment of his gar-
ments, that when the audience called for Mr. Bancroft
he informed them that Mr. Bancroft was prevented from
coming forward by modesty, but that Mrs. Bancroft—
and here Mrs. Bancroft came forward smiling; and the
audience naturally chuckled hugely.

May I suggest that soap and water is an excellent
cosmetic for the arms, and that it does not mark coats?
Also that this whitewashing malpractice has become an
intolerable absurdity, and that there is at least one critic
who means to try whether ridicule can kill it.

TWO PLAYS

Macaire: a melodramatic farce in three acts. By William Ernest Henley and Robert Louis Stevenson. In the *New Review,* June, 1895.

La Femme de Claude. By Alexandre Dumas *fils.* Drury Lane Theatre, 5 June, 1895.

I SEE that Mr. William Henley has just published in the *New Review* the version of "Robert Macaire" which he made in collaboration with the late R. L. Stevenson. I read the work myself for the first time before the revival of the old version at the Lyceum Theatre; and it has always struck me as a pat illustration of the divorce of the stage from literature that we should have had, on the one hand, a famous writer of fiction collaborating with a born master of verse to rescue a famous old harlequinade from obsolescence, and, on the other, a revival of this harlequinade by our leading actor managing our leading theatre; yet that there was no thought of combining the two opportunities, the revival at the theatre proceeding contentedly with the old cheap and common dialogue, written originally with the idea that the play was a serious blood-and-thunder melodrama, whilst the new version circulated quietly in private as a booklet, and finally appears as a magazine contribution. It is a pity that Mr. Henley could not very well print the old version in his *Review* side by side with the new, in order to show, not only that the old is quite unreadable, and the new so wittily and whimsically turned that every phrase tickles, but that even the stage technique of the new is hugely superior to that of the old. Instead of

two elaborate scenes, causing a long interval which a
harlequinade will not bear, and entailing extra labor and
expense, there is one scene all through, enabling the curtain to be dropped for a moment to point the situations
and express conventionally the change from morning to
bedtime, and from bedtime to murder-time, without per-
ceptibly breaking the continuity of the extravaganza. The
incongruous relics of the original folly of the author are
swept away, and the whole brought into the vein of the
fantastic variation by which Lemaître rescued the theme
from obscurity. The effective situations are preserved
and improved; Macaire retains all his old business except
the creaking snuff-box, in exchange for which he acquires
an epigrammatic philosophy expressed in lines which a
distinguished actor need not be ashamed to speak; the
ridiculous long-lost wife disappears; the gendarme and
the innkeeper become amusing; the murder has the true
touch of nightmare: in short, the two "literary men" have
beaten the bungling stage "author" at his own craft in
every point; outwritten him, outwitted him, outstaged
him, and erased him from all future possibility in the
eyes of every person of ordinary culture and intelligence
who makes the comparison. And yet I have a grim conviction that actors will feel a mysterious "suitability to
the stage" in the old version which is missing in the new.
This divination of mine is not due to my unaided insight
and sympathy, but to the fact that my education as a
critic has not been confined to West End theatres. I
remember finding myself one evening in the Whitechapel
Road with a company of active-minded people, including
two well-known ladies of distinguished attainments in
oratory and poetry, and a few gentlemen addicted, like
myself, to art, literature, and politics. Presently we came

different air. And it is because Stevenson and Mr. Henley substituted for the low cunning and the cynical experience which makes effective melodramas out of such calculations, the higher qualities of wit, imagination, romance, and humor, applied with a literary workmanship which is at once curiously skilful and carelessly happy, that even the Lyceum Theatre dared not rise to their level.

Now that the collaboration of the authors of "Macaire" is broken up by the death of Stevenson, who must, I think, be admitted to have gone on without the managers rather better than the managers have gone on without him, one wonders whether Mr. Henley will carry on the business alone. The charm of the pair was their combination of artistic faculty with a pleasant boyishness of imagination. Stevenson, always the older of the twain, showed signs of growing up, and could even, when kept to the point by the collaboration of his stepson, produce stories that were not obviously the penny numbers of our boyhood rewritten by a fine hand. But Mr. Henley defies the ravages of time. That amusing mixture of pedantry and hero-worship which marks the schoolboy's cult of athletics survives unabated and unenlightened in Mr. Henley's cult of literature. He delights in puerile novels about prize-fighters, like "Cashel Byron's Profession"; he has imagination without sense; he not only adores his literary and artistic heroes, but is violently jealous for their sakes of the reputations of all the others; his attitudes are reverently traditional; experience means to him the works of fiction he has read; at every turn of his pen he shows that cardinal quality of youth, its incapacity for apprehending life at first hand as distinguished from appreciating its presenta-

tions and formulations in art and social or scientific
theory. And yet he has the romantic imagination and
the fine gift of poetic speech which only need some con-
crete subject-matter—for really plays cannot, like poems
or even articles, be made out of purely abstract indignation, scorn, defiance, and so on—to provide "Macaire,"
"Admiral Guinea," and the rest with more than worthy
successors.

The appearance of Duse at Drury Lane on Wednesday
in "La Femme de Claude," is too recent for my judgment to have recovered from the emotional disturbance
produced by such an appeal as she made to my passion
for very fine acting. The furthest extremes of Duse's
range as an artist must always, even in this greatest art
center in the world, remain a secret between herself and
a few fine observers. I should say without qualification
that it is the best modern acting I have ever seen, were
it not that the phrase suggests a larger experience of
first-rate acting in this department than I possess. I have
only seen Salvini and Ristori in their historic-heroic parts,
or in Shakespeare; and my experience of Coquelin is
limited to Molière and such plays of our own day as
"Les Surprises de Divorce." The work of these three
great artists seemed to me (humanly speaking) quite
thorough and perfect in its application to their conception of the parts they played; and their conception was,
for the most part, adequate, and more than adequate, to
the culture of their generation. But their incubatory
period was the period before the theatre had advanced
to the point at which Wagner and Ibsen became its master spirits. Duse is the first actress whom we have seen
applying the method of the great school to characteristically modern parts or to characteristically modern con-

ceptions of old parts. Her style is not, to the attentive observer of the stage, entirely new: nothing arrives at such perfection without many tentative approaches to it. I remember, years ago, when "The Lady of Lyons" was first produced at the Lyceum, being struck with two things about it: first, the fact that Henry Irving, after much striving and, if I may be allowed the expression, not a little floundering, had at last discovered the method of heroic acting; and, second, that in the scene where Claude brings Pauline home after their wedding, Miss Ellen Terry, by a number of delicate touches, slipped into the scene a play of subtle emotion quite foreign to its traditions, with such effect that I can conjure up those moments perfectly to this day, though my utmost effort of memory cannot bring back the very faintest adumbration of any other scene in Pauline's part, which was as useless as material for Miss Terry's peculiar genius as most of those twenty-three Lyceum heroines—Catherine Duval in "A Dead Heart," and so forth—of which Mr. Clement Scott has made a list for my benefit, evidently to make me cry afresh over the wicked waste of so rare a talent. Of course the twenty-three parts are not all bad parts as parts are reckoned conventionally; and equally of course Miss Terry has not exactly played any of them badly. But neither is Shakespeare's Cleopatra a bad part; and neither did Duse exactly play it badly. Yet who on earth would know that Duse was a great actress if he had never seen her play anything but Cleopatra? And who on earth will ever know what Miss Terry can do if we are never to see her except in plays that date, in feeling if not in actual composition, from the dark ages before the Married Women's Property Act? I can only guess at her powers myself from my recollections of the old Court Theatre, and the little interpolations in the Lyceum parts by which her genius so often instinctively thrusts through the old play to the new style, only, of course, to be beaten back by the giving out of the material. Still, just in these thrustings you could see Duse's style coming. Long after the "Lady of Lyons" came Miss Janet Achurch, whose playing as Alexandria, in Voss's play, came nearer to Duse's work in subtlety, continuity and variety of detail, and in beauty of execution, than anything I have seen on the English stage. But Duse has been helped to her supremacy by the fortunate sternness of Nature in giving her nothing but her genius. Miss Ellen Terry is a woman of quite peculiar and irresistible personal charm. Miss Achurch has been kept in constant danger of missing the highest distinction in her art by having, as an extra and cheaper string to her bow, an endowment of conventional good looks, and a large share of that power of expressing all the common emotions with extraordinary intensity which makes the vulgar great actress of the Bernhardt school. Consequently you have two Miss Achurches: the Miss Achurch of Nora and Alexandra, and the Miss Achurch of Adrienne and Forget-me-not; and there are moments when the two get mixed. But in Duse you necessarily get the great school in its perfect integrity, because Duse without her genius would be a plain little woman of no use to any manager, whereas Miss Terry or Miss Achurch, if they had no more skill than can be acquired by any person of ordinary capacity in the course of a few years' experience, would always find a certain degree of favor as pretty leading ladies. Duse, *with* her genius, is so fascinating that is is positively difficult to attend to the play. instead of attending wholly to her. The extraordinary richness of her art can only be understood by those who have studied the process by which an actress is built up. You offer a part to a young lady who is an enthusiastic beginner. She reads it devoutly, and forms, say, half a dozen great ideas as to points which she will make. The difficulty then is to induce her to do nothing between these points; so that the play may be allowed at such moments to play itself. Probably when it comes to the point, these intervals will prove the only effective periods during her performance, the points being ill chosen or awkwardly executed. The majority of actresses never get beyond learning not to invent new points for themselves, but rather to pick out in their parts the passages which admit of certain well worn and tried old points being reapplied. When they have learnt to make these points smoothly and to keep quiet between whiles with a graceful air of having good reasons for doing nothing, they are finished actresses. The great actress has a harder struggle. She goes on inventing her points and her business determinedly, constantly increasing the original half-dozen, and constantly executing them with greater force and smoothness. A time comes when she is always making points, and making them well; and this is the finishing point with some actresses. But with the greatest artists there soon commences an integration of the points into a continuous whole, at which stage the actress appears to make no points at all, and to proceed in the most unstudied and "natural" way. This rare consummation Duse has reached. An attentive study of her Marguerite Gauthier, for instance, by a highly trained observer of such things, will bring to light how its apparently simple strokes are combinations of a whole series of strokes, separately conceived originally, and added one by one to the part, until finally, after many years of evolution, they have integrated into one single highly complex stroke. Take, as a very simple illustration, the business of Camille's tying up the flowers in the third act. It seems the most natural thing in the world; but it is really the final development of a highly evolved dance with the arms—even, when you watch it consciously, a rather prolonged and elaborate one. The strokes of character have grown up in just the same way. And this is the secret of the extraordinary interest of such acting. There are years of work, bodily and mental, behind every instant of it—work, mind, not mere practise and habit, which is quite a different thing. It is the rarity of the gigantic energy needed to sustain this work which makes Duse so exceptional; for the work is in her case highly intellectual work, and so requires energy of a quality altogether superior to the mere head of steam needed to produce Bernhardtian explosions with the requisite regularity. With such high energy, mere personal fascination becomes a thing which the actress can put off and on like a garment. Sarah Bernhardt has nothing but her own charm, for the exhibition of which Sardou contrives love scenes—save the mark. Duse's own private charm has not yet been given to the public. She gives you Césarine's charm, Marguerite Gauthier's charm, the charm of La Locandiera, the charm, in short, belonging to the character she impersonates; and you are enthralled by its reality and delighted by the magical skill of the artist without for a moment feeling any complicity either on your own part or hers in the passion represented. And with that clue to the consistency of supreme admiration for the artist with perfect respect for the woman—a combination so rare that some people doubt its possibility—I must leave discussion of the plays she has appeared in this week to my next article.

DUSE AND BERNHARDT

15 June, 1895.

Mr. William Archer's defence of the dramatic
critics against Mr. Street's indictment of them
for their indifference to acting appears to be
falling through. Mr. Archer pleads that whereas Hazlitt
and Leigh Hunt had frequent opportunities of comparing
ambitious actors in famous parts, the modern dramatic
critic spends his life in contemplating "good acting plays"
without any real people in them, and performers who
do not create or interpret characters, but simply lend their
pretty or popular persons, for a consideration, to fill up
the parts. Mr. Archer might have added another reason which applies to nearly all modern works: to wit,
the operation of our copyright laws, whereby actors and
actresses acquire the right not only to perform new plays
but to prevent any one else from performing them. Nevertheless we critics can now at last outdo Hazlitt and
Leigh Hunt if we have a mind to; for we have just had
two Mrs. Ebbsmiths to compare, besides a fourth Fedora,
and Duse and Sarah Bernhardt playing "La Dame aux
Camellias" and Sudermann's "Heimat" against one
another at Daly's Theatre and at Drury Lane. Clearly
now or never is the time for triumphant refutation of
the grievance of the English actor against the English
Press: namely, that hardly any critic knows enough about
acting to be able to distinguish between an effective part
and a well played one, or between the bag of tricks which
every old hand carries and the stock of ideas and sense

of character which distinguish the master-actor from the mere handy man.

This week began with the relapse of Sarah Bernhardt into her old profession of serious actress. She played Magda in Sudermann's "Heimat," and was promptly challenged by Duse in the same part at Drury Lane on Wednesday. The contrast between the two Magdas is as extreme as any contrast could possibly be between artists who have finished their twenty years apprentice-ship to the same profession under closely similar condi-tions. Madame Bernhardt has the charm of a jolly ma-turity, rather spoilt and petulant, perhaps, but always ready with a sunshine-through-the-clouds smile if only she is made much of. Her dresses and diamonds, if not exactly splendid, are at least splendacious; her figure, far too scantily upholstered in the old days, is at its best; and her complexion shows that she has not studied mod-ern art in vain. Those charming roseate effects which French painters produce by giving flesh the pretty color of strawberries and cream, and painting the shadows pink and crimson, are cunningly reproduced by Madame Bernhardt in the living picture. She paints her ears crimson and allows them to peep enchantingly through a few loose braids of her auburn hair. Every dimple has its dab of pink; and her finger-tips are so delicately incarnadined that you fancy they are transparent like her ears, and that the light is shining through their del-icate blood-vessels. Her lips are like a newly painted pillar box; her cheeks, right up to the languid lashes, have the bloom and surface of a peach; she is beautiful with the beauty of her school, and entirely inhuman and increditable. But the incredibility is pardonable, because, though it is all the greatest nonsense, nobody believing in it, the actress herself least of all, it is so artful, so clever, so well recognized a part of the business, and carried off with such a genial air, that it is impossible not to accept it with good-humor. One feels, when the heroine bursts on the scene, a dazzling vision of beauty, that instead of imposing on you, she adds to her own piquancy by looking you straight in the face, and saying, in effect: "Now who would ever suppose that I am a grandmother?" That, of course, is irresistible; and one is not sorry to have been coaxed to relax one's notions of the dignity of art when she gets to serious business and shows how ably she does her work. The coaxing suits well with the childishly egotistical character of her acting, which is not the art of making you think more highly or feel more deeply, but the art of making you admire her, pity her, champion her, weep with her, laugh at her jokes, follow her fortunes breathlessly, and applaud her wildly when the curtain falls. It is the art of finding out all your weaknesses and practising on them—cajoling you, harrowing you, exciting you—on the whole, fooling you. And it is always Sarah Bernhardt in her own capacity who does this to you. The dress, the title of the play, the order of the words may vary; but the woman is always the same. She does not enter into the leading character; she substitutes herself for it.

All this is precisely what does not happen in the case of Duse, whose every part is a separate creation. When she comes on the stage, you are quite welcome to take your opera-glass and count whatever lines time and care have so far traced on her. They are the credentials of her humanity; and she knows better than to obliterate that significant handwriting beneath a layer of peach-bloom from the chemist's. The shadows on her face are grey, not crimson; her lips are sometimes nearly grey also; there are neither dabs nor dimples; her charm could never be imitated by a barmaid with unlimited pin money and a row of footlights before her instead of the handles of a beer-engine. The result is not so discouraging as the patrons of the bar might suppose. Wilkes, who squinted atrociously, boasted that he was only quarter of an hour behind the handsomest man in Europe: Duse is not in action five minutes before she is quarter of a century ahead of the handsomest woman in the world. I grant that Sarah's elaborate Monna Lisa smile, with the conscious droop of the eyelashes and the long carmined lips coyly disclosing the brilliant row of teeth, is effective of its kind—that it not only appeals to your susceptibilities, but positively jogs them. And it lasts quite a minute, sometimes longer. But Duse, with a tremor of the lip which you feel rather than see, and which lasts half an instant, touches you straight on the very heart; and there is not a line in the face, or a cold tone in the grey shadow that does not give poignancy to that tremor. As to youth and age, who can associate purity and delicacy of emotion, and simplicity of expression, with the sordid craft that repels us in age; or voluptuous appeal and egotistical self-insistence with the candor and generosity that attract us in youth? Who ever thinks of Potiphar's wife as a young woman, or St. Elizabeth of Hungary as an old one? These associations are horribly unjust to age, and undeserved by youth: they belong of right to differences of character, not of years; but they rule our imaginations; and the great artist profits by them to appear eternally young. However, it would be a critical blunder as well as a personal folly on my part to suggest that Duse, any more than Sarah Bern-

but as a right which it has to the services of the females
as abject slaves. In fact, there is not the slightest reason
to suspect Madame Bernhardt of having discovered any
such theme in the play; though Duse, with one look at
Schwartze, the father, nailed it to the stage as the subject of the impending dramatic struggle before she had
been five minutes on the scene. Before long, there came
a stroke of acting which will probably never be forgotten
by those who saw it, and which explained at once why
those artifices of the dressing-table which help Madame
Bernhardt would hinder Duse almost as much as a screen
placed in front of her. I should explain, first, that the
real name of the play is not "Magda" but "Home."
Magda is a daughter who has been turned out of doors
for defying her father, one of those outrageous persons
who mistake their desire to have everything their own
way in the house for a sacred principle of home life.
She has a hard time of it, but at last makes a success as
an opera singer, though not until her lonely struggles
have thrown her for sympathy on a fellow student, who
in due time goes his way, and leaves her to face mother-
hood as best she can. In the fullness of her fame she
returns to her native town, and in an attack of home-
sickness makes advances to her father, who consents to
receive her again. No sooner is she installed in the house
than she finds that one of the most intimate friends of
the family is the father of her child. In the third act
of the play she is on the stage when he is announced as
a visitor. It must be admitted that Sarah Bernhardt
played this scene very lightly and pleasantly: there was
genuine good fellowship in the way in which she reassured the embarrassed gallant and made him understand
that she was not going to play off the sorrows of Gretchen

on him after all those years, and that she felt that she owed him the priceless experience of maternity, even if she did not particularly respect him for it. Her self-possession at this point was immense: the peach-bloom never altered by a shade. Not so with Duse. The moment she read the card handed her by the servant, you realized what it was to have to face a meeting with the man. It was interesting to watch how she got through it when he came in, and how, on the whole, she got through it pretty well. He paid his compliments and offered his flowers; they sat down; and she evidently felt that she had got it safely over and might allow herself to think at her ease, and to look at him to see how much he had altered. Then a terrible thing happened to her. She began to blush; and in another moment she was conscious of it, and the blush was slowly spreading and deepening until, after a few vain efforts to avert her face or to obstruct his view of it without seeming to do so, she gave up and hid the blush in her hands. After that feat of acting I did not need to be told why Duse does not paint an inch thick. I could detect no trick in it: it seemed to me a perfectly genuine effect of the dramatic imagination. In the third act of "La Dame aux Camellias," where she produces a touching effect by throwing herself down, and presently rises with her face changed and flushed with weeping, the flush is secured by the preliminary plunge to a stooping attitude, imagination or no imagination; but Magda's blush did not admit of that explanation; and I must confess to an intense professional curiosity as to whether it always comes spontaneously.

I shall make no attempt to describe the rest of that unforgettable act. To say that it left the house not only

I read Alexandrines, I cook them, in spite of myself, so as to make them scan like the last line of a stanza in "Childe Harold": for instance, if I may illustrate by combining Rostand and Byron:

> "Te voyant accoutré d'une manière telle,
>   He rushed into the field, and, foremost fighting, fell,
>   Pour porter monseigneur vers sa Dame Lointaine
>   And fertilize the field that each pretends to gain."

This, I know, is deplorable; but it would be useless for me to attempt to conceal my hopeless deficiencies as a linguist. I am very sorry; but I cannot learn languages. I have tried hard, only to find that men of ordinary capacity can learn Sanscrit in less time than it takes me to buy a German dictionary. The worst of it is that this disability of mine seems to be most humiliatingly exceptional. My colleagues sit at French plays, German plays, and Italian plays, laughing at all the jokes, thrilling with all the fine sentiments, and obviously undestanding the finest shades of the language; whilst I, unless I have read the play beforehand, or asked somebody during the interval what it is about, must either struggle with a sixpenny "synopsis" which invariably misses the real point of the drama, or else sit with a guilty conscience and a blank countenance, drawing the most extravagantly wrong inferences from the dumb show of the piece. The torture of this can only be adequately apprehended when it is considered that in ordinary novels, or plays, or conversations, the majority of sentences have no definite meaning at all; and that an energetic intellectual effort to grapple with them, such as one makes in trying to understand a foreign language, would at once discover their inconclusiveness, inaccuracy, and emptiness. When

I listen to an English play I am not troubled by not understanding when there is nothing to understand, because I understand at once that there is nothing to understand. But at a foreign play I do not understand this; and every sentence that means nothing in particular—say five out of six in the slacker moments of the action— seems to me to be a sentence of which I have missed the meaning through my unhappy and disgraceful ignorance of the language. Hence torments of shame and inefficiency, the betrayal of which would destroy my reputation as a critic at one blow. Of course I have a phrase or two ready at the end of my tongue to conceal my ignorance. My command of operatic Italian is almost copious, as might be expected from my experience as a musical critic. I can make love in Italian; I could challenge a foe to a duel in Italian if I were not afraid of him; and if I swallowed some agonizing mineral poison, I could describe my sensations very eloquently. And I could manage a prayer pretty well. But these accomplishments are too special for modern comedy and ordinary conversation. As to French, I can neither speak it nor understand it when spoken without an impracticably long interval for reflection; and I am, besides, subject to a curious propensity, when addressed by Italian or French people, to reply in fluent German, though on all other occasions that language utterly baffles me. On the whole, I come off best at the theatre in such a case as that of "Magda," where I began by reading the synopsis, then picked up a little of the play in French at Daly's Theatre, then a little more in Italian at Drury Lane, then a little more in German from the book, and finally looked at Duse and was illuminated beyond all the powers of all the books and languages on earth.

I may now return to M. Rostand's play with an easy conscience, since I have made it plain that my sense that its versification is a drawback to it may be the effect of pure ignorance on my part. Certainly it made it verbose, and destroyed the illusion of the seafaring scenes by setting all the sailors monotonously bawling their phrases like street cries, in the manner of M. Mounet Sully and the Comédie Française, though of course they stopped short of the worst declamatory horrors of that institution. And in some subtle way, it led on the two troubadours, Joffroy Rudel and Bertrand d'Allamanon, to make themselves ridiculous. About Joffroy (M. de Max) there was no mistake from the very beginning. As he lay moribund on his litter, his large dark eyes were fixed in profound pity for himself; and his lips were wreathed in a smile of ineffable complacency at the thought of how well his eyes looked. He smiled all poor M. Rostand's poetry overboard within a minute of his entrance; and it then became a question whether Bertrand (M. Guitry) could raise it from the depths in the second and third acts, in which Joffroy does not appear. But though M. Guitry did not smile at all, being, in fact, as serious a man as any poet could desire, the audience laughed outright at Bertrand. In vain did Madame Bernhardt work up his entrance by tearing off her white sleeves and throwing them out of the window to him, enjoining him to redden them in the gore of the gigantic green knight. In vain did he dash in spinning with the impetus of his charge, whirling his falchion in the air, and bearing on his brow a gash which suggested that the green knight, before succumbing, had sliced the top off his head like the lid of a saucepan. The audience only laughed. They laughed again when he fainted; they shrieked when Sorismonde (the inevitable confidante) said "He is better"; and they might have ended by laughing the piece off the stage had he not reminded Melissinde that she had no sleeves on, whereupon she became conscious of herself, and a blushing silence fell on the house. It was really not M. Guitry's fault: for the life of me I cannot see what he could have done other than what he did; but I cannot pretend that I take a very severe view of the bad manners of the audience in laughing. However, his entrance, like several of the exciting events on the ship in the first act, might have been better stage-managed. The great modern master of such effects is Richard Wagner, with regard to whom the French nation is still in a comparatively benighted condition. The stage manager who wishes to work up the arrival of a champion or the sighting of land from a ship had better go to Bayreuth and watch the first acts of "Lohengrin" and "Tristan," unless he is content to run the risk of making modern audiences laugh. But I do not think very much could be done with M. Rostand's scene leading up to Bertrand's arrival in any case. Melissinde and Sorismonde describing the attack from the window—"Oh, quel superbe élan!" and so on— is not to be compared either to Rebecca describing the onslaught of the black knight to Ivanhoe, or Klingsor's running commentary to Kundry on the havoc made by Parsifal among the knights of the flower maidens.

As to Madame Bernhardt's own performance, it is not humanly possible for an actress to do very much with a play in which, when the other characters are not describing what a peerlessly beautiful and wonderful creature she is, she is herself on the stage accepting that ridiculous position. But the moment Madame Bernhardt entered one very welcome reform was evident. The elaborate make-up which I took the liberty of describing in some detail in my last article, and which made Gismonda and Magda so impossibly like goddesses in a Tiepolesque ceiling, had all but disappeared. Melissinde had a face, not a stucco mask: she was a real woman, not a hairdresser's shop-window image. And what an improvement it was! How Madame Bernhardt can ever have supposed that her face is less interesting or attractive than the complexion which she carries in her dressing-bag, or that she has anything to gain by trying to make herself look like the silliest sort of lady of fashion, would be a mystery to me if it were not only too evident that she no longer brings to her art the immense pressure of thought and labor which earns for the greatest artists that rarest of all faiths, faith in their real selves. She looked much better; but there was very little thought, very little work, and consequently very little interest in her performance. Fortunately for her, she still has exceptional nervous power; and she has not altogether forgotten those situations in her old parts which repeat themselves with more or less inessential modification in her new ones. This, to so clever a woman, with such a reputation, is enough to enable her to play the great actress still. But it should not satisfy London criticism. Take, for example, the end of the third act of this "Princesse Lointaine," which she selects as her opportunity for one of those displays of vehemence which are expected from her as part of the conventional Bernhardt exhibition. It is pure rant and nothing else. When once she begins to tear through her lines at the utmost pitch and power of her voice, she shows no further sense of what she is saying, and is unable to recover herself when, in the final speech, the feeling changes. As her physical endurance threatens to fail she tears along the faster, and finally rushes off the stage in a forced frenzy. I do not deny that there is something very exciting in a blind whirlwind of roaring energy. I have seen a working-class audience spring to their feet and cheer madly for three minutes at it. But then the artist was Mr. John Burns, who can give Madame Bernhardt a start of several miles at that particular sort of effect, and beat her easily. And I am bound to say, in justice to Mr. Burns, that I have never seen him bring down the curtain in this fashion until the play was really over, or substitute the peroration for the business part of the speech, whereas Madame Bernhardt does deliberately substitute rant for the business of the play. Again, Mr. Burns does it to amuse an election meeting of working men who are tired of sitting still: he does not offer it as serious political oratory in the House of Commons. I need hardly say that it is not the sort of effect that improves as the artist grows older, since it can only be produced by sustained physical violence. It is quite different from those effects which great players produce at a dramatic climax by working up the scene, through sheer force of acting, to the pitch at which, when the crucial moment comes, the effect makes itself, the artist's work being then over, though the audience is persuaded that some stupendous magnetic explosion has taken place. No doubt some of my readers have witnessed that scene in which Queen Elizabeth and her court seemed to vanish miraculously from the stage, apparently swept into nothingness when Ristori let loose her wrath as Marie Stuart; or they may have seen the same effect produced by Salvini when the king flies in disorder from the play scene in "Hamlet." But it is only the critic, watching and listening with the same intensity with which the performer acts, who, when asked what extraordinary thing Ristori or Salvini did at that supreme moment to work such a miracle, is able to reply that they did nothing. Elizabeth and Claudius ran off the stage with their courts after them: that was all. Ristori and Salvini simply looked on, having already wrought the scene to the point at which the flight of the rest produced the necessary effect on the imagination of the audience. I need hardly refer again to the effect made last week by the third act of Sudermann's "Home," as Duse played it. I only ask any one who saw that performance to try to imagine—if he has the heart to do it—such an artistic scandal as that great actress suddenly throwing her part to the winds and substituting for it a good two minutes' rant, like the finish to the third act of "La Princesse Lointaine." The public should learn to distinguish in these matters consciously as well as unconsciously. Ranting is not, as it is generally assumed to be, bad acting. It is not acting at all, but the introduction of an exhibition of force for the sake of force. And let us not affect to deny that when the performer has strength enough to raise the pressure to hurricane pitch, a successful rant is attractive and exciting, provided only the performer is clearly doing it on purpose, and is not an epileptic or a lunatic. But it takes not only purpose but reason to humanize force and raise it to the rank of a factor in fine art. It is the strength that is completely controlled and utilized that takes the crown: it is your Ristori, your Salvini, your Duse, with their unfailing hold and yet exquisitely delicate touch upon their parts, their sleeplessly vigilant sense of beauty of thought, feeling, and action, and their prodigious industry, that are recognized as the real athletes of the stage, compared with whom the ranters are weaklings and sluggards. That, at least, must be the judgment of London. Artists of international fame do not come to this capital of the world for money, but for reputation; and the London critic should be jealous above all things of letting that reputation go cheaply. When Duse gives us her best work, we cannot be too emphatic in declaring that it is best of the best and magnificent; so that our hall-mark may be carried through the nations on a piece of sterling gold. But when Madame Bernhardt gives us pinchbeck plays and acting that is poor in thought and lazily eked out with odds and ends stripped from her old parts; when she rants at us and brings down the house in a London theatre just as she brings it down in a provincial American one, we must tell her that she can do better than that, and that we will have nothing less than her best. When she offers us her reputation instead of first-rate acting, we must reply that we give reputations instead of taking them, and that we accept nothing in exchange except first-rate acting down on the counter, without a moment's credit. Already there are signs that she is waking up to the situation. The failure of Gismonda to elicit any expression of the deep respect which really fine work imposes, even on those who prefer something cheaper; the sudden and complete obliteration of her Magda by Duse's first five minutes in the part; the fatal compliments by which her most enthusiastic champions have exposed the commonness and obviousness of the intellectual material of her acting: something of all this may have penetrated to her through the barrier of language and the incense-clouds of flattery; for it looked as if on Monday the disappearance of the Gismonda make-up were only a symptom of a more serious attitude towards London. I suggest, now, that the rant should be discarded as well, and replaced by a genuine study and interpretation of the passages which are sacrificed to it. I further suggest, as a musical critic, that the shallow trick of intoning which sets so many of my musically neglected colleagues babbling about the "golden voice" should be discarded too. Miss Rehan, who is coming next week, will expose the musical emptiness of Madame Bernhardt's habit of monotonously chanting sentences on one note, as effectually as Duse has exposed the intellectual emptiness of her Magda. Of course, intoning is easy —as easy as holding down one key of an accordion and keeping up a mellifluous smile all the time; but it dehumanizes speech, and after some minutes becomes maddening, so that a flash of fun or a burst of rage is doubly welcome because it for a moment alters that eternal pitch and timbre. Some critics speak of "the melody" of it, as to which I can only say that the man who finds melody in one sustained note would find exquisite curves in a packing case. I therefore respectfully urge Madame Bernhardt to add a complete set of strings to her lyre before Miss Rehan comes. Otherwise there will be fresh comparisons of the most disparaging kind.

MR. DALY FOSSILIZES

The Railroad of Love: a comedy in four acts. Adapted by Augustin Daly from the German of Frau von Schönthan. Daly's Theatre, 25 June, 1895.

YET another foreign language—that of Amurrica! And Mr. Augustin Daly again! What is to be done with Mr. Daly? How shall we open his mind to the fact that he stands on the brink of the twentieth century in London and not with Mr. Vincent Crummles at Portsmouth in the early Dickens days? I have in my hand the programme of last Tuesday's performance. One character is described as "a polished relic of wasted energies," another as "not half a bad sort of parent, and an excellent judge—of Latour '70." A lady is catalogued as "a goldfish of much experience—not to be caught on the fly." This programme measures twenty-one inches by seven and a quarter, and the decorative printing is in blue ink. Why is it not printed on tissue paper; why does not the blue come off on my fingers; why did I not buy it from an orange seller outside the theatre? Not, I am sure, from any desire on Mr. Daly's part to break with the tradition of my boyhood, but doubtless because the manufacture of the old playbill is a lost art here. I picture Mr. Daly, vainly searching London for that particular sort of tissue paper and that crayon-like blue ink, trembling lest the public should think him outlandish and unprofessional without them. Bless your innocence, dear Mr. Daly, such things have not been

Fan," "The Second Mrs. Tanqueray," and "The Case of Rebellious Susan" with the repertory whose gems, from the box-office point of view, were "The Ironmaster" and "A Scrap of Paper," not to repeat my former instances! The change is evident at once. In short, a modern manager need not produce "The Wild Duck"; but he must be very careful not to produce a play which will seem insipid and old-fashioned to playgoers who have seen "The Wild Duck," even though they may have hissed it.

This is the lesson that Mr. Daly has not learnt. When he first came, there was nothing more old-fashioned about his productions than the archaic playbills, the horseplay at the ends of the acts, and the doggerel tags before the final curtain. But nowadays the plays themselves are old-fashioned with the most dangerous sort of old-fashionedness: that is, they are ten years out of date, whereas the playbill smartnesses and the doggerel, being fifty years out of date, have a certain rococo quaintness about them which appeals to our indulgence. All that can be said for "The Railroad of Love" now is that it is not an absolute outrage on the public and on Miss Rehan's genius, as "Dollars and Cents" was, and that in the third act the part of Valentine Osprey can still be raised, by a rapture of over-acting on Miss Rehan's part, to the point of rescuing the play from utter impossibility. But that terrible milliterry lewt'nent, with his company manners, his badinage and repartee, and his dashing manner of chucking the parlor-maid under the chin, is hard to bear, especially now that Mr. Drew has left the company, and no successor can be found with his grace of style and his apologetic humor. And then the fathers, with their interminable "preeliminerries" and explanations! Except when Miss Rehan or Mr. Lewis or Mrs. Gilbert is on the stage the play is hardly tolerable—the less so because Mr. Daly's stage management is of the most fatal kind, being founded throughout on a boyish sense of fun instead of on a sense of comedy and character. What he calls acting I should call larking. For example, the part of Benny Demaresq, described in the bill as "condemned by the judge and waiting sentence from the judge's daughter," is taken by an actor who, though young and not as yet very proficient, could quite easily do himself credit in the part under artistic guidance. But he has been apparently encouraged to set about it in the broadly burlesqued, rough-and-ready, physically violent style of the circus. We do not accept that sort of thing in first-rate theatres in London; and when Mr. Otis Skinner made the part agreeable years ago he did it by making the least, and not the most, of the tomfoolery (the expression is really unavoidable) laid out for him. The same criticism, in a greater or less degree, applies to all those members of the company who do not know their business better than Mr. Daly does. The comic negro servant and the parlor-maid who flirts with the visitors discharge their duty of destroying the illusion without adding to the entertainment, with the fellest efficiency, and, I doubt not, with the warmest approval of the manager. The whole atmosphere of the play is one of stale pleasantry of a kind for which we are not just now in the humor.

As to Miss Rehan, without whom the performance would be a hopeless failure, I should prefer to speak more fully of her when we have seen the play which Mr. Daly has founded on Shakespeare's "Two Gentlemen of Verona" (for Mr. Daly shows himself a thorough disciple of the old school in his conviction that Shakespeare was a wretchedly unskilful dramatic author). The scene of

POOR SHAKESPEARE!

The Two Gentlemen of Verona. Daly's Theatre, 2
July, 1895.

THE PIECE founded by Augustin Daly on Shakespeare's "Two Gentlemen of Verona," to which I
looked forward last week, is not exactly a comic
opera, though there is plenty of music in it, and not exactly a serpentine dance, though it proceeds under a play
of changing colored lights. It is something more old-
fashioned than either: to wit, a vaudeville. And let me
hasten to admit that it makes a very pleasant entertainment for those who know no better. Even I, who know
a great deal better, as I shall presently demonstrate rather
severely, enjoyed myself tolerably. I cannot feel harshly
towards a gentleman who works so hard as Mr. Daly does
to make Shakespeare presentable: one feels that he loves
the bard, and lets him have his way as far as he thinks
it good for him. His rearrangement of the scenes of the
first two acts is just like him. Shakespeare shows lucidly
how Proteus lives with his father (Antonio) in Verona,
and loves a lady of that city named Julia. Mr. Daly, by
taking the scene in Julia's house between Julia and her
maid, and the scene in Antonio's house between Antonio
and Proteus, and making them into one scene, convinces
the unlettered audience that Proteus and Julia live in the
same house with their father Antonio. Further, Shakespeare shows us how Valentine, the other gentleman of
Verona, travels from Verona to Milan, the journey being
driven into our heads by a comic scene in Verona, in
which Valentine's servant is overwhelmed with grief at

leaving his parents, and with indignation at the insensibility of his dog to his sorrow, followed presently by another comic scene in Milan in which the same servant is welcomed to the strange city by a fellow-servant. Mr. Daly, however, is ready for Shakespeare on this point too. He just represents the two scenes as occurring in the same place; and immediately the puzzle as to who is who is complicated by a puzzle as to where is where. Thus is the immortal William adapted to the requirements of a nineteenth-century audience.

In preparing the text of his version Mr. Daly has proceeded on the usual principles, altering, transposing, omitting, improving, correcting, and transferring speeches from one character to another. Many of Shakespeare's lines are mere poetry, not to the point, not getting the play along, evidently stuck in because the poet liked to spread himself in verse. On all such unbusinesslike superfluities Mr. Daly is down with his blue pencil. For instance, he relieves us of such stuff as the following, which merely conveys that Valentine loves Silvia, a fact already sufficiently established by the previous dialogue:

"My thoughts do harbor with my Silvia nightly;
   And slaves they are to me, that send them flying:
Oh, could their master come and go as lightly,
   Himself would lodge where senseless they are lying.
My herald thoughts in thy pure bosom rest them,
   While I, their king, that thither them importune,
Do curse the grace that with such grace hath blessed them,
   Because myself do want my servant's fortune.
I curse myself, for they are sent by me,
   That they should harbor where their lord would be."

Slaves indeed are these lines and their like to Mr. Daly, who "sends them flying" without remorse. But when he comes to passages that a stage manager can understand, his reverence for the bard knows no bounds. The following awkward lines, unnecessary as they are under modern stage conditions, are at any rate not poetic, and are in the nature of police news. Therefore they are piously retained.

> "What halloing, and what stir, is this to-day?
> These are my mates, that make their wills their law,
> Have some unhappy passenger in chase.
> They love me well; yet I have much to do,
> To keep them from uncivil outrages.
> Withdraw thee, Valentine: who's this comes here?"

The perfunctory metrical character of such lines only makes them more ridiculous than they would be in prose. I would cut them out without remorse to make room for all the lines that have nothing to justify their existence except their poetry, their humor, their touches of character—in short, the lines for whose sake the play survives, just as it was for their sake it originally came into existence. Mr. Daly, who prefers the lines which only exist for the sake of the play, will doubtless think me as great a fool as Shakespeare; but I submit to him, without disputing his judgment, that he is, after all, only a man with a theory of dramatic composition, going with a blue pencil over the work of a great dramatist, and striking out everything that does not fit his theory. Now, as it happens, nobody cares about Mr. Daly's theory; whilst everybody who pays to see what is, after all, advertised as a performance of Shakespeare's play entitled "The Two Gentlemen of Verona," and not as a demonstration of Mr. Daly's theory, does care more or less about the art of Shakespeare. Why not give them what they ask for, instead of going to great trouble and expense to give them something else?

In those matters in which Mr. Daly has given the rein to his own taste and fancy: that is to say, in scenery, costumes, and music, he is for the most part disabled by a want of real knowledge of the arts concerned. I say for the most part, because his pretty fifteenth-century dresses, though probably inspired rather by Sir Frederic Leighton than by Benozzo Gozzoli, may pass. But the scenery is insufferable. First, for "a street in Verona" we get a Bath bun colored operatic front cloth with about as much light in it as there is in a studio in Fitzjohn's Avenue in the middle of October. I respectfully invite Mr. Daly to spend his next holiday looking at a real street in Verona, asking his conscience meanwhile whether a manager with eyes in his head and the electric light at his disposal could not advance a step on the Telbin (senior) style. Telbin was an admirable scene painter; but he was limited by the mechanical conditions of gas illumination; and he learnt his technique before the great advance made during the Impressionist movement in the painting of open-air effects, especially of brilliant sunlight. Of that advance Mr. Daly has apparently no conception. The days of Macready and Clarkson Stanfield still exist for him; he would probably prefer a watercolor drawing of a foreign street by Samuel Prout to one by Mr. T. M. Rooke; and I dare say every relic of the original tallow candle-light that still clings to the art of scene-painting is as dear to him as it is to most old playgoers, including, unhappily, many of the critics.

As to the elaborate set in which Julia makes her first entrance, a glance at it shows how far Mr. Daly prefers the Marble Arch to the loggia of Orcagna. All over the scene we have Renaissance work, in its genteelest stages of decay, held up as the perfection of romantic elegance and beauty. The school that produced the classicism of the First Empire, designed the terraces of Regent's Park and the façades of Fitzroy Square, and conceived the Boboli Gardens and Versailles as places for human beings to be happy in, ramps all over the scenery, and offers as much of its pet colonnades and statues as can be crammed into a single scene, by way of a compendium of everything that is lovely in the city of San Zeno and the tombs of the Scaligers. As to the natural objects depicted, I ask whether any man living has ever seen a pale green cypress in Verona or anywhere else out of a toy Noah's Ark. A man who, having once seen cypresses and felt their presence in a north Italian landscape, paints them lettuce color, must be suffering either from madness, malice, or a theory of how nature should have colored trees, cognate with Mr. Daly's theory of how Shakespeare should have written plays.

Of the music let me speak compassionately. After all, it is only very lately that Mr. Arnold Dolmetsch, by playing fifteenth-century music on fifteenth-century instruments, has shown us that the age of beauty was true to itself in music as in pictures and armor and costumes. But what should Mr. Daly know of this, educated as he no doubt was to believe that the court of Denmark should always enter in the first act of "Hamlet" to the march from "Judas Maccabæus?" Schubert's setting of "Who is Silvia?" he knew, but had rashly used up in "Twelfth Night" as "Who's Olivia." He has therefore had to fall back on another modern setting, almost supernaturally devoid of any particular merit. Besides this, all through the drama the most horribly common music repeatedly

breaks out on the slightest pretext or on no pretext at all.
One dance, set to a crude old English popular tune,
sundry eighteenth and nineteenth century musical banal-
ities, and a titivated plantation melody in the first act
which produces an indescribably atrocious effect by coming in behind the scenes as a sort of coda to Julia's curtain
speech, all turn the play, as I have said, into a vaudeville.
Needless to add, the accompaniments are not played on
lutes and viols, but by the orchestra and a guitar or two.
In the forest scene the outlaws begin to act by a chorus.
After their encounter with Valentine they go off the stage
singing the refrain exactly in the style of "La Fille de
Madame Angot." The wanton absurdity of introducing
this comic opera convention is presently eclipsed by a
thunderstorm, immediately after which Valentine enters
and delivers his speech sitting down on a bank of moss,
as an outlaw in tights naturally would after a terrific
shower. Such is the effect of many years of theatrical
management on the human brain.

Perhaps the oddest remark I have to make about the
performance is that, with all its glaring defects and blunders, it is rather a handsome and elaborate one as such
things go. It is many years now since Mr. Ruskin first
took the Academicians of his day aback by the obvious
remark that Carpaccio and Giovanni Bellini were better
painters than Domenichino and Salvator Rosa. Nobody
dreams now of assuming that Pope was a greater poet
than Chaucer, that "Mozart's Twelfth Mass" is superior
to the masterpieces of Orlandus Lassus and Palestrina,
or that our "ecclesiastical Gothic" architecture is more
enlightened than Norman axe work. But the theatre is
still wallowing in such follies; and until Mr. Comyns
Carr and Sir Edward Burne-Jones, Baronet, put "King

Arthur" on the stage more or less in the manner natural
to men who know these things, Mr. Daly might have
pleaded the unbroken conservatism of the playhouse
against me. But after the Lyceum scenery and architecture I decline to accept a relapse without protest.
There is no reason why cheap photographs of Italian
architecture (six-pence apiece in infinite variety at the
bookstall in the South Kensington Museum) should not
rescue us from Regent's Park Renaissance colonnades on
the stage just as the electric light can rescue us from
Telbin's dun-colored sunlight. The opera is the last place
in the world where any wise man would look for adequate
stage illusion; but the fact is that Mr. Daly, with all his
colored lights, has not produced a single Italian scene
comparable in illusion to that provided by Sir Augustus
Harris at Covent Garden for "Cavalleria Rusticana."

Of the acting I have not much to say. Miss Rehan
provided a strong argument in favor of rational dress by
looking much better in her page's costume than in that
of her own sex; and in the serenade scene, and that of
the wooing of Silvia for Proteus, she stirred some feeling
into the part, and reminded us of what she was in
"Twelfth Night," where the same situations are fully
worked out. For the rest, she moved and spoke with
imposing rhythmic grace. That is as much notice as so
cheap a part as Julia is worth from an artist who, being
absolute mistress of the situation at Daly's theatre, might
and should have played Imogen for us instead. The two
gentlemen were impersonated by Mr. Worthing and Mr.
Craig. Mr. Worthing charged himself with feeling without any particular reference to his lines; and Mr. Craig
struck a balance by attending to the meaning of his
speeches without taking them at all to heart. Mr. Clarke,

as the Duke, was emphatic, and worked up every long speech to a climax in the useful old style; but his tone is harsh, his touch on his consonants coarse, and his accent ugly, all fatal disqualifications for the delivery of Shakespearean verse. The scenes between Launce and his dog brought out the latent silliness and childishness of the audience as Shakespeare's clowning scenes always do: I laugh at them like a yokel myself. Mr. Lewis hardly made the most of them. His style has been formed in modern comedies, where the locutions are so familiar that their meaning is in no danger of being lost by the rapidity of his quaint utterance; but Launce's phraseology is another matter: a few of the funniest lines missed fire because the audience did not catch them. And with all possible allowance for Mr. Daly's blue pencil, I cannot help suspecting that Mr. Lewis's memory was responsible for one or two of his omissions. Still, Mr. Lewis has always his comic force, whether he makes the most or the least of it; so that he cannot fail in such a part as Launce. Miss Maxine Elliot's Silvia was the most considerable performance after Miss Rehan's Julia. The whole company will gain by the substitution on Tuesday next of a much better play, "A Midsummer Night's Dream," as a basis for Mr. Daly's operations. No doubt he is at this moment, like Mrs. Todgers, "a dodgin' among the tender bits with a fork, and an eatin' of 'em"; but there is sure to be enough of the original left here and there to repay a visit.

TOUJOURS DALY

Madame Sans-Gêne. Garrick Theatre, 8 July, 1895.
A Midsummer Night's Dream. Daly's Theatre, 9
July, 1895.

BEFORE Madame Sans-Gêne I think it best to retire
in good order without committing myself. I have
never seen a French play of which I understood
less; and that, for me, is saying a good deal. Many of
the sallies of Rejane which provoke the loudest laughter
are just those which escape me. Napoleon is an inscrutable person, as becomes the Man of Destiny. I do not
catch a solitary word he says, no doubt because of his
Corsican accent. With the rest I can pick my way along
sufficiently to be almost as much bored as if the play were
in English. Surely the twenty minutes or so of amusement contained in the play might be purchased a little
more cheaply than by the endurance of a huge mock
historic melodrama which never for a moment produces
the faintest conviction, and which involves the exhibition
of elaborate Empire interiors requiring half an hour between the acts to set, and not worth looking at when they
are set. Of course I admire the ingenuity with which
Sardou carries out his principle of combining the maximum of expenditure and idle chatter with the minimum
of drama; but I have admired that so often that it is beginning to pall on me. And I think something better
could be done with Rejane's talent than this business,
funny as it is for once in a way, of playing the washerwoman like a real duchess and the duchess like a stage
washerwoman. Rejane, to say the least, is not exacting
as to the quality of her parts provided they are popular;

and it rests with the dramatists to make the best or worst
of her. How Sardou proceeds when he has *carte blanche*
in that way may be learnt from the pages of the Sardou-
Bernhardt repertory—though please observe that I do
not imply that he ever makes the worst of anything; because to go to that extreme requires a good deal of conviction, which is just the sort of force that he lacks. I
can no more believe in Madame Sans-Gêne than in Theodora or La Tosca. She is more amusing: that is all.

"The Two Gentlemen of Verona" has been succeeded
at Daly's Theatre by "A Midsummer Night's Dream."
Mr. Daly is in great form. In my last article I was rash
enough to hint that he had not quite realized what could
be done with electric lighting on the stage. He triumphantly answers me by fitting up all his fairies with portable
batteries and incandescent lights, which they switch on
and off from time to time, like children with a new toy.
He has trained Miss Lillian Swain in the part of Puck
until it is safe to say that she does not take one step,
strike one attitude, or modify her voice by a single in-
flexion that is not violently, wantonly, and ridiculously
wrong and absurd. Instead of being mercurial, she poses
academically, like a cheap Italian statuette; instead of
being impish and childish, she is elegant and affected; she
laughs a solemn, measured laugh, like a heavy German
Zamiel; she announces her ability to girdle the earth in
forty minutes in the attitude of a professional skater, and
then begins the journey awkwardly in a swing, which
takes her in the opposite direction to that in which she
indicated her intention of going: in short, she illustrates
every folly and superstition that still clings round what
Mr. Daly no doubt calls "the legitimate." Another stroke
of his is to make Oberon a woman. It must not be sup-

of these absurdities are part of a systematic policy of sacrificing the credibility of the play to the chance of exhibiting an effective "living picture."

I very soon gave up the attempt to keep a record of the outrages practised by Mr. Daly on the text. Everyone knows the lines:

> "I swear to thee by Cupid's strongest bow,
>   By his best arrow with the golden head,
>   By the simplicity of Venus' doves,
>   By that which knitteth souls and prospers loves," etc.

Mr. Daly's powerful mind perceived at a glance that the second and third lines are superfluous, as their omission does not destroy the sense of the passage. He accordingly omitted them. In the same scene, Shakespeare makes the two-star-crossed lovers speak in alternate lines with an effect which sets the whole scene throbbing with their absorption in one another:

> "LYSANDER: The course of true love never did run smooth.
>   But either it was different in blood—
>   HERMIA: O cross! too high to be enthralled to low!
>   LYSANDER: Or else misgraffed in respect of years,
>   HERMIA: O spite! too old to be engaged to young!
>   LYSANDER: Or else it stood upon the choice of friends,
>   HERMIA: O hell! to choose love by another's eye!
>   LYSANDER: Or if there were a sympathy in choice,
>   War, death, or sickness did lay siege to it," etc.

With a Hermia who knew how to breathe out these parentheses, the duet would be an exquisite one; but Mr. Daly, shocked, as an American and an Irishman, at a young lady using such an expression as "Oh hell!" cuts out the whole antiphony, and leaves Lysander to deliver a long lecture without interruption from the lady. At such moments, the episode of the ass's head rises to the dignity of allegory. From any other manager I should accept the excuse that the effects of verse for which I am pleading require a virtuosity of delivery on the part of the actor which is practically not to be had at present. But Mr. Daly has Miss Rehan, who is specially famous for just this virtuosity of speech; and yet her lines are treated just as the others are. The fact is, beautiful elocution is rare because the managers have no ears.

The play, though of course very poorly spoken in comparison with how it ought to be spoken, is tolerably acted. Mr. George Clarke, clad in the armor of Alcibiades and the red silk gown of Charlie's Aunt, articulates most industriously, and waves his arms and flexes his wrists in strict accordance, not for a moment with the poetry, but with those laws of dramatic elocution and gesture which veteran actors are always willing to impart to novices at a reasonable price per dozen lessons. Mr. Lewis as Bottom is not as funny as his part, whereas in modern plays he is always funnier than his part. He seemed to me to miss the stolid, obstinate, self-sufficient temperament of Bottom altogether. There is a definite conception of some particular sort of man at the back of all Shakespeare's characters. The quantity of fun to be got out of Bottom and Autolycus, for instance, is about the same; but underneath the fun there are two widely different persons, of types still extant and familiar. Mr. Lewis would be as funny in Autolycus as he is in Bottom; but he would be exactly the same man in both parts.

As to Miss Rehan, her scenes in the wood with Demetrius were very fine, although, in the passage where Hermia frightens her, she condescended to arrant clowning. Her treatment of Shakespearean verse is delightful after the mechanical intoning of Sarah Bernhardt. She

body can persuade me that if she says "Cymbeline," Mr. Daly can say "The Two Gentlemen of Verona," or that if she says Sudermann or Ibsen, Mr. Daly can insist on the author of "Dollars and Cents." But the self-culture which has produced her superb graces of manner and diction seems to have isolated her instead of quickening her sympathy and drawing closer her contact with the world. Every woman who sees Duse play Magda feels that Duse is acting and speaking for her and for all women as they are hardly ever able to speak and act for themselves. The same may be said of Miss Achurch as Nora. But no woman has ever had the very faintest sensation of that kind about any part that Miss Rehan has yet played. We admire, not what she is doing, but the charm with which she does it. That sort of admiration will not last. Miss Rehan's voice is not henceforth going to grow fresher, nor her dignity less conscious, nor her grace of gesture less studied and mannered, nor her movements swifter and more spontaneous. Already I find that young people who see her for the first time cannot quite agree that our raptures about her Katherine and her Rosalind are borne out by her Julia and Helena. Five years hence she will be still more rhetorical and less real: further ahead I dare not look with Barry Sullivan in my mind. There is only one way to defy Time; and that is to have young ideas, which may always be trusted to find youthful and vivid expression. I am afraid this means avoiding the company of Mr. Daly; but it is useless to blink the fact that unless a modern actress can and will force her manager, in spite of his manly prejudices, to produce plays with real women's parts in them, she had better, at all hazards, make shift to manage for herself. With Grandfather Daly to choose her plays for her, there is no future for Ada Rehan.

THE SEASON'S MORAL

27 July, 1895.

NOW THAT the theatrical season is over, is there any moral to be drawn? I do not mean by literary factions—Ibsenites and anti-Ibsenites and the like—but by, let us say, a manager with enough money at stake to make him anxious to get some guidance for next season. To him, as far as I can see, the season has been like Ibsen's plays: the moral is that there is no moral. The outcry against Ibsen has been deferred to carefully. "Little Eyolf" has been boycotted; and none of the older plays have been touched in English, whilst there has been a plentiful supply of what was described the other day, in contradistinction to Ibsen's work, as "the drama that the public likes and the public pays for." Need I add that in most cases the public has not liked it and has declined to pay for it. What is a manager to do? He responds to the demand for honest, wholesome, English murder, suicide and adultery, by commissioning M. Sardou to supply those solid native articles; and lo! bottomless disaster, worse than the worst Ibsen ever threatened. He tries the newest English psychological drama, with an interestingly improper heroine who throws the Bible into the fire. The press proclaims a masterpiece—where is that masterpiece now? The infallible Mrs. Tanqueray is revived, and does not draw a sixpence. Mr. Grundy, as an expert in "construction," with daring views on the great marriage question, is called in; but his "Slaves of the Ring" perishes without having enjoyed a seventieth part of the popularity of "A Doll's House." Even Henry Arthur Jones, the strong and successful, has no more than a Norwegian success: the manager might have produced "The League of Youth" instead of "The Triumph of the Philistines" without being any the poorer. What a muddle it all seems! That safe old hand Sardou, playing the safe old game according to the safe old rules, fails ignominiously. Those safe old hands, Pinero, Grundy, and Jones, cautiously playing the new game according to the safe old rules, fail to retrieve the situation. One must not forget, however, that performances have to be taken into account as well as plays. Sardou's contribution, "Delia Harding," was adequately acted—much better than it deserved in Miss Marion Terry's case—and may be dismissed as having failed hopelessly on its merits. "Mrs Ebbsmith," badly cast and badly acted except for Mrs. Campbell's Agnes and Mr. Hare's Duke of St. Olpherts, did not begin to flag until the withdrawal of Mrs. Campbell brought out all the defects in the performance. "Slaves of the Ring," though better cast, was worse acted than "Mrs. Ebbsmith"; and "The Triumph of the Philistines" never got fairly on to the stage, the strong and sympathetic parts being just enough underplayed to take the edge off the performance. This points to the difficulty which has been apparent for the last five or six years: namely, that the public are getting tired of the old-fashioned plays faster than the actors are learning to make the new ones effective. The unfortunate new dramatist has, therefore, to write plays so extraordinarily good that, like Mozart's operas, they succeeded in spite of inadequate execution. This is all very well for geniuses like Ibsen; but it is rather hard on the ordinary purveyor of the drama. The managers do not seem to me yet to grasp this feature of the situation. If they did, they would only meddle with the strongest specimens of the

new drama, instead of timidly going to the old firms and
ordering moderate plays cut in the new style. No doubt
the success of "The Second Mrs. Tanqueray" and "The
Case of Rebellious Susan" seemed to support the view
that the new style had better be tried cautiously by an
old hand. But then "Mrs. Tanqueray" had not really
the faintest touch of the new spirit in it; and recent
events suggest that its success was due to a happy cast
of the dice by which the play found an actress who
doubled its value and had hers doubled by it. For we
have this season seen the play without the actress and the
actress without the play, with disappointing results in
both cases. As to "Rebellious Susan" it was, on the outside, an amusing and naughty comedy, acted by the company which has since made a success of Mr. Carton's
scatterbrained and conventionally sentimental "Home
Secretary." The fact that "The Triumph of the Philistines," in which the element of social criticism was pushed
well to the front of the play, and in which the element
of amusing and naughty comedy was confined to one
part, only succeeded in respect of this very part, and did
not hold the stage long, completes the demonstration that
the moral drawn from the success of Mrs. Tanqueray and
Rebellious Susan was the wrong moral, and that for the
present it is dangerous to meddle with plays of the new
type unless they are strong enough to be "actor proof."
Thus it would appear that Mr. Alexander was ill advised
to produce "The Triumph of the Philistines" with such
a work as Sudermann's "Home" ("Magda") up his
sleeve. "Home" will hold as much acting as even Duse
can put into it; but the play was handicapped in Duse's
hands by a language that the audience did not understand. The general complaints made that the situation

in the last act was strained and weak, were due, I suspect, to the failure of the audience to catch the meaning, or at least the full force, of the speech which brings about the catastrophe. Magda, after many years of work and finally of great success as an independent woman, working as a public singer, becomes reconciled to her father, a fanatical believer in the old ideals of family honor and manly supremacy. She has a child whose father turns up among the intimate friends of the family. Her father demands that she shall marry this man as a point of honor. She submits to this and to the sacrifice of her profession until the man demands also that she shall part with the child in order to save appearances. Magda then turns on him and overwhelms him with scorn. Her father insists. She defies her father, who attempts to kill her and is struck down by paralysis in the act. To any one who is only following in a general way what is happening, this catastrophe must indeed appear inadequately motived and over-strained. So would the story of Othello under the same circumstances. But when the dialogue is fully understood, there are few strokes of drama more effective and convincing than the climax of the final scene between the father and daughter, when she at last asks him the terrible question, "How do you know that he was the only one?" After that, the catastrophe comes quite inevitably; and there is no reason to doubt that in an English version it would justify itself fully. Mr. Alexander could not easily have got Magda played as Duse played her; but he could have got her played well enough to make much more effect than those parts in Mr. Jones's play which missed fire through underacting. In truth, Magda is so excellent an acting part that it would be very hard for an actress of any standing to fail in it. All this,

however, is wisdom after the event. At the beginning of
the season Sudermann was an unknown quantity; and
everything pointed to the expediency of producing "The
Triumph of the Philistines." Besides, Mr. Alexander
had already made an heroic contribution to the cause of
art by venturing on Mr. Henry James's "Guy Domville,"
and producing it with great care and unstinted liberality,
though the result was one for which he could hardly have
been quite unprepared. The play, delicately written and
admirably performed, was too fine for the audience; and
the gallery first-nighters behaved very badly, as they did
subsequently, more excusably, at "Delia Harding," though
after that they happily pulled themselves together, and
conducted themselves decently during the rest of the
season. The production of "Guy Domville" was an attempt to conquer new territory by a *coup de main;* and
that sort of enterprise needs a heavier weapon than Mr.
Henry James forges. Then, too, Mr. Henry James's intellectual fastidiousness remains untouched by the re-
surgent energy and wilfulness of the new spirit. It takes
us back to the exhausted atmosphere of George Eliot,
Huxley, and Tyndall, instead of thrusting us forward
into the invigorating strife raised by Wagner, Ibsen, and
Sudermann. That verdant dupe of the lunacy specialists,
Dr. Max Nordau, would hardly recognize in Mr. Henry
James the "stigmata of degeneration," which no dramatist at present can afford to be without. Mr. Alexander
should have struck his blow with the arm of Ibsen or
Sudermann, or else kept to the old ground. And it ap-
pears that neither Mr. Pinero, Mr. Grundy, nor Mr.
Jones could have helped him any better than Mr. Henry
James. Moral, apparently: those who make half revolu-
tions dig their own graves.

But it must be remembered, as a check to the folly of moralizing, that the plays which belong to no "movement," and in which the authors have gratified their fancies without reference to any views, have prospered—at least, they have not been withdrawn. In "The Passport," "The Prude's Progress," and "The Strange Adventures of Miss Brown," you have imagination, humor, and a sense of character within the limits of good fellowship. These qualities will carry a good deal of psychology and social doctrine about the unhappiness of marriage, the emancipation of woman, and so forth, if the loading be judiciously done. But the psychology and the doctrine can be done without, whereas the imagination, the humor, the sympathetic sense of character, whether blunt and vulgar or acute and subtle, are indispensable. It was the purest snobbery of criticism which this season reverently hailed "The Notorious Mrs. Ebbsmith" as a masterpiece, and saluted "The Prude's Progress" with a supercilious nod. I rather congratulate myself on having been polite to the three unpretending successes, and on having cut Mrs. Ebbsmith dead at first sight.

Here again it should be noted that these three successful plays, unlike "Mrs. Ebbsmith" and "The Philistines," are very well cast and very well acted, "The Passport" especially being played for all it is worth by an exceptionally strong and well suited company. Another apparently successful play was Mr. Carton's "Home Secretary." Mr. Carton, beside the pleasant gift of lightness of heart, has at least imagination and humor enough to assimilate the imaginative and humorous work of other authors, and to make up a pasticcio of the parts in which a London audience delights to see certain favorite artists: Mr. Lewis Waller as Captain Swift, Miss Neilson as the austerely angelic wife of an erring mortal man, Miss Moore as a bewitching flirt, Mr. Sydney Brough as a good-hearted young gentleman with a sympathetically comic love affair, and Mr. Wyndham as a reformed rake. For my part, I wish Mr. Wyndham had never reformed. In the old days, when he sipped every flower and changed every hour, when he sowed acres of wild oats and violated every moral obligation, one foresaw that the pace would not last, and one hoped that he would presently go deeper into life and art, and do the fullest justice to his admirable talent as an actor. Unhappily, instead of doing this, he played the insufferable John Mildmay, became serious, and gave up acting altogether to exhibit himself as a quiet gentleman, who can act in the old scandalous fashion if he likes, but prefers, as a man of heart, to refrain. The refraint is no doubt impressive; but it is getting tiresome as a pose, though I should be delighted to see it in a real part. Rosmer, for instance, would be an excellent part for Mr. Wyndham in his latest vein.

I now propose to banish the theatre from my mind for a couple of months at least. Since January I have devoted to it far too much of what was meant for mankind. I could hardly have gone back to it even for the above retrospect had I not been led gently by Miss Cissie Loftus, whose imitations of popular actors I studied with much interest at the Palace Theatre the other evening. Nothing teaches a critic more than a study of how far a great artist can be imitated. As a musical critic I learnt a great deal from a comparison of Miss Nettie Carpenter with Sarasate, and Miss Szumowska with Paderewski; and I am the wiser now for seeing how much more of Sarah Bernhardt Miss Loftus can reproduce than of Miss Rehan. But it is not as a mimic that Miss Loftus fascinates the public. The imitation, clever and delicate as it is, is only an excuse for the reality, which is Miss Loftus herself; and I shall not analyze the qualities which go to make up her very attractive personality until I see her on another stage acting at first hand. Among other artists whom I saw at the Palace were Miss Clara Wieland and the illustrious Miss Lottie Collins. Miss Wieland is very interesting from the critic's point of view. Her singing, her dancing, her pantomime, her ogling, her cleverness, even her plump sort of prettiness, are as smart and artistic as they need be; and yet it is impossible to detect in her any enjoyment of what she does, or any sympathetic sense of its charm. She seems to have observed that such things are effective, and to have industriously learnt to do and to be accordingly. Miss Lottie Collins, on the other hand, has still her Tarararesque *diable au corps;* but all the music has gone from her singing, because, in her determination to deliver her lines pointedly, she forgets to keep up the swing of the tune, and allows her comic-song singing to decay into mere seventh-rate character acting. A tune treated in that way is a tune spoilt; and the words of a music-hall song are never worth spoiling the tune for. I respectfully assure Miss Collins that unless she promptly recaptures the art of keeping the musical lilt perfectly in step with every syllable of the words, she will soon find her popularity degringolading from the summit on which the Tarara craze exalted it.

ROMEO AND JULIET

Romeo and Juliet. Lyceum Theatre, 21 September, 1895.

How we lavish our money and our worship on Shakespeare without in the least knowing why! From time to time we ripen for a new act of homage. Great preparations are made; high hopes are raised; every one concerned, from the humblest *persona muta* on the stage to the sworn first-nighter in the gallery, is full of earnest belief that the splendor of the Swan will be revealed at last, like the Holy Grail. And yet the point of the whole thing is missed every time with ludicrous ineptitude; and often a ruined actor-manager spends the rest of his life, like the Ancient Mariner, in telling the tale of what it cost, and how So-and-So got his (or her) first chance in it, and how such and such other eminent people declared that nothing like it had ever been done before, and so on and so forth. Still, there is nothing for it but to try and try and try again. Every revival helps to exhaust the number of possible ways of altering Shakespeare's plays unsuccessfully, and so hastens the day when the mere desire for novelty will lead to the experiment of leaving them unaltered. Let us see what there is to learn from Mr. Forbes Robertson's revival of "Romeo and Juliet," before that goes the way of all the other revivals. I hardly like to call Mr. Forbes Robertson an artist, because he is notoriously an Englishman with a taste for painting, and the two things are usually incompatible. Your Englishman always conceives that to be romantic and to have a susceptible imagination

inferred, that the scenery is enormously in advance of that to which Mr. Augustin Daly treated us for "The Two Gentlemen of Verona." No doubt Mr. Daly paid as much as Mr. Forbes Robertson; but Mr. Daly's scene-painters copied bad work, and Mr. Forbes Robertson's have copied good. That makes all the difference.

Of course, in criticizing the general effect, the play and the acting cannot be altogether left out of account, though it would be unfair to lay too much stress on them. Perhaps the most difficult character in the play as far as finesse of execution goes is Mercutio. We see Mercutio in his first scene as a wit and fantasist of the most delicate order. In his next, apparently without any shock to the Elizabethan sense of congruity, he is a detestable and intolerable cad, the exact prototype of our modern 'Arry. The change gives such another glimpse into the manners of that time as you get in "Much Ado" from the astonishment which Benedick creates by taking to washing his face every day. By stage tradition, Mercutio is as much a leading part as Romeo, if not more so. Therefore, when the manager chooses Romeo, he should be particularly careful to choose a good Mercutio, lest he should appear to have that part purposely underplayed. Perhaps this was why Mr. Forbes Robertson went so far out of his way as to cast Mr. Coghlan for the part. If so, he over-reached himself; for he could not possibly have made a worse choice. I really cannot express myself politely on the subject of Mr. Coghlan's performance. He lounges, he mumbles, he delivers the Queen Mab speech in a raffish patter which takes, and is apparently deliberately meant to take, all beauty of tone and grace of measure out of it. It may be that Mr. Coghlan has studied the part carefully, and come to the conclusion that since the visit of the Montagues to Capulet's ball is a young bloods' escapade, Mercutio should be represented as coming half drunk and lolling on the stone seat outside to repeat a tipsy rigmarole about nothing. In that case I must express my entire disagreement with Mr. Coghlan's reading. Shakespeare never leaves me in any doubt as to when he means an actor to play Sir Toby Belch and when to play Mercutio, or when he means an actor to speak measured verse and when slipshod colloquial prose.

Far better than Mr. Coghlan's Mercutio, and yet quite the worst impersonation I have ever seen of a not very difficult old woman's part, was Miss Dolores Drummond's Nurse. Tybalt's is such an unmercifully bad part that one can hardly demand anything from its representative except that he should brush his hair when he comes to his uncle's ball (a condition which he invariably repudiates) and that he should be so consummate a swordsman as to make it safe for Romeo to fall on him with absolute abandonment, and annihilate him as Jean de Reszke used to annihilate Montariol. This is one of the great sensations of the play: unless an actor is capable of a really terrible explosion of rage, he had better let Romeo alone. Unfortunately, the "fire-eyed fury" before which Tybalt falls lies outside the gentlemanly limits of Mr. Forbes Robertson's stage instinct; and it may be that his skill as an actor is not equal to the task of working-up the audience to the point at which they will imagine an explosion which cannot, of course, be real. At all events the duel scene has none of the murderous excitement which is the whole dramatic point of it: it is tamed down to a mere formal pretext for the banishment of Romeo. Mr. Forbes Robertson has evidently no sympathy with Shakespeare's love of a shindy: you see his love of law and order coming out in his stage management of the fighting scenes. Nobody is allowed to enjoy the scrimmage: Capulet and Montague are silenced; and the spectators of the duel are women—I should say ladies—who look intensely shocked to see gentlemen of position so grossly forgetting themselves. Mr. Forbes Robertson himself fights with unconcealed repugnance: he makes you feel that to do it in that disorderly way, without seconds, without a doctor, showing temper about it, and actually calling his adversary names, jars unspeakably on him. Far otherwise have we seen him as Orlando wrestling with Charles. But there the contest was in the presence of a court, with measured ground and due formality —under Queensberry rules, so to speak. For the rest, Mr. Forbes Robertson is very handsome, very well dressed, very perfectly behaved. His assortment of tones, of gestures, of facial expressions, of attitudes, are limited to half a dozen apiece; but they are carefully selected and all of the best. The arrangements in the last scene are exceedingly nice: the tomb of the Capulets is beautifully kept, well lighted, and conveniently accessible by a couple of broad steps—quite like a new cathedral chapel. Indeed, when Romeo, contemplating the bier of Juliet (which reflected the utmost credit on the undertaker) said:

> "I still will stay with thee,
> And never from this palace of dim night
> Depart again,"

I felt that the sacrifice he was making in doing without a proper funeral was greatly softened. Romeo was a gentleman to the last. He laid out Paris after killing him as carefully as if he were folding up his best suit of clothes. One remembers Irving, a dim figure dragging a

horrible burden down through the gloom "into the rotten
jaws of death," and reflects on the differences of imaginative temperament that underlie the differences of acting and stage-managing.

As to Juliet, she danced like the daughter of Herodias.
And she knew the measure of her lines to a hairsbreadth.
Did I not say, long ago, that Mrs. Tanqueray's piano-
playing was worth all the rest of her? And yet I was
taken in by Mrs. Tanqueray—also by Mrs. Ebbsmith, as
we all were. Woman's great art is to lie low, and let the
imagination of the male endow her with depths. How
Mrs. Patrick Campbell must have laughed at us whilst
we were giving her all the credit—if credit it were—for
our silly psychologizing over those Pinero parts! As
Juliet she still fits herself into the hospitable manly heart
without effort, simply because she is a wonderful person,
not only in mere facial prettiness, in which respect she is
perhaps not superior to the bevy of "extra ladies" in the
fashionable scenes in the new Drury Lane play, not even
in her light, beautifully proportioned figure, but in the
extraordinary swiftness and certainty of her physical self-
command. I am convinced that Mrs. Patrick Campbell
could thread a needle with her toes at the first attempt
as rapidly, as smoothly, as prettily, and as with as much
attention to spare for doing anything else at the same
time as she can play an arpeggio. This physical talent,
which is seldom consciously recognized except when it
is professedly specialized in some particular direction (as
in the case, for instance, of Miss Letty Lind), will, when
accompanied by nimbleness of mind, quick observation,
and lively theatrical instinct, carry any actress with a
rush to the front of her profession, as it has carried Mrs.
Patrick Campbell. Her Juliet, nevertheless, is an im-

mature performance at all the exceptional points, which, please remember, are not very numerous, much of Juliet's business being of a kind that no "leading lady" of ordinary ability could possibly fail in. All the conscious ideas gathered by her from the part and carried out in planned strokes of her own are commonplace. There is not a touch of tragedy, not a throb of love or fear, temper instead of passion: in short, a Juliet as unawakened as Richard III., one in whose death you don't believe, though you would not cry over it if you did believe. Nothing of it is memorable except the dance—the irresistible dance.

It should never be forgotten in judging an attempt to play "Romeo and Juliet" that the parts are made almost impossible, except to actors of positive genius, skilled to the last degree in metrical declamation, by the way in which the poetry, magnificent as it is, is interlarded by the miserable rhetoric and silly logical conceits which were the foible of the Elizabethans. When Juliet comes out on her balcony and, having propounded the question, "What's in a name?" proceeds to argue it out like an amateur attorney in Christmas-card verse of the "rose by any other name" order, no actress can make it appear natural to a century which has discovered the art of giving prolonged and intense dramatic expression to pure feeling alone, without any skeleton of argument or narrative, by means of music. Romeo has lines that tighten the heart or catch you up into the heights, alternately with heartless fustian and silly ingenuities that make you curse Shakespeare's stagestruckness and his youthful inability to keep his brains quiet. It needs a great flowing tide of passion, an irresistibly impetuous march of music, to carry us over these pitfalls and stumbling-blocks, even when we are foolish enough to mistake the good for the bad, and to reverently accept Mr. Coghlan as an authority on the subject of Mercutio. It would be folly to hold out any such hopes of rescue at the Lyceum. Of the whole company there is only one member who achieves artistic respectability as a Shakespearean player, and that is Mr. Warde as Capulet. For the most part, one has to listen to the music of Shakespeare—in which music, I repeat again and again, the whole worth and charm of these early plays of his lies—as one might listen to a symphony of Beethoven's with all the parts played on the bones, the big drum, and the Jew's-harp. But the production is an unsparing effort, and therefore as honorable to Mr. Forbes Robertson's management as the highest artistic success could make it. The more efforts of that kind we have, the sooner we shall have the artistic success.

PINERO AS HE IS ACTED

The Benefit of the Doubt: a new and original comedy, in three acts. By Arthur W. Pinero. Comedy Theatre, 16 October, 1895.

Poor Mr. Potton: a new and original farce, in three acts. By Clarence Hamlyn and H. M. Paull. Vaudeville Theatre, 10 October, 1895.

THIS time Mr. Pinero has succeeded. "The Benefit of the Doubt" is worth "The Profligate," "Mrs. Tanqueray," and "Mrs. Ebbsmith" rolled into one and multiplied by ten. It is melancholy to have to add that it has broken the back of our London stage, and may even fail through the sniffing monotony and dreary ugliness of the acting; but about the merit of the play there can be no question. Mr. Pinero, concentrating himself on a phase of life and sentiment which he thoroughly understands, has extracted abundant drama from it, and maintained it at an astonishingly high and even pressure for two hours, without for a moment being driven back on the woman with a past, the cynical libertine peer, the angel of purity, the Cayley Drummle confidant, or any other of the conventional figures which inevitably appear in his plays whenever he conceives himself to be dealing as a sociologist with public questions of which he has no solid knowledge, but only a purely conventional and theatrical conceit. In "The Benefit of the Doubt" he keeps within the territory he has actually explored; and the result is at once apparent in the higher dramatic pressure, the closer-knit action, the substitution of a homogeneous slice of life for the old theatrical sandwich of

sentiment and comic relief, and the comparative originality, naturalness, and free development of the characters. Even in the machinery by which the persons of
the play are got on and off the stage there is a marked
improvement. It is artificial enough—Mr. Pinero has
not exactly been born again—but at least there are no
intercepted letters, or sendings of one set of people to
France and another to India in order to enable a lady
to arrive unexpectedly or a gentleman to walk in by
night at the drawing-room window. There certainly is
one nocturnal visit through a window; but it is pardonable; and for the rest, the people come and go in a normal and respectable manner. The play is of a frivolous
widow with three fast, slangy, pretty daughters, two of
them married. An amiable young gentleman named John
Allingham, tormented by a frightfully jealous wife, con-
fides his miseries to one of the married daughters, a Mrs.
Fraser (Fraser being much away from home). The
jealous Mrs. Allingham sues for a judicial separation,
and the play opens at the point where her petition is
refused. Mrs. Fraser, however, only escapes very narrowly, as the Judge comments strongly on her indiscretion, and suggests nothing more complimentary for
her than "the benefit of the doubt." When Mr. Fraser
comes home, he acts on this suggestion so very grudg-
ingly that Mrs. Fraser rushes off to throw herself upon
the more sympathetic Allingham. But that ill-starred
example of the perils of excessive good-nature has meanwhile succumbed to his wife's appeal for a reconciliation,
she being nearly as violent in her remorse as in her jealousy, and much less reasonable. There you have your
drama: first, in the suspense of awaiting the verdict,
ended by the return of Mrs. Fraser from the divorce

court to face out her disgrace before her family and be driven to desperation by the rebuff from her husband; and second, her arrival at Allingham's house just as the demon of jealousy has been reinstalled there on the domestic throne. In handling all this Mr. Pinero is never at a loss. He knows what pretty daughters and frivolous mothers are like in those circles which used to be called *demi-mondaine* before that distinction was audaciously annexed by people who are not *mondaine* at all; he knows what the divorce court and the newspapers mean to them; he knows what a jealous woman is like; and he has dramatized them with an intensity never attained by him before. Consciously or unconsciously, he has this time seen his world as it really is: that is, a world which never dreams of bothering its little head with large questions or general ideas. He no longer attempts to dress up Mrs. Ponsonby de Tompkins like Mrs. Besant, and to present the ridiculous result as a portrait of a typical modern "advanced" woman: he sticks to the Bayswater-Kensington *genre,* of which he is a master. He does not even adulterate it with conventional stage sentiment: for instance none of Mrs. Emptage's fast and rather raffish daughters burst into tears at the thought of the holy purity of their sixteenth year, when they could look angels in the face unashamed, as Paula Tanqueray did. His early weaknesses have disappeared along with his late affectations; and the happy issue is the best serious play he has yet produced.

The subject of the acting is almost too painful to face. The second act, which lasts for more than an hour, is pervaded by the violently jealous wife. She only leaves the stage to give place to her wearied and desperate rival, who ends by drinking champagne cup to save herself from fainting, and, having fed on nothing all day but excitement, naturally gets tipsy and hysterical. Such scenes, however, moving and interesting they may be, and however skilfully written, can only be made tolerable by sheer beauty of execution. Tact and experience —the best substitutes our unfortunate stage can offer— may do something to steer the performance clear of positive offensiveness; but tact and experience are not enough: unless the lines are spoken by voices of which the ear never tires, with gestures and action which never lose their fascination, the result can be no better than a disagreeable experience, drawing a crowd and holding it only as a street accident does. The reason why the second act made the audience uneasy was that long before the end of it we had had enough, and more than enough, not of the play, but of the performers. We all know the melodramatic style which grew up in the days when actors who played "emotional" parts habitually got themselves into the requisite maudlin condition by making themselves half drunk. This was the true origin of the detestable veiled voice and muzzy utterance which no longer produce any illusion except that of the odor of spirits. The actor of the past will not walk across the stage to open the door: he plunged headlong at the handle, and, when he had safely grasped it, rolled his eye round to give some pretense of dramatic significance to an action which really expressed nothing but his doubts as to his ability to walk straight. He hung over the furniture, leant against the staircase, wallowed, collapsed tragically when he sat down, did everything, in short, to conceal his condition and cover up the absence of that clear, sober, elegant speech and movement which mark the self-possessed and accomplished artist. The old drunken habits have nearly passed away—at least, I hope future generations of critics will not often have to write sympathetic obituary notices deploring the "breakdown in health" of actors and actresses who notoriously drank themselves first off the stage and then out of the world—but the style of acting that arose in the days when everybody drank remains with us as a senseless superstition, and is still laboriously acquired and cultivated by perfectly sober actors. Unhappily for Mr. Pinero's play, Mr. Leonard Boyne, who probably has no suspicion of the real origin of the traditional style of play of which he has made himself, next to Mr. Charles Warner, the most popular exponent, played John Allingham as he would have played an Adelphi or Drury Lane hero. Miss Lily Hanbury, as the jealous Mrs. Allingham, soon proved the weakness of our system of promoting young ladies to leading parts on the strength of good looks and general intelligence and address. Miss Hanbury acted as acting is understood on the London stage. That is, she expressed emotion by catching the left side of her under lip between her front teeth, and twisting the right corner as much out of its natural place as possible. She cried, and declared that she was "bad," meaning that she was mad. Her voice, which careful cultivation might by this time have made a very agreeable one, still has all its girlish, nasal character. Five minutes of Mr. Boyne and Miss Hanbury, doing some light and pleasant work in an ordinary play, would leave the impression that they were charming and clever people, and encourage our fatuous satisfaction with the most incompetent profession in the world; but half an hour with them—such a half-hour as Mr. Pinero has set them —may I never spend such another! They did their best;

but they were hopelessly overparted. As to Miss Winifred Emery, she received boundless applause; but as it
burst out in all its enthusiasm in the first act, before she
had uttered a word or made a gesture, it may safely be
discounted. All the same, Miss Emery played astonishingly well, considering that she is virtually a beginner
at work so difficult as that cut out for her by Mr. Pinero.
She was, of course, powerfully aided by her natural
charm, and by the confidence in it which experience has
given her. The champagne scene and the passages of
querulous lassitude were frankly realistic; and I rather
doubt whether a less pretty and popular lady dare have
treated them so without greater art to help her. Even
as it was, Miss Emery sometimes lost her style and allowed her intonation to become decidedly disagreeable.
But for the most part, and especially in the first act, she
got far beyond any point I have seen her reach before,
and, indeed, beyond any point that is commonly reached
by our London "leading ladies." She evidently only
wants plenty of that sort of work to make her, within
the limits of her temperament, a highly accomplished
actress.

Miss Rose Leclercq, not this time condemned to play
the usual caricature of herself, had a real part, and
played it with real distinction. The other parts are of
the usual type; that is to say, they require a certain professional habit for their effective presentation, but involve
little knowledge of the art of acting. The best of them
are in the hands of Miss Esme Beringer, Mr. Cyril
Maude, and Mr. Aubrey Fitzgerald. Mr. Pinero, always
a bad hand at casting a play, has not fitted Miss Beringer
very happily—more's the pity, as she is one of the few
young actresses now on the stage who have studied their

profession, or even realized that there is anything to study in it.

"Poor Mr. Potton," at the Vaudeville, is called a farce, even a new and original farce; but it is hardly more than a romp. However, it is tolerably good fun of its kind, childish fun mostly as regards the action, clever fun occasionally as regards the lines. The scenes, especially the last act, are not at all ill-planned: there is a certain incongruity between the jejune flimsiness of the general notion of the play and the comparative solidity and intelligence with which it is put together. Probably this is a natural consequence of the collaboration between Mr. Clarence Hamlyn and Mr. Paull. From the critical point of view the play is chiefly interesting as an example of the extent to which brutality and silliness are still in demand in our theatres, just as the performance is an example of the impudent artlessness with which long scenes can be gabbled through on the London stage without provoking as much criticism as a company of children performing in a nursery would receive from their parents. The brutality is, of course, unconscious, though that is an excellent reason for a critical attempt to induce some consciousness of it. The fun of the play lies in the engagement of Mr. Potton (Mr. Weedon Grossmith) to an elderly and several times widowed heroine (Miss Gladys Homfrey). Miss Gladys Homfrey is a lady of very ample proportions. I shall not attempt to estimate the excess of her weight over that of Mr. Weedon Grossmith with precision: let me put it roughly and safely at not less than fifty pounds. Need I add that the main joke in "Poor Mr. Potton" is the spectacle of Miss Homfrey throwing herself ponderously on Mr. Grossmith's neck, and being petted and kissed and courted by him. I am obliged to make the strange confession that I do not enjoy this sort of stage effort; though I admit that the guffaws which it invariably elicts show that London audiences do not agree with me. Mr. Gilbert quite understood his public when he furnished his operas so carefully with stout and mature ladies for the express purpose of making fun of their age and figure. Such fun has always revolted me; and I am waiting for the time when it will revolt the public too. I have by me a book called "The Elizabethan Hamlet," by Mr. John Corbin, published by Mr. Elkin Mathews, in which the author succeeds in fully driving home the fact, not of course hitherto unknown, but certainly hitherto underestimated, that Hamlet first became popular on the stage as a madman: that is, as a comic person according to the ideas of that time. I say of that time as a matter of politeness to my contemporaries, though any one who has ever seen a village idiot at large must have seen also a crowd of villagers teasing him, encouraging him to make uncouth sounds and cut deplorable capers, and laughing at him with gross enjoyment as at one of Nature's primest jokes. It has always been so, I am afraid. The old-fashioned king's jester was not a clever, satirical, able person like Dumas's Chicot: he was a zany, a poor idiot, a butt, not a wit. Fortunately we have at last reached a point at which the old Hamlet play is out of the question, whilst the masterpiece which Shakespeare built on it is the most popular play we have. But is there any distinction, except in degree of atrocity, between the old brutal laughter at "Hamblet's" madness and murderous cunning, and our laughter to-day at the Lady Janes of Mr. Gilbert, and at certain comedians and music-hall artists who are commercially fortunate enough to be abnormally small or grotesque in appearance? And if Shakespeare, in a much coarser age, could take subjects which were reeking with the vilest stage traditions, and lift them at one stroke to the highest tragic dignity, is it too much to ask that our modern dramatists should habitually assume that "the British public" consists of humane persons with developed sympathies, and not of rowdy undergraduates and street Arabs? I presume that Miss Gladys Homfrey has an honorable ambition to distinguish herself in the art of acting, as Mrs. Stirling and Mrs. Gilbert have distinguished themselves. Why then should she be condemned to merely exhibit herself as a fat lady? I am not pretending to ignore the fact that personality is an element in the qualification of an actor or actress as well as skill, and that our stage affords so little training that practical dramatic authorship has become the art of exploiting the personalities of popular favorites instead of setting tasks to the executive skill of accomplished artists. If a young author were to come to me and announce his intention of striving to win fame by creating an imaginary heroine who should survive millions of real women as Imogen and Gretchen have, I should, in the paternal character of a man of the world, immediately reply, "Bless your innocence, you mustn't do that. You must vamp up a serious part that will fit Mrs. Patrick Campbell, and a serio-comic part that will fit Miss Fanny Brough, bearing carefully in mind that neither of these ladies ever acts anybody but herself, nor indeed dare to do it, since the public goes to the theatre to see them playing themsleves and not to enjoy dramatic poetry or fine acting." Still, there are limits even to the compulsory cynicism of dramatic authorship. The author may be forced to exploit a lady's temperament and appearance because she cannot act; but he need not condescend to exploit her circumference. Characters like Falstaff are not added to dramatic literature by any process so cheap as the simple making game of the stoutest member of the profession.

Two parts in "Poor Mr. Potton" are well played. Mr. Weedon Grossmith succeeds in making Potton perfectly real, and quite a different person from the other characters of his creation. His perplexed conviction, the apparent unconsciousness with which he allows his funniest points to make themselves, the art with which he takes care that they shall make themselves, and the adroitness of his execution, leave nothing for the critic to say except that the part is as well done as it can be done. Miss Haydon, as Mrs. Potton, makes a charming old lady, preserving her own dignity and that of her art, as well as the verisimilitude of the play, without losing a scrap of comic effect. I will not say that none of the rest were amusing; but they certainly were often quite as annoying as amusing, gabbling and guying as if the play were being performed for their entertainment much more than for that of the audience. Accustomed as I am becoming to see important parts given to clowning novices and to young women whose flippant personal vanity, bad manners, vulgarly titivated costumes, and slipshod carelessness of speech and action would not be tolerated from a parlor-maid by the people who are expected to pay half a guinea for a seat at the theatre, it hardly now seems worth while to complain of an outrage more or less in this direction. The Vaudeville company, apart from Mr. Grossmith and Miss Haydon, is neither better nor worse than I expected to find it. The exceptions were Miss Beet, who gave a capital sketch of an irritable general servant, and Mr. Tom Terriss, whose father has endowed him handsomely with an admirable voice and an attractive figure and face, disinheriting him only in the matter of his chin, which is a comparatively unfamiliar figure. If Mr. Terriss's part was not a very exacting one, he at least got a thorough grip on it, and would have pleased the audience even if his name had been an unknown one.

THE CHILI WIDOW

12 October, 1895.

The Chili Widow. Adapted by Arthur Bourchier and Alfred Sutro from *Monsieur le Directeur,* by MM. Bisson and Carré.   Royalty Theatre.

ON PAYING a somewhat belated visit to "The Chili Widow" the other evening, I was astonished to find that Mr. Bourchier has not only taken the Royalty Theatre—many have done that before him, and some have repented it—but has actually founded there, with apparent success, a new school of stage art. At least it is new to the regular professional stage, though not to the country house or the university dramatic club. It is the school of the romping, gleeful amateur, not he with the contracted brow, the Elizabethan imagination, and the patent method of voice production, but the facetious undergraduate who dresses up for a lark, the awfully jolly girl who can act like anything, and the funny man with accomplishments, including the banjo.

I am not intolerant of such sportiveness: the majesty of criticism can unbend on occasion and enjoy a bit of fun, served up with ridiculous home-made art, as much as the humblest member of the domestic staff admitted to the drawing-room to see the daughters of the house in their stage glory. Even at the Royalty Theatre I do not object to it: only, it is my duty to be perfectly explicit with the public as to the nature of the entertainment. Let me therefore explain.

The accomplishments which distinguish the trained actor from the amateur are not the same as the qualities which distinguish great actors from ordinary ones. Take, first, the difference between the trained actor and the man in the street—the layman. When the layman walks, his only object is to get to Charing Cross; when he makes a gesture, it is to attract the attention of a cab-driver or bus-conductor; when he speaks, it is to convey or demand information, or tell a lie, or otherwise further his prosaic ends; when he moves his hands, it is to put up his umbrella or take out his handkerchief. On the stage these merely utilitarian purposes are only simulated: the real purpose is to produce an effect on the senses and imagination of the spectator. The actor's walk is addressed to the spectator's sense of grace, dignity, or strength of movement, and his voice to the listener's sense of expressive or beautiful tone. Impersonations even of ugly or deformed creatures with harsh voices have the same artistic character, and are agreeably disagreeable, just as the most extreme discords in a symphony or opera are distinctly musical, and perfectly different to the random cacophonies which arise from the tuning of the orchestra. Now, the power of complying with artistic conditions without being so preoccupied by them as to be incapable of thinking of anything else is hard to acquire, and can be perfected only by long practise. Talma estimated the apprenticeship at twenty years. The habit can never become as instinctive as keeping one's balance, for instance, because failure in that for even an instant means a fall, so that the practise in it is lifelong and constant; whereas the artistic habit lapses more or less in the absence of an audience, and even on the stage can be forgotten for long periods without any worse consequences than a loss of charm which nothing may bring to the actor's attention. The real safeguard against such lapses is a sense of beauty—the artistic sense—cultivated to such a degree of sensitiveness that a coarse or prosaic tone, or an awkward gesture, jars instantly on the artist as a note out of tune jars on the musician. The defect of the old-fashioned systems of training for the stage was that they attempted to prescribe the conclusions of this constantly evolving artistic sense instead of cultivating it and leaving the artist to its guidance. Thus they taught you an old-fashioned stage-walk, and old-fashioned stage-voice, an old-fashioned stage way of kneeling, of sitting down, of shaking hands, of picking up a handkerchief, and so on, each of them supposed to be the final and perfect way of doing it. The end of that was, of course, to discredit training altogether. But neglect of training very quickly discredits itself; and it will now perhaps be admitted that the awakening and culture of the artistic conscience is a real service which a teacher can render to an actor. When that conscience is thoroughly awakened and cultivated, when a person can maintain vigilant artistic sensitiveness throughout a performance whilst making all the movements required by the action of a drama, and speaking all its dialogue graphically without preoccupation or embarrassment, then that person is a technically competent artistic actor, able to play a part of which he hardly comprehends one line, in a play of which he knows nothing except his own words and speeches and the cues thereto, much more intelligibly and effectively, as well as agreeably, than a statesman with ten times his general ability could. He can only be beaten, in fact, by the professional rival who has equal skill in execution, but has more numerous and valuable ideas to execute. The finest actors—Jefferson, Coquelin, Salvini, Duse—carry this technical skill to such a point that though they act so beautifully that you cannot take your eyes off them even when you do not understand what they are saying, yet the beauty seems so spontaneous and inevitable that it is generally quite impossible to persuade their admirers that there is any art or study in their acting at all.

The effect on an ordinary man of making him suddenly conscious of the artistic aspect of his movements and speech is to plunge him into a condition of terror and bewilderment in which he forgets how to do anything. It gives him stage fright, in short. Take a humble tradesman who has demolished his boiled mutton and turnips for half a century without misgiving. Invite him to meet a peer or two at dinner in Grosvenor Square, and he will refuse dish after dish because he no longer feels sure of how he ought to eat it. Take a lady who habitually talks the heads off all her acquaintances, and put her on a platform to make the simplest statement to an audience, and she will be struck dumb. The nervous agonies of the young have caused more discomfort in the world than the torments of the Inquisition If this happens on the large stage of the world to people who have all had at least some social training, what must be the anguish of the wretch who, with his face absurdly painted, and dressed in outlandish costume that does not fit him, is thrust on a stage for the first time in his life to speak Elizabethan stage English as Rosencrantz or Guildenstern, or even to stand a mute courtier and look on at some fellow creature making the like horrible exhibition of himself!

All this, however, presupposes that the victim has an artistic conscience, only just born and still blind. There are plenty of people who have either no artistic conscience at all or else one which is very easily satisfied. Just as you have soldiers who are not frightened under fire because they have not imagination enough to conceive their danger, whilst your imaginative Napoleon or Nelson turns pale, and your serene Goethe sees yellow, so there are debutters, both on the social and theatrical stage, who get through their ordeal easily because they are only imperfectly conscious of it. And there are happy people whose artistic conscience has always been awake, and to whom sufficient conscious grace and beauty to begin with are second nature. There is also the person with high animal spirits, a strong sense of fun, and a turn for mimicry. He, with an utterly unawakened artistic conscience, will flourish greatly at private theatricals, and sometimes also at public ones. With a good ear for musical pitch and tune and measure, and some physical agility, he will do excellently at the music-halls; but he very often has no ear to speak of; and then, incapable of singing, dancing, fine diction or graceful movement, he delights himself with tomfoolery, and is hugely pleased with himself when the people laugh. And since the people do laugh, there is a constant tendency to substitute tomfoolery for artistic comedy on the stage, since artistic comedians are in the nature of things much scarcer than buffoons. Then it is that the skilled critic must act as the watchdog of art, and begin to bark vigorously. Unfortunately, he can only bark: it is the manager who must bite. The artistic manager, as distinguished from the man who merely takes a theatre and puts up a play, is also a critic, and, knowing the difference between finished stage execution and mere larking, picks and drills his company accordingly. That is how theatres come to have styles as well as individuals.

The nature of my criticism of the Royalty performance will now be intelligible. I do not deny that it is amusing —sometimes; but I do most emphatically deny that the performance, as a whole, has any artistic character. I go further: I sorrowfully profess my conviction, based on an attentive examination of the stage business, that the performers have been not only encouraged, but positively ordered, to clown as much as possible so as to keep the fun going and make the play lively. The back drawing-room has never produced a company of comedians so intensely and ostentatiously conscious of their own funniness. Squawking voices, grinning faces, foolish antics, pervade the play to such an extent that though, as I have admitted (very magnanimously, believe me), the second act amused me, yet I could not face the third, having lost my old robust schoolboy appetite for large doses of that sort of merriment. The jar on my nerves began in "Harmony," a litle play by Mr. Henry Arthur Jones, one of his early pieces, in which you can plainly see the feeling, imagination, and humor of the future author of "The Crusaders" and "Rebellious Susan," along with the stage asides and soliloquies of a cruder period. The gentleman who played the youthful lover in this nearly drove me out of my senses with his determination to be breezy and not to let the play down. His voice rattled and his figure bounded, until I gave up trying to imagine that I was looking at a scene in a primitive country parish, and fell to wondering what quality over and above a cheerful effrontery can be needed to make any able-bodied young gentleman into an actor in three weeks nowadays. Mr. Kinghorne hardly improved matters by doing his business as the blind organist in the safest of old stage styles, piling it on and working it up tremendously, and never touching nature at any point. And Miss Ettie Williams, pretty, self-possessed, and resolutely metropolitan, gave the final blow to the illusion. But it was not until "The Chili Widow" came on that I began to suspect that breeziness, and rattle, and intense comic consciousness were parts of the managerial policy. Mr. Bourchier seemed determined that there should be no mistake about our being there to make a regular evening of it; and it is possible that the profound depression into which this attitude naturally threw me—as I think it would any reasonable person— may have made me somewhat captious. At all events, I soon felt that I could willingly mow down the whole of that stage Home Office staff with a Maxim gun. It was not mere extravagance of caricature that annoyed me; for Mr. Blakeley and Miss Larkin, who are hardened veterans in broad caricature, managed their business smoothly and easily, and at least did not play the part of the audience as well by laughing at their own performances; whilst Miss Phillips clowned only when a silly part absolutely forced her to, and made the most of the rest. What was wrong with the performance was its persistent Philistinism. It is fortunate for Mr. Bourchier and for Miss Violet and Miss Irene Vanbrugh that they are such very pleasant people, and that the play is such an amusing play. Mr. Bourchier is a born comedian: he has ease, humor, geniality, and plenty of natural grace of speech and manner. Happy in these endowments, he insists on sharing the fun himself, and is evidently quite persuaded that if all the others will only rattle along in the same careless way, the result will be as pleasant in their case as in his. He enjoys himself so robustly that the audience cannot help feeling good-humored. The very thoughtlessness of his performance is an element in its popularity: one feels that a thoroughly healthy person never thinks. Miss Violet Vanbrugh is very attractive; but she is much more conscious of Miss Violet Vanbrugh than of her part: in other words, she lacks conviction. The fact is, she is not a comedian: all this man-killing archness does not belong to her: one sees that it is only her fun, not her nature; and the result is, not an artist at work, but a pretty lady at play, a spectacle always agreeable, but not to the purpose of the connoisseur in dramatic art. Miss Irene Vanbrugh has more genuine comic force, and is better fitted in her part; but as far as I saw the play she only appeared in the first act, which might with great advantage be cut out. Mr. Kinghorne plays the office-keeper much more naturally than the organist in the first piece, and much more entertainingly. The others funnify their parts more or less blatantly, the whole ill-concerted attempt to produce a facetious atmosphere without any reference to the finer artistic conditions being, as I have said, discordant and amateurish. Even the audience struck me as a somewhat unsophisticated, not to say chuckleheaded one; but I am glad to be able to add that it was numerous and well pleased. It had the air of having at last discovered a play which was better fun than a smoking concert.

On a point of pronunciation may I be allowed to say that Ballymacklerush, with a strong stress on the rush, is a credible Irish name, but that Bally McKillrush, with the stress on the kill, is impossible. The only safe rule about the pronunciation of an Irish name is that whatever way comes naturally to an Englishman is quite certain to be the wrong way.

MORE MASTERPIECES

The Rise of Dick Halward: a new play in three acts. By Jerome K. Jerome. Garrick Theatre, 19 October, 1895.

WITH every possible disposition to tolerate all views of life on the stage, I cannot quite keep my patience with the pessimism of Mr. Jerome K. Jerome and his school. I can endure, for a strictly limited time, the splenetic, cynical pessimist, who lashes and satirizes the abundant follies and weaknesses of mankind to excuse himself for giving it up as a bad job. But your maudlin pessimist who, like Mr. Jerome K. Jerome, says, "We are all hopeless scoundrels; so let us be kind and gentle to one another": him I find it hard to bear. Mr. Jerome's hero, Dick Halward, is called Dick because that is a less harsh term than Richard. A judge might say, "Richard Halward: after a patient trial, and upon evidence which must convince every reasonable person of the justice of the verdict, you have been found guilty of one of the meanest frauds that has ever come before a court of law. By selling your professional honor and robbing your friend at one stroke, you have shown yourself void alike of character in your public capacity and of feeling in your private relations. You are a dishonest and worthless fellow; and the sentence of the court is, &c., &c." Not thus Mr. Jerome K. Jerome. He grasps the culprit's hand, and, in a voice husky with emotion, says: "Dick, old chap, not another word about that money. Not a man of us but would have done just as you did, Heaven help us, if we got the chance. You were tempted, and you fell; but you sent £5 to your sisters when you were poor; you never had a hard word for the housemaid at your chambers; and in the sterling simplicity of your heart you hid your pipe and slippers in the coal-scuttle when you had lady visitors. How many of us would do as much? You have sinned; but you have suffered; and it was love that led you astray. Let the cold world say what it will, you shall have a happy ending, Dick, dear old man. God bless you, Dick, God bless you. Go and live happily ever after. It's unmanly to— dash it, I think I'll go and smoke a pipe outside, if you don't mind, Dick." Ibsen might have been a rich man to-day if he had only taken that view of things. Perhaps, however, it is only fair that it should bring dramatic authors money; for it will assuredly not bring them anything else.

A criminal is not necessarily a despicable person. The man who is strongly, ably, egotistically and therefore self-respectingly wicked may be crowned or hung, as the case may be, according to his failure or success; but he is not despised. The only one insufferable and unpardonable thing for a criminal to do is to confess before he is found out. When a man goes to a police station and gives himself up for an undiscovered murder, the first uncontrollable impulse of every healthy person is one of impatient exasperation with a fool who cannot bear his cross and hold his tongue, but must tear open a healed wound for the sake of having his miserable conscience soothed by the hangman. Mr. Jerome K. Jerome, by way of carrying to its possible extreme his pessimistic theory that the baser a man is, the more intensely human and sympathetic he is, completes the infamy of Dick Halward by making him volunteer a quite exceptionally gratuitous and dastardly confession at the moment when he believes he is going to commit suicide by taking his father's patent headache cure. Under such circumstances a man with any decency left in him would surely make a stage will leaving his property to the person he had robbed of it, and then slip quietly overboard, so to speak. But Halward cannot deny himself a dram of sympathy at the price of leaving everybody disgusted, ashamed, and miserably uncomfortable. He pours the headache cure into a tumbler (by the way, it is quite a genuine cure, and may be relied on not only for headache, but for ailments of all kinds—nineteen drops of hydrocyanic acid), and summons to his presence his two most intimate friends, one of whom, it is hardly necessary to say, is the youth whose inheritance he has stolen. His own betrothed and that of the young man are also sent for. He then baldly confesses; and the play immediately collapses like a punctured tire, Mr. Jerome's stagecraft collapsing visibly with it. For the unhappy four witnesses of the confession are so totally unequal to the occasion that they simply drift off the stage one after another flabbergasted, only one of them having the presence of mind to explain that he must go and think about it a little before committing himself. Fortunately for Mr. Jerome, the five parties to this unexampled stage effect were artists no less popular than Miss Marion Terry, Miss Annie Hughes, Mr. Willard, Mr. Esmond, and Mr. Barnes. If Mr. Jerome will try it at the Independent Theatre with five comparatively unknown performers, he will probably be made acutely conscious of his own originality. When the disabled quartet had melted from the gaze of a dumbfounded audience, Halward proceeded to bid the world farewell and raise the headache cure to his lips. We all remembered how, in "The Dancing Girl," when Mr. Tree was in the like extremity, Miss Norreys slid down the banisters and seized the fatal goblet at the last moment. We were therefore not surprised to see Miss Marion Terry come back. Since it was Miss Terry's objection to marrying a man with less than five thousand a year that had given Dick his excuse for his crime, the attitude of pure derision in which we should otherwise have contemplated the heroine's reappearance was suspended in view of the possibility that the play might after all end heroically by the lady insisting on sharing the poison, and the two dying together by their own condemnation, Rosmersholmwise. But Mr. Jerome knew better than that. Miss Terry did her duty according to Mr. Jerome's lights—the footlights. She weaned her lover from his fell purpose, and promised to go across the seas with him and begin a new life regardless of income. At which unspeakable crisis of Mr. Jerome's attempt to hold the mirror up to nature, the curtain fell.

I find it very hard to believe that Mr. Jerome, in writing this play, or Mr. Willard in producing it, had any

other object than to make money in the cheapest possible
way. So hard, in fact, that I shall not try to believe it.
No doubt I shall be told that

> "The drama's laws the drama's patrons give;
> And those who live to please must please to live."

But you cannot get out of an argument by simply telling
a lie in a heroic couplet. The drama's laws the drama's
patrons do *not* give, nor ever can give: that is the pre-
rogative of the dramatist, and of the dramatist alone.
Nor need anybody "please to live": on the contrary, the
person who is willing to do anything to please everybody
is a universally and deservedly despised and disastrous
person. The public cannot do without the theatre; and
the actor and the dramatist are therefore in a position to
insist on honorable terms. The managers who are at
present flinging all professional honor and artistic faith
to the winds by competing with one another as to who
shall secure the vulgarest and foolishest play are no more
under any compulsion to do so than Sir Henry Irving is
to swallow swords, balance straws on his nose, or bounce
up through star-traps. Suppose Sir Henry were to join
the ignoble scramble after big pecuniary successes, and
to abandon the comparatively high ground on which he
is now securely planted, what would be the result? Only
that on the low ground he would be easily beaten by the
music-halls; so that he would debauch his audiences only
to lose them. That is just what too many of our managers
are doing at the present time. They deliberately select
melodramas of the Surrey and Marylebone types, and
engage first-rate performers to present them at west end
houses at west end prices. In due course these pieces are
sent "on tour" through the provinces. Now "the prov-

inces" include suburban London; and at this very moment the people who like shoddy melodrama are waking up to the fact that if they do their playgoing at the suburban houses, they can see, at reasonable prices, exactly the same plays as they are now paying exorbitant prices to see worse acted at west end houses. Take this play of Mr. Jerome's, "The Rise of Dick Halward." The part of Dick, from its ridiculous invocation of Mephistopheles in the first act to its sham farewell to earth in the last, is arrant fustian, better than the fustian of twenty years ago, no doubt, but still, judged by the literary and artistic standards of to-day, very sorry fustian. Mr. Willard does not play it more effectively than a strong transpontine leading man would: he plays it less effectively. As to Miss Marion Terry, I could name half a dozen young ladies, not to be compared to her for a moment in artistic power and accomplishment, who might replace her with advantage as the heroine. The part in her hands is only a bad misfit. Miss Hughes, Mr. Esmond, and the rest are equally, if less grotesquely, thrown away on their parts. "The Prude's Progress" was far more successfully represented, not only because it was a better play, but because it had a weaker cast. When "The Rise of Dick Halward" is performed by actors just fit for the class of people to whose level the play has been written down, it will go ten times better than it does at the Garrick, although the sums paid to the leading performers will be less by about five-sixths.

In Mr. Oscar Wilde's "Ideal Husband" there was a remarkable scene in which the fraudulent Cabinet Minister reproached his wife with idealizing and worshipping his moral virtues instead of loving his very self as he loves her. This so exactly suits Mr. Jerome's sentimental pessimism that he flourishes it in a crude state all over his love scenes. The lady reproves Dick for loving her in spite of her demerits: he replies by laboriously explaining Mr. Oscar Wilde's point to her, thereby very effectually reducing it to absurdity. Fortunately for the play, Mr. Jerome has a vein of shrewd fun, and has discovered that in working the familiar but safe stage trick of *dénouement* by coincidence, the long arm cannot be too long, in spite of the certainty that the critics will immediately fill up their notices with futile complaints of improbability. So what with Mr. Jerome's jokes, and his manipulation of a camera and a microscope, the play passes the time. But it is as much inferior to "The Prude's Progress" as that play, I hope, will prove to Mr. Jerome's next.

THE NEW MAGDALEN AND THE OLD

The New Magdalen. By Wilkie Collins. (Revival.) Theatre Metropole, 28 October, 1895.

THE RISE of the suburban theatre into artistic importance is a phenomenon which I have been expecting for many years. If the suburban population went to the theatre with anything like the assiduity with which it goes to church and chapel, I should not have had so long to wait. Even now there are districts of London, larger than many German towns which have their theatre and their grand ducal opera-house, where the inhabitants must come to the Strand district to find a theatre tolerable by people of the most moderate culture. But the signs of change in this respect are thickening. Whilst west end management is getting more and more desperately precarious, theatres like the Grand at Islington, the Lyric at Ealing, and the Metropole at Camberwell apparently prosper steadily. Still, until this week, I had never been invited by a suburban manager to a first night, because the suburban manager has usually nothing to show except a piece already produced and criticized at a west end theatre. Now, however, Mr. Mulholland, the manager of the Metropole, has taken a step forward by producing a play on his own account, the said play being no less a work than Wilkie Collins's "New Magdalen," in which the late Ada Cavendish became famous twenty years ago. "It is a curious fact in connection with the recent craze for problem and sex plays," says Mr. Mulholland, in a little manifesto circulated last Monday night in his theatre, "that the bold initiation of Wilkie Collins in this respect has been practically ignored. The existence alike of such a work as 'The New Magdalen,' and the creation of Mercy Merrick in this relation, has never been adequately acknowledged. It is in some sense with a view to showing the influence of this work on the so-called 'new movement' in dramatic literature, and placing dramatic facts in their true perspective, that the present revival has been undertaken."

On that let me say, respectfully but firmly, that "The New Magdalen" is no more a modern "sex play" than Mercy Merrick is a real Magdalen, or, for the matter of that, a real woman. Mercy is the old-fashioned man made angel-woman. She is only technically a liar, an impostor, and a prostitute; for the loss of her reputation occurs through no fault of her own; and the fraud by which she attempts to recover her place in society is so contrived as to seem quite harmless when she enters on it. Mercy is interesting, not because she is specifically feminine, or what Lombroso calls "sexually psychopathic," but because certain ideally and nobly human impulses are personified in her; so that she gains our sympathies in spite of inconsistent and improbable circumstances. To invent such an ideal figure; to thrust her into a refuge by a string of novelist-manufactured accidents, and then bring on a Christian Socialist clergyman to raise her up and hail her as "the noblest of God's creatures" before an audience perfectly well aware that the typical women in our refuges are not in the least like her except in point of the susceptibility to sentimental sermons and the superficially amiable emotional facility which are only the symptoms of their weakness of character—to do all this was not to anticipate "the new movement," but to provoke it. Where Wilkie Collins really struck the new movement was in his sketch of the Reverend Julian Grey, who might have been a stagey forecast of the Reverend Stewart Headlam, though he was probably a reminiscence of some earlier pioneer of Christian Socialism. You will find hundreds of such parsons now: in fact, the Guild of St. Matthew is a Guild of St. Julian Grey. The scene in which Julian Grey describes all the little sallies by which he horrifies his bishop already falls flat because by this time the bishop himself might perpetrate them all, and worse, without scandalizing anybody.

The stage has moved as well as the world since Ada Cavendish created Mercy Merrick. Then "The New Magdalen" was a fashionable and well-made piece: to-day its innumerable asides and soliloquies, each more absurd and impossible than the last, are quite out of the question.

In other respects it is still a strong play as plays go, hugely superior to the modern work of Messrs. Carton, Frith, and Jerome, but presenting the fatal disqualification from the point of view of the west end manager of to-day that it requires acting, and powerful acting, too. It is a significant fact that the return of "The New Magdalen" to the London stage has involved the return of Miss Janet Achurch, the only tragic actress of genius we now possess. After seeing Miss Achurch in the third act of "The New Magdalen," I quite understand why she has not recently been let loose in modern plays. The other evening even the comparatively quiet and adaptable talent of Miss Marion Terry, in spite of all her tact and charm, nearly knocked "Dick Halward" to pieces; and I hardly expect to see Miss Terry on the stage again except on occasions when the supply of ladies who can be depended on not to act runs short. Miss Winifred Fraser, the English creator of Ibsen's Hedwig Ekdal, was cautiously admitted on that occasion as a Temple laundress, in which capacity she could hardly do much harm. What would happen to a play of the "Dick Halward" class with Miss Achurch in it is hardly to be imagined—it is like trying to conceive a successful gunpowder plot. The supreme test of tragic acting is that indescribable disturbance of soul in which the spectator finds himself when the curtain comes down, a sensation from which I have usually found myself perfectly safe in London theatres except when Duse is at large here. How Miss Achurch managed to produce it with the execrable support she had, I do not know—it is hardly too much to say that in the most difficult scenes every speech of hers was followed by some ineptitude or obvious blunder which reduced the whole play to absurdity until she rescued it again—but she certainly did produce it. Three magnificent strokes in particular remain vividly in my memory: the gleam of rage through the hungry tenderness of her demand to Horace Holmcroft whether his love for her would stand the test of the loss of her social position; her annihilation of Grace Roseberry with the contemptuous "mad, you're mad," the words striking the woman in the face like a hammer; and the superb movement with which she swept herself to the feet of Julian Grey as the penitent Magdalen. This last would have been a fine piece of art even if there had been anything resembling a Julian Grey on the stage. As there was nothing but an unfortunate gentleman who was not within a fortnight of knowing his part, and not within five years of being able for it, the feat was all but miraculous. Miss Achurch actually persuaded the audience, between her efforts to prompt him, that he was acting rather well; and after one memorable scene, during which she had borne him with a strong hand through a troubled ocean of forgetfulness, unpreparedness, inexpertness, and general ignominy and confusion, he received a hearty round of applause from an audience which rightly felt that he had been taking part in a very powerfully acted scene. Comparing Miss Achurch's play in this third act, and in the first act at the point where the possibility of impersonating Grace Roseberry first strikes her, with the few squalls of temper which made Mrs. Tanqueray's reputation, I am compelled to admit that our playgoing digestion has been rather weak of late.

For all that, the New Magdalen is not her old self at the Metropole, and never can, perhaps, be her old self again. When Ada Cavendish made her great success in it, she did no violence to the author. She gathered sympathy, first as the good hospital nurse on the battlefield, and then as the nice young lady at Mablethorpe House, quite as Wilkie Collins meant her to. Even the memorable fit of hysterics which swept away the audiences of the seventies with the undercurrent of rich, passionate, indignant emotion which was Ada Cavendish's chief gift, was ladylike in its form and conventional in its symptoms. But Miss Achurch belongs to an age which has little sympathy with the doves, soiled or unsoiled, of the age of Wilkie Collins. Mercy Merrick and Tom Hood's drowned young lady "fashioned so slenderly; young, and *so* fair" were not rebels against society: they were its victims, always conveying a faint suggestion that they were probably the daughters of distressed clergymen. And as victims, they were pitied. What has happened since is that we have changed sides to a great extent; and though we may not all care to say so, yet it is the rebel against society who interests us; and we want to see the rebel triumphant rather than crushed or reconciled, conventional society being just now in the pillory as a collective fool with whom we have lost patience. Miss Achurch, as might be expected from an actress who became famous as Nora Helmer in "A Doll's House," presents Mercy Merrick as rebel rather than victim. Middle-aged playgoers will still remember the deep conviction and pathos of Ada Cavendish's "I can't get back: I can't get back" (into society), when she told her story at the beginning of the play. Miss Achurch made no such effect in this line: the effort of trying to imagine a woman in the honorable employment and heroic activity of Florence Nightingale, yearning like the Peri at the gate of paradise for a permanent situation as parlormaid in a respectably prejudiced family, was too much for her; and the once famous line came out almost with suppressed impatience and contempt. I can as easily conceive a tigress settling down in a dairy as Miss Achurch's Mercy Merrick domesticating herself with Lady Janet Roy, and receiving an offer of marriage from such a sample of good form as Mr. Horace Holmcroft. She has dignity and charm, but not the dignity and charm that Lady Janet would have recognized or liked: she has tenderness, but not quite the tenderness that soothes the fevered brow of the wounded soldier of the stage. She reproduced for me an old experience of the days when, as a musical critic, I gained from contact with great works and a living art the knowledge I am now losing and the finely trained sense I am now blunting in our silly and vulgar theatres. Just as Giula Ravogli first, and then Calve, in the exuberance of their dramatic talent, wrecked an innocently pretty opera by suddenly springing upon the delicate romance of Bizet's and Prosper Merimée's fancy the worthless, fierce, sensual, reckless, rapscallionly Carmen of real life, so, precisely, has Miss Achurch taken this innocent old figment of Wilkie Collins's benevolent and chivalrous imagination, and played into it a grim truth that it was never meant to bear—played it against the audience, so that the curious atmosphere of reluctance and remonstrance from which Calve used to wring the applause of the huge audiences at Covent Garden when the curtain fell on her Carmen, arose more than once when Miss Achurch disturbed and appalled us at moments when Ada Cavendish, looking at the part from an older point of view, would have soothed and pleased us. Only, Miss Achurch, unlike Calve in Carmen, preserved the heroic element in Mercy's character. The clergyman's line, when her betrothed repudiates her, "Horace: I pity you," had its full value.

This incongruity between the New Woman and the Old was accentuated in an irresistibly comic way by the representative of Grace Roseberry, an actress with apparently no idea of any part but that of the heroine of a popular melodrama. Grace Roseberry is, from the professional point of view, an excellent part. Detestable as she is made to appear by her utter lack of charity, this odious defect of hers is dramatically so important at the crisis of the play, that an actress who plays the part forcibly and faithfully can make herself remembered as surely as Mercy Merrick herself can. Unfortunately the Grace Roseberry at the Metropole, a young lady with a promising appearance and temperament, to which she has added nothing except a presentable diction and a meaningless mannerism or two, proved so deficient in dramatic intelligence as actually to play for the sympathy of the audience, thereby not only destroying her own opportunity, but disabling the play at its most critical points to an extent which would have ensured a disastrous failure if Miss Achurch had not been sufficiently powerful to create the illusion which her incompetent colleague was feebly contradicting. The effect at the end of the second act (counting the prologue as the first), when Miss Achurch was not on the stage, nearly upset the whole performance. Grace Roseberry, instead of entering so as to make every one hate her instinctively at once, thereby excusing her cool reception by Lady Janet, came in pale, slow, and pathetic, only needing a patch of snow on her cloak, and a sentimental strain from the band, to draw tears from the gallery as the long-lost, cruelly wronged heroine. As it was, they waxed indignant at Lady Janet's inhuman coldness to this sweet young creature. The curtain descended on Grace Roseberry, the one unsympathetic female character in the play, as its heroine, and all the sympathetic characters as brutal and uppish conspirators against an innocent maiden's happiness. She was loudly applauded amid the suppressed convulsions of the critics who knew the play, and what was coming in the next act. But it must have been extremely poor fun for Miss Achurch, who had to fight her way all through her great act against this silly blunder, instead of having its most powerful situation perfectly prepared for her, and needing only the touch of the match to the gunpowder, as Ada Cavendish always had.

Miss Ada Neilson as Lady Janet, and Mr. Herbert Pearson as Horace Holmcroft, knew their parts, and got steadily and competently, if not very brilliantly, through them. But the play was in a desperately unprepared condition. In spite of a busy prompter, and considerable activity in that direction by Miss Achurch, appalling and irretrievable omissions occurred. A stupid cut in the first act, spoiling the introduction of Mercy's narrative, was, I am afraid, intentional. The stage-manager managed to get the curtain up and down punctually; but that was all. Grace Roseberry had to wait a long and weary time for the shell that was to strike her down; and when, after loud and long remonstrances by the authorities behind the scenes, the catastrophe at last came tardy off, the window was blown in first, and the shell exploded afterwards. I hope I have made it clear that my disposition towards the suburban theatre is altogether friendly.

TRILBY AND "L'AMI DES FEMMES"

Trilby: an entertainment in four acts based by Paul Potter on Du Maurier's novel. Haymarket Theatre, 30 October, 1895.

The Squire of Dames. Adapted from "L'Ami des Femmes" of Dumas *fils* by R. C. Carton. Criterion Theatre, 5 November, 1895.

I OBSERVE that some of my honored colleagues in dramatic criticism, not having read "Trilby," explain that they were not lazy, but that they felt bound to present their minds in the condition of a *tabula rasa* to the Haymarket performance. Now I *am* lazy; and I never read anything; yet I have read "Trilby" and enjoyed it greatly. It is a no mere novel with illustrations; it is a homogeneous work of art in which the master, like a composer who sets his own poem to music, shows us his people by the art of the draughtsman, and tells us their story by the art of the fabulist. What Thackeray, with his enslaved mind and clumsy hand, tried to do in vain, is here brought happily off by the pleasantest of free-thinkers and the most charming of artists. Oddly enough, the successful artist has taken the unsuccessful one for his model, greatly improving on him in every respect save one: to wit, honesty. Thackeray saved his reputation and forced his oppressive books like sentences of penal servitude on the reading public by telling the truth in spite of himself. He may protest against it, special plead against it, exaggerate the extenuating circumstances, be driven into pessimism by it; but it comes raging and snivelling out of him, all the same, within the limit of his sense of decency. He exhausts all his feeble pathos in trying to make you sorry for the death of Colonel Newcome, imploring you to regard him as a noble-hearted gentleman instead of an insufferable old fool, developing into a mischievous old swindler; but he gives you the facts about him faithfully. Nothing can be more pitiable than Thackeray chuckling over his poor little stroke of genius in making Becky Sharp admire Rawdon Crawley when he assaults Lord Steyne, in which stroke he shows about as much knowledge of Becky-Sharpness as Prosper Merimée's dragoon did when he went to Carmen to boast how he killed her hateful old husband-proprietor in single combat by a clever knife thrust. "You fool," said Carmen: "your thrust is all stuff. Why couldn't you buy me honestly? He'd have sold me for fifteen shillings." Rawdon Crawley's figure would have been higher; but he would have sold Becky for all that. Still worse is Thackeray's exultation over the success with which Major Pendennis quells the rebellion of his wretched valet; and there is something pathetically foolish in his attempt to convince himself that his pulses stirred at the thought of Waterloo, and in his absolutely sincere sense of the international gravity of a newspaper paragraph stating that a certain letter written from abroad was, "strange to say, on club paper" (implying the unspeakably awful accusation against a west end clubman of putting a quire of that commodity into his portmanteau). But he tells you no lies; and if you want to know Rawdon Crawley and Major Pendennis as they appeared to their own set, and their servants as they appeared to their masters, there they are, as no artist-author could ever give them to you.

Mr. du Maurier, on the other hand, has all the artist's charm, and all his dishonesty. His Taffy is an attempt at the Colonel-Newcome-Dobbin sympathy catcher; but Mr. du Maurier does not tell you the truth about Taffy, except for a moment when his professional point of honor is touched, when he is constrained to confess that Taffy was an impostor in art. There is not a character in the book which is not obviously drawn to please the author's imagination. For all we know, George Eliot may have been the original of Trilby: at all events, if she really had been, he would have altered her age and her face and her circumstances and profession in just the same way to please himself and please us. If I want to respect Thackeray, I must think of his veracity and forget his workmanship: if I would respect Mr. du Maurier, I must think of his workmanship and forget his veracity. I know well that there never was any such person as Trilby— that she is a man's dream; but I am a man myself, and delight in her. Happily, truth and good-nature do not always clash. I am convinced as well as touched by Little Billee with the dead heart, going about and making himself affectionately agreeable in his remorse for being secretly unable to care for anybody. And I like an imagination without gall, to which poor Svengali is *not* a villain, but only a poor egotistical wretch who provokes people to pull his nose, although he has better grounds for egotism than any one else in the book except Little Billee and Trilby (I must except the adorable Trilby). Besides, the philosophy of the book is humane and enlightened: Mr. du Maurier is not afraid to write of religion and morals and the nude in art just as he would speak of them in the society of people whom he respects.

"Trilby" is the very thing for the English stage at present. No need to act or create character: nothing to do but make up after Mr. du Maurier's familiar and largely popular drawings, and be applauded before uttering a word as dear old Taffy, or the Laird, or darling Trilby, or horrid Svengali. Mr. Paul Potter has done his business with considerable knowledge of what was wanted of him, especially by the actor-manager. Nearly all the favorite pictures and passages from the book are worked in, without violence, if possible, but at all events worked in. Thus, though the play ends with Trilby's death, Gecko is allowed to have his "Ich habe geliebt und gelebet" in the third act. Still, let nobody suppose that the play gives any idea of the book. Imagine Trilby, the incarnation of womanly sympathy, with Baratier and Besson and old Monsieur Penque cut out of her record for the sake of making a correct young English girl of her! Imagine little Billee pared down and painted up into the most futile of "juvenile leads!" Imagine, above all, Svengali taken seriously at his own foolish valuation, blazed upon with limelights, spreading himself intolerably over the whole play with nothing fresh to add to the first five minutes of him—Svengali defying heaven, declaring that henceforth he is his own God, and then tumbling down in a paroxysm of heart disease (the blasphemer rebuked, you see), and having to be revived by draughts of brandy. I derived much cynical amusement from this most absurd scene; but if I were Mr. du Maurier, I should ask whether the theatre is really in such an abject condition that all daintiness and seriousness of thought and feeling must be struck out of a book, and replaced by vulgar nonsense before it can be accepted on the stage. I grant that the public deserves nothing better from Mr. Tree. It has done its silly best to teach him that it wants none of his repeated and honorable attempts to cater for people with some brains. But surely even the public

would just as soon—nay, rather—have the original Svengali, the luckless artist-cad (a very deplorable type of
cad, whom Mr. du Maurier has hit off to the life), understanding neither good manners nor cleanliness, always
presuming, and generally getting snubbed and nose-
pulled and bullied, but taking Trilby's headache into his
own elbows and making a great artist of her. Mr. Tree
began excellently with this: why, then, should he absurdly
decline into the stagey, the malignant, the diabolic, the
Wandering-Jewish, and vainly endeavor to make our
flesh creep, besides making the play one act too long?
No doubt Mr. Potter, familiar with the ways of the American actor-manager, wrote the part for Mr. Tree as he
thought Mr. Tree would like it. But he spoiled the book
and very nearly spoiled the play in doing it.

With the exception of the sham serious episodes,
"Trilby" is very bright and pleasant. There is no acting
in it to speak of: Miss Rosina Filippi alone gets in a
stroke of genuine art in the *ouvreuse* scene. Miss Baird's
Trilby is a very pretty performance by a very pretty girl;
but it is no more possible to base an estimate of her future
on it than it was on the early performances of Miss
Mary Anderson or Miss Dorothy Dene. The older ladies
in the audience, dating from the age of reclining boards
and straight backs, were of opinion that Miss Baird
carried herself too creepily; and I will not deny that
there may be some truth in this. As to Mr. Tree, I
should no more dream of complimenting him on the
Svengali business than Sir Henry Irving on "A Hero
of Waterloo." The studio, the quadrille, Zouzou and
Dodor, and all the rest of it, are great fun; and although
the whole affair not only adds nothing to the merit of
Mr. du Maurier's original production of the book and

the drawings, but steals a good deal from it, I imagine that every one will enjoy a visit to the Haymarket just now. Let me, however, warn musicians that they will find Schubert represented by the notoriously spurious "Addio."

At the Criterion Mr. Wyndham has resumed his exhibitions of acting, an art now become so rare that people flock to see him, no matter what the play may be. This time, however, he has a tolerably good part—that of De Ryons in "L'Ami des Femmes," transmuted by Mr. Carton into Mr. Kilroy in "The Squire of Dames." "L'Ami des Femmes" is a bad play with good material in it. The material is what we now call Ibsenite: the technique is that of Scribe. In it, accordingly, we have serious characters philosophically discussing themselves and one another quite undramatically in long speeches, and at the same time senselessly carrying on an irrelevant comedy of intrigue of the old kind in five "well-made" acts. The dialogue and characterization of "Emperor or Galilean" tacked on to the action of "Cheer, boys, Cheer" would not be a whit more incongruous. De Ryons is a high-minded, chivalrous, delicate gentleman-philosopher in theory, in practise a busy-body and go-between—Benedick and Figaro in one. De Montégre talks like Hernani, and behaves like the weak, vain fop in Thackerary's "Vanity Fair" (Osborne, if I recollect aright), who was shot at Waterloo. And so on. Mr. Carton had therefore not merely to adapt the piece from French to English life, but to get rid of its incongruities and make a fairly homogeneous, compact drama of it. Necessarily, he has done this by discarding the serious side of the characterization, and retaining only that which is proper to the ignoble and commonplace action, since if he had taken the alternative course, he must have provided the piece with a different action—in short, written a new play, which was not what he was commissioned to do. He has not done his work consistently—Mr. Carton never does anything consistently: a certain pleasant scatter-brainedness is of the very essence of his talent. He has retained a good deal that belongs to the side of the play which he has discarded, and has discarded some things (in Leverdet's part, for example) which would strengthen the side which he has retained. This inconsequence has landed him in four acts where three would have sufficed; in dull and vague parts for Miss Mary Moore and Mr. Bernard Gould; and here and there in a speech producing an effect belonging to the original play and not to the adaptation. Occasionally he does not take the trouble to adapt: he translates literally. In the original, Jane tells De Ryons that she detests him, to which he replies coolly "Ça passera," the equivalent of which, I take it, is "Ah, you will get over that." Mr. Carton has made Mr. Wyndham say "That will pass," a perfectly impossible speech for an Englishman, except when giving his opinion of a doubtful coin. Another speech of Mr. Wyndham, in his great scene with Zoë Nuggetson, "What game are we playing at?" is an excellent school-girl translation of "Queljeujouons-nous, mademoiselle?" but it is not what an Englishman would say under such circumstances.

The acting is a good deal better than most theatres provide at present. Mr. Wyndham's success as De Ryons Kilroy is genuine and unprepared. No books have been written about his part; no pictures of his make-up and attitudes have been circulated; no preliminary conversations between the other characters give the audience's imagination its cue. Mr. Wyndham goes to work as the curtain rises, and creates his character by pure acting. There was no leaning on stage tricks and effects which any experienced actor could produce, nor any of that feeble need of being constantly played to by the rest, which is so often put down to the vanity of the actor-manager, though it is really due to his incompetence. Mr. Wyndham is always playing to somebody, and getting double value out of it, for himself as actor and artist, by making the most of his own part, and for himself as manager by getting the most out of the fellow-artist whose salary he pays. Everybody acts better at the Criterion than at most other theatres; and yet Mr. Wyndham, whether he has the worst part in the piece, as in "The Home Secretary," or the best, as in the present instance, comes out further ahead than the actor managers who obviously dread competition. Miss Mar_ Moore, though much on the stage, has no part and no chance. The proud, half Greek Jane de Simerose, so ill prepared for marriage that she is shocked by it into driving her husband into the arms of another woman, and ꝯ fine witted that she is able to deal her jealous Hernani lover such strokes as, "I suppose, when I have answered all your questions—when I have proved to you that I am an honest woman, you will then demand that I shall cease to be one to prove that I love you"—this distinguished person becomes the merest cipher in "The Squire of Dames." Fräulein Hackendorf survives very healthily in an American millionairess, played by Miss Fay Davis, who made an unmistakable hit in the part. The part of the lovesick schoolgirl Balbine, originally played by Chaumont, becomes a mere piece of tomfoolery in English. Miss Beatrice Ferrars amuses herself with it laughably enough. Chantrin, the hero of the beard, is more fortunate. He has survived the Channel passage without alteration; so that the part is as dangerous in English as in French: that is, it remains the part of a bore who actually is a bore, and not an unconscious humorist. Mr. De Lange, however, averted the peril with great art and was very funny and very finished at the same time, a combination rather scarce on our stage. Mr. Bernard Gould was in the same difficulty as Miss Moore: his part was not very intelligible, and led to nothing but a paltry piece of spite, unrelieved by the tragic pretension with which, in the original, it is contrasted, Ibsen fashion, by Dumas *fils*. Nevertheless Mr. Gould, always *persona grata,* but hitherto one of the most experimental of amateurs, begins to show signs of serious formation as an artist with a definite style. As Sir Douglas Thorburn (Montégre) all he could do was to tow the wreck of his part into harbor without a catastrophe. Mr. Frank Fenton did precisely what was wanted as the husband. A man so abjectly in love with his wife is hardly a decent spectacle; but it is the actor's business to supply sentiment when the drama demands it, and Mr. Fenton certainly rose to the occasion, under no easy conditions, with remarkable efficiency. Mr. Alfred Bishop and Miss Granville are also in the cast; but their parts have been adapted into unredeemed commonplace.

THE CASE FOR THE CRITIC-DRAMATIST

16 November, 1895.

A DISCUSSION has arisen recently as to whether a dramatic critic can also be a dramatic author without injury to his integrity and impartiality. The feebleness with which the point has been debated may be guessed from the fact that the favorite opinion seems to be that a critic is either an honest man or he is not. If honest, then dramatic authorship can make no difference to him. If not, he will be dishonest whether he writes plays or not. This childish evasion cannot, for the honor of the craft, be allowed to stand. If I wanted to ascertain the melting-point of a certain metal, and how far it would be altered by an alloy of some other metal, and an expert were to tell me that a metal is either fusible or it is not—that if not, no temperature will melt it; and if so, it will melt anyhow—I am afraid I should ask that expert whether he was a fool himself or took me for one. Absolute honesty is as absurd an abstraction as absolute temperature or absolute value. A dramatic critic who would die rather than read an American pirated edition of a copyright English book might be considered an absolutely honest man for all practical purposes on that one particular subject—I say on that one, because very few men have more than one point of honor; but as far as I am aware, no such dramatic critic exists. If he did, I should regard him as a highly dangerous monomaniac. That honesty varies inversely with temptation is proved by the fact that every additional penny on the income-tax yields a less return than the penny before it, showing that men state their incomes less honestly for the purposes of taxation at sevenpence in the pound than sixpence. The matter may be tested by a simple experiment. Go to one of the gentlemen whose theory is that a man is either honest or he is not, and obtain from him the loan of half-a-crown on some plausible pretext of a lost purse or some such petty emergency. He will not ask you for a written acknowledgment of the debt. Return next day and ask for a loan of £500 without a promissory note, on the ground that you are either honest or not honest, and that a man who will pay back half a crown without compulsion will also pay back £500. You will find that the theory of absolute honesty will collapse at once.

Are we then to believe that the critic-dramatist who stands to make anything from five hundred to ten thousand pounds by persuading a manager to produce his plays, will be prevented by his honesty from writing about that manager otherwise than he would if he had never written a play and were quite certain that he never should write one? I can only say that people who believe such a thing would believe anything. I am myself a particularly flagrant example of the critic-dramatist. It is not with me a mere case of an adaptation or two raked up against me as incidents in my past. I have written half-a-dozen "original" plays, four of which have never been performed; and I shall presently write half-a-dozen more. The production of one of them, even if it attained the merest success of esteem, would be more remunerative to me than a couple of years of criticism. Clearly, since I am no honester than other people, I should be the most corrupt flatterer in London if there were nothing but honesty to restrain me. How is it, then, that the most severe criticisms of managers come from me and from my fellow critic-dramatists, and that the most servile puffery comes from writers whose every sentence proves that they have nothing to hope or fear from any manager? There are a good many answers to this question, one of the most obvious being that as the respect inspired by a good criticism is permanent, whilst the irritation it causes is temporary, and as, on the other hand, the pleasure given by a venal criticism is temporary, and the contempt it inspires permanent, no man really secures his advancement as a dramatist by making himself despised as a critic. The thing has been tried extensively during the last twenty years; and it has failed. For example, the late Frank Marshall, a dramatist and an extravagantly enthusiastic admirer of Sir Henry Irving's genius, followed a fashion which at one time made the Lyceum Theatre a sort of court formed by a retinue of literary gentlemen. I need not question either their sincerity or the superiority of Canute to their idolatry; for Canute never produced their plays: "Robert Emmett" and the rest of their masterpieces remain unacted to this day. It may be said that this brings us back to honesty as the best policy; but honesty has nothing to do with it: plenty of the men who know that they can get along faster fighting than crawling, are no more honest than the first Napoleon was. No virtue, least of all courage, implies any other virtue. The cardinal guarantee for a critic's integrity is simply the force of the critical instinct itself. To try to prevent me from criticizing by pointing out to me the superior pecuniary advantages of puffing is like trying to keep a young Irving from going on the stage by pointing out the superior pecuniary advantages of stockbroking. If my own father were an actor-manager, and his life depended on his getting favorable notices of his performance, I should orphan myself without an instant's hesitation if he acted badly. I am by no means the willing victim of this instinct. I am keenly susceptible to contrary influences—to flattery, which I swallow greedily if the quality is sufficiently good; to the need of money, to private friendship or even acquaintanceship, to the pleasure of giving pleasure and the pain of giving pain, to consideration for people's circumstances and prospects, to personal likes and dislikes, to sentimentality, pity, chivalry, pugnacity and mischief, laziness and cowardice, and a dozen other human conditions which make the critic vulnerable; but the critical instinct gets the better of them all. I spare no effort to mitigate its inhumanity, trying to detect and strike out of my articles anything that would give pain without doing any good. Those who think the things I say severe, or even malicious, should just see the things I do *not* say. I do my best to be partial, to hit out at remediable abuses rather than at accidental shortcomings, and at strong and responsible people rather than weak and helpless ones. And yet all my efforts do not alter the result very much. So stubborn is the critic within me, that with every disposition to be as good-natured and as popular an authority as the worst enemy of art could desire, I am to all intents and purposes incorruptible. And that is how the dramatist-critic, if only he is critic enough, "slates" the actor-manager in defiance of the interest he has in conciliating him. He cannot help himself, any more than the ancient mariner could help telling his story. And the actor-manager can no more help listening than the wedding guest could. In short, the better formula would have been, that a man is either a critic or not a critic; that to the extent to which he is one he will criticize the managers in spite of heaven or earth; and that to the extent to which he is not, he will flatter them anyhow, to save himself trouble.

The advantage of having a play criticized by a critic who is also a playwright is as obvious as the advantage of having a ship criticized by a critic who is also a master shipwright. Pray observe that I do not speak of the criticism of dramas and ships by dramatists and shipwrights who are not also critics; for that would be no more convincing than the criticism of acting by actors. Dramatic authorship no more constitutes a man a critic than actorship constitutes him a dramatic author; but a dramatic critic learns as much from having been a dramatic author as Shakespeare or Mr. Pinero from having been actors. The average London critic, for want of practical experience, has no real confidence in himself: he is always searching for an imaginary "right" opinion, with which he never dares to identify his own. Consequently every public man finds that as far as the press is concerned his career divides itself into two parts: the first, during which the critics are afraid to praise him; and the second, during which they are afraid to do anything else. In the first, the critic is uncomfortably trying to find faults enough to make out a case for his timid coldness: in the second, he is eagerly picking out excellences to justify his eulogies. And of course he blunders equally in both phases. The faults he finds are either inessential or are positive reforms, or he blames the wrong people for them: the triumphs of acting which he announces are stage tricks that any old hand could play. In criticizing actresses he is an open and shameless voluptuary. If a woman is pretty, well dressed, and self-satisfied enough to be at her ease on the stage, he is delighted; and if she is a walking monument of handsome incompetence, so much the better, as your voluptuary rarely likes a woman to be cleverer than himself, or to force him to feel deeply and think energetically when he only wants to wallow in her good looks. Confront him with an actress who will not condescend to attack him on this side—who takes her work with thorough seriousness and self-respect—and his resentment, his humiliation, his sense of being snubbed, break out ludicrously in his writing, even when he dare not write otherwise than favorably. A great deal of this nonsense would be taken out of him if he could only write a play and have it produced. No dramatist begins by writing plays merely as excuses for the exhibition of pretty women on the stage. He comes to that ultimately perhaps; but at first he does his best to create real characters and make them pass through three acts of real experiences. Bring a critic who has done this face to face with the practical question of selecting an actress for his heroine, and he suddenly realizes for the first time that there is not such a galaxy of talent on the London stage as he thought, and that the handsome walking ladies whom he always thought good enough for other people's plays are not good enough for his own. That is already an immense step in his education. There are other steps, too, which he will have taken before the curtain falls on the first public representation of his play; but they may be summed up in the fact that the author of a play is the only person who really wants to have it well done in every respect, and who therefore has every drawback brought fully home to him. The man who has had that awakening about one play will thenceforth have his eyes open at all other plays; and there you have at once the first moral with the first technical qualification of the critic—the determination to have every play as well done as possible, and the knowledge of what is standing in the way of that consummation. Those of our critics who, either as original dramatists or adapters and translators, have superintended the production of plays with paternal anxiety, are never guilty of the wittily disguised indifference of clever critics who have never seen a drama through from its first beginnings behind the scenes. Compare the genuine excitement of Mr. Clement Scott, or the almost Calvinistic seriousness of Mr. William Archer, with the gaily easy what-does-it-matterness of Mr. Walkley, and you see at once how the two critic-dramatists influence the drama, whilst the critic-playgoer only makes it a pretext for entertaining his readers. On the whole there is only as much validity in the theory that a critic should not be a dramatist, as in the theory that a judge should not be a lawyer nor a general a soldier. You cannot have qualifications without experience; and you cannot have experience without personal interest and bias. That may not be an ideal arrangement; but it is the way the world is built; and we must make the best of it.

MANXSOME AND TRADITIONAL

The Manxman: in four acts. Adapted from Hall
Caine's celebrated novel. Shaftesbury Theatre, 18
November, 1895.

The Rivals: a revival of Sheridan's comedy. Court
Theatre, 11 November, 1895.

I N THE bill "The Manxman" is described as "adapted
from HALL CAINE'S celebrated novel." Who is
Hall Caine? How did he become celebrated? At
what period did he flourish? Are there any other Manx
authors of his calibre? If there are, the matter will soon
become serious; for if that gift of intolerably copious
and intolerably common imagination is a national characteristic in the Isle of Man, it will swamp the stage with
Manx melodramas the moment the islanders pick up the
trick of writing for the stage.

Whether the speeches in "The Manxman" are inter-
polated Wilson Barrett or aboriginal Hall Caine I cannot
say, as I have not read the celebrated novel, and am
prepared to go to the stake rather than face the least
chapter of it. But if they correctly represent the colloquial habits of the island, the Manx race are without
a vernacular, and only communicate with one another
by extracts from Cassell's National Library, the Chandos
Classics, and the like. In the Isle of Man you do not use
the word "always": you say "Come weal come woe, come
life come death." The most useful phrases for the tourist
are "Dust and ashes, dust and ashes," "Dead sea fruit,"
"The lone watches of the night," "What a hell is conscience!" "The storm clouds are descending and the

tempest is at hand," and so on. The Manx do not speak of a little baby, but of a baby "fresh from God." Their philosophy is that "love is best—is everything—is the cream of life—better than worldly success"; and they conceive woman—or, as they probably call her, "the fair sex"—as a creature "giving herself body and soul, and never thinking what she gets by it. That's the glory of Woman!" And the Manxwoman rather deserves this. Her idea of pleasantry is to sit on a plank over a stream dangling her legs; to call her young swain's attention to her reflection in the water; and then, lest he should miss the coquetry of the exhibition, to cut off the reflected view of her knees by wrapping her skirt round her ankles in a paroxysm of affected bashfulness. And when she sprains her ankle, and the gentleman tenders some surgical aid, she requests him to turn his head the other way. In short, the keynote of your perfect Manxman is tawdry vulgarity aping the heroic, the hearty, the primevally passionate, and sometimes, though here the show of vigor in the affectation tumbles into lame ineptitude, the gallant and humorous.

Even when I put my personal distaste for "The Manxman" as far as possible on one side, I cannot persuade myself that it is likely to live very long, although no device is spared to move the audience, from a cascade of real water to a poor little baby, which is exploited as shamelessly as if it had been let out on hire to an organ-grinder or a beggar. Thirty years hence, no doubt, we shall have some newly risen star telling the interviewers of a first appearance as the baby in "The Manxman"; but that interesting possibility cannot reconcile me to the meanness of such ways of fishing for sympathy. In the great "Doll's House itself," where children are introduced

with so serious a purpose that no one can have any sense
of their being unworthily used, I always feel that I should
prefer the baby to be an amateur. At the Shaftesbury
melodrama, where there was no serious purpose, but only
an ostentatious cradling and cuddling and dandling and
bless-its-little-hearting in order to work up the greatest
possible quantity of sentiment on the cheapest possible
terms, I felt thoroughly ashamed of the business. What
with the real water, the infant, and the well-worn incident of the fond and simple-hearted husband returning
home to find his wife gone, the drama passes the time
tolerably up to the end of the second act. The rest of
it is as null and dull as the most cautious manager could
desire. The third act is nothing but a "front scene"
bulked out to fill up the evening; and the fourth act, with
its offensively noisy street music, does not produce a
moment's illusion. The play, originally designed for an
actor-manager who played Quilliam, has evidently been
a good deal botched in altering it to fit another actor-
manager who plays Christian; but it never can have been
a good play, because it is not really a drama at all, but
an acted narrative. Any competent playwright could
make the third act effectively dramatic if only he were
released from all obligation to consult "the celebrated
novel." As it is, it is a chapter in a story, not an act in
a drama.

As to the acting, most of the sixteen parts are so in-
definite in spite of their portentous names—Black Tom,
Ross Christian, Jemmy y Lord, and so on—that there is
nothing to act in them. Mr. Cockburn is just the man
for Pete Quilliam, a rather fortunate circumstance for
him, as there is little art and no husbandry in his acting,
though his natural equipment is first-rate of its kind.

Miss Kate Phillips, with much greater skill, divided the honors with him. There were no other personal successes. Mr. Fernandez, in one of those characters which the celebrated Hall Caine apparently copies very vilely from Sir Walter Scott, mouthed texts of Scripture in a manner which exposed him to the most serious risk of being described as "a sound actor." Professional methods were also illustrated by Mr. Hamilton Knight as the Manxsome governor. He, having to leave the stage with the innocent words, "Come and see us as soon as you can," showed us how the experienced hand can manufacture an effective exit. He went to the door with the words "Come and see us as soon." Then he nerved himself; opened the door; turned dauntlessly; and with raised voice and sparkling eyes hurled the significant words "as you can" in the teeth of the gallery. Naturally we were all struck with admiration, because it was just the thing that none of us would have thought of or known how to do.

Mr. Lewis Waller managed to get a moment of real acting into the end of the first act, and then relapsed into nonsensical solemnity for the rest of the evening. I do not know what he was thinking of; but it can hardly have been of the play. He delivered his lines with the automatic gravity of a Brompton Cemetery clergyman repeating the burial service for the thousandth time. He uttered endless strings of syllables; but he did not divide them into words, much less phrases. "I cannotIwillnotlistentothisIwonthearofit," was the sort of thing he inflicted on us for three mortal acts. As to Miss Florence West, if she persists in using her privilege as the manager's wife to play melodramatic heroines, she will ruin the enterprise. Some years' hard and continuous work might make her an accomplished performer in artificial comedy or in the Sardou-Bernhardt line of sensational drama. At present she is obviously a highly civilized modern London lady, whose natural attitude towards melodramatic sentiment is one of supercilious incredulity. There is about as much sense in casting her for Kate Cregeen as there would be in casting Mr. Waller himself for Tony Lumpkin.

Of "The Rivals" at the Court Theatre, I can only say that Mrs. John Wood's Mrs. Malaprop is so good that it almost atones for the atrocity of the rest of the performance. I am sorry to say that the shortcomings are not all due to "the traditions," insufferable as they are. In more than one instance, a leading part has been deliberately given to a mere pupil, coached up to the requisite business gesture by gesture and phrase by phrase. Most of the rest of the acting is forced, noisy, and tiresome beyond description. The cackling, boisterous, mirthless laughter; the racketing and swaggering; the ostentatious consciousness of Sheridan's reputation; the tomfoolish stage business, which might have been invented by Pierce Egan, and would not now be tolerated in a modern play at any leading theatre: all this wearies me, disgusts me, jars on me unbearably. I will do Mr. Sidney Brough the justice to admit that he tries to dehumanize himself, in the manner unhappily expected of him, without being offensive, and succeeds as far as that is possible; and that Mr. Brandon Thomas plays Sir Lucius agreeably and even with dignity, mainly by not doing what is expected of him. But the others fall an unresisting prey to the traditions, which, as far as the stage business is concerned, are simply the coarse methods and Mohawk manners of Sheridan's day thrust on to our stage. Mr. Farren, as Sir Anthony Absolute, is one of the worst offenders. He does not succeed in making the part live for a moment. Mr. Farren can play Sir Peter Teazle adequately, because any polished elderly actor of comedy has only to repeat Sheridan's lines intelligently to be Sir Peter. But Sir Anthony, a well-marked choleric character type, demands a genuine feat of impersonation; and this Mr. Farren does not give us. Of course, he is applauded in the part—I am convinced that if he had substituted the lines and costume of the ghost in "Hamlet" for Sir Anthony's, everybody would have gone into the customary raptures sooner than venture to use their own judgment when Mr. Farren and Sheridan were in question—but to me there was no Sir Anthony there, nothing but an obsolete formula for old comedy worked out with plenty of technical address, but without verisimilitude or relevance to the peculiar temperament indicated in the play. Mrs. John Wood's sincerity, and the genuine comic effect it produced, ought to have convinced the rest that her policy of never laughing at herself, or at Sheridan, or to persuade the audience that old comedy is immensely funny, was the right policy; but the lesson was quite lost on them.

The band played a maddening string of old English airs all the evening. If Mr. Edward Jones will cut them all out except his variation on "The Banks of Allan Water," which is effective and ingenious, all musicians will be grateful to him. Old English airs are all very well; but a couple of hundred of them on end is more than any reasonable person can be expected to endure at one sitting.

THE DIVIDED WAY

The Divided Way: an original play in three acts. By H. V. Esmond. *The Misogynist:* an original one-act play. By G. W. Godfrey. St. James's Theatre, 23 November, 1895.

"A T LAST a noble deed," says Hedda Gabler. "At last a charming play," I was able to exclaim at the St. James's, last Saturday, after weeks of splenetic denunciation of the theatre and everything connected with it. "The Divided Way" is a romantically tragic love drama, written with a delicate freshness of feeling, and here and there a pardonable and even pleasant touch of exaggeration and indiscretion, which gives the work an air of boyish genius and surrounds it with an atmosphere of hope. That the author, Mr. Esmond, is youthful in appearance, we all know. Whether he is a young man really, I have no idea. I have known men just like Mr. Esmond, and treated them as children of genius—Chattertons, in fact —for fifteen years, during which period their appearance has not altered in the least, only to be finally invited by them to celebrate the tenth birthday of their second eldest grandchild. Consequently until I see Mr. Esmond's certificate of birth, I shall suspend my judgment as to whether his years are those of Cayley Drummle or Little Billee. Fortunately age is not a matter of years only, but of evolution. A man of forty-eight is younger in body than a dog of twelve; and in the same way one man at sixty is sometimes younger in mind than another at twenty: at all events it is certain that anyone who chooses his friends from among the brightest spirits of his time will soon become familiar with fathers who are younger than their sons and mothers who are younger than their daughters. Therefore when I say that Mr. Esmond's charm is a youthful one, I imply neither patronage nor disparagement: I am perfectly prepared to learn that he is old enough to be my father, and to venerate him in private life whilst envying him in his public aspect.

I call "The Divided Way" tragically romantic because it ends with death, in unquestioning obedience to the law of the realm of romance, that love is strong as death and jealousy cruel as the grave. In real life this law does not hold. As I have already had to point out in criticizing romantic dramas, love can be more easily baffled and jealousy more safely braved than any of the other passions, in spite of the fact that both social discipline and criminal law are sentimentally relaxed to an alarming degree in favor of people who act on the romantic theory, even to the extent of committing murder. In Mr. Esmond's play a young lady falls in love with a young gentleman named Gaunt Humeden, who goes to Africa and gets killed. Thereupon the lady, acting on the celebrated view of the Grand Duchess of Gerolstein, that if you cannot have the man you love you must love the man you have, marries Jack, brother to the deceased. This is no sooner settled than the deceased comes back from Africa to contradict the news of his death, and settles down at Humeden Grange with the rest of the family. He allows the old flirtation to pass as a joke; and so does the lady, each believing that the other no longer cares. Enter to them one day Jay Grist, not, as one would expect, an unscrupulous American financier, but an African traveller. To the lady he reveals the fact that Gaunt, whilst dying in the African desert, raved continually of her: to Gaunt, who explains that the lady no longer cares for him, and that he is pretending not to care for her, he puts the question, "How do you know that she is not pretending also?" Then all the fat is in the fire. The lady takes a practical view of the case, the gentleman an idealistic one. She says, "I agreed to spend my life with Jack under the impression that you were not available. Now that it appears you *are* available, I propose to spend my life with you. If I stay with Jack I shall make him miserable, make you miserable, and be miserable myself. Clearly it is better economy to make Jack miserable and make you and myself happy." Gaunt is too conventionable to be able to explain to her that this is the logic of romance, not of life, and that a broken heart is a much more healthy complaint than she imagines. He threatens to run away to the East again. She trumps that card by threatening to follow him. He then says, "Very good: I shall poison myself; and you can follow me there if you like." This is the logic of romance with a vengeance. Vanquished, she declines the ordeal; and it is agreed that he is to return to the East and that she is not to follow him, but to go home like a good wife. At this point Jack comes in; and for some reason which escaped me at the performance, and which I confess I can trace neither in the logic of romance nor life, is informed of the whole situation. The lady, seeing that this makes the future, romantically speaking, impossible for her, suddenly drinks the poison and ends the play. The moral, apparently, is that which the French assassin offered on the scaffold as the lesson of his experience: "Never confess." But of course the ending, being a romantic ending, exists for its own sake, and not as a peg to hang a moral on.

Like all romantic plays which create a strong illusion, this one irresistibly raises the question how its final situation would do for the starting-point of a realistic play. All Ibsen's later plays, from "Pillars of Society" to "Little Eyolf," are continuations of this kind, a fact which wrought so powerfully with Mr. Austin Friars that he actually wrote and put on the stage the drama which lies implicit in the exposition of "Rosmersholm," perhaps the most singular dramatic exploit of modern times, and one which, whether it was intended merely to teach Ibsen the right place to begin, or, as I believe, out of a perfectly genuine impulse to put the pathos of the story of Mrs. Rosmer on the stage without the merciless philosophy of Ibsen behind it, had its value as an object lesson. It seems to me that if Mr. Esmond would reverse the procedure of Mr. Austin Friars, and, having already brought Gaunt Humeden to life after killing him, were to bring Mrs. Gaunt to life also, we should have a remarkably interesting realistic play on top of the romantic one. Any one who has attentively watched the world for some years past must by this time be aware that conventional solutions of such situations are growing extremely dangerous and unstable in practice, and that unconventional ones are growing more practicable than they used to be. What exceptional people do in one generation average people are generally found doing in the next. About twenty-six years ago a somewhat similar dilemma to that in Mr. Esmond's play arose between three persons no less famous than Wagner, Hans von Bulow, and Liszt's daughter, Cosima von Bulow. Madame von Bulow preferred to spend her life with Wagner, just as

Mrs. Humeden in the play preferred to spend her life with Gaunt. The change was effected with the happiest results: at least I am not aware that anybody was a penny the worse—certainly not Madame Wagner, who holds her court at Bayreuth with a dignity which many actual princesses might, and probably do, envy. Far be it from me to suggest anarchical violations of our marriage laws rather than an orderly agitation for constitutional reform of them in harmony with the higher morality of our own times; but I do venture to remark that people who decline to carry obedience to that law too far are at least as interesting dramatically as people who forge and murder, and that the notion that the consequences of such disobedience, when carried out in good faith by respectable people (George Eliot, for example) are necessarily so awful that suicide is the more reasonable alternative, is a piece of nonsense that might as well be dropped on the stage. No human institution could stand the strain of the monstrous assumptions on which our existing marriage laws proceed if we were really sincere about them; and though there is much to be said for our English method of maintaining social order by collectively maintaining the sacredness of our moral ideas whilst we individually mitigate their severity by evasion, collusion, and never seeing anything until our attention is compelled by legal proceedings, yet the abuse of this system of toleration by people whose conduct we are not prepared to excuse, but who cannot very well be exposed if the excusable people are to be spared, is landing us in looser views than we ever bargained for. Already we have an aimlessly rebellious crusade against marriage altogether, and a curious habit of circumspection on the part of the experienced man of the world, who, when newly introduced to an English household, picks his way very cautiously until he has ascertained whether the husband and wife really would be husband and wife in France or Germany or South Dakota, and, if his conclusion is unfavorable, which friend of the family is Mr. Gaunt Humeden, so to speak. Not that the domestic situations which are not white are all necessarily jet black or even disagreeably grey; but the fact that under the English law a mistake in marriage cannot be effectively remedied except by the disgrace of either party—that is to say, cannot be remedied at all by decent people, divorce being thus a boon reserved to reward the dissolute—is continually producing a supply of cases not at all dissimilar to that which is the subject of Mr. Esmond's play. Most of them are settled, not by suicide, nor by flights into Egypt, but by the parties drifting along, nobody doing anything wrong, and nobody doing anything right, all seeing enough of one another to make them contented *faute de mieux*, whilst maintaining their honor intact. Whether this customary and convenable solution is really better—say in its effect on the children who grow up observing it—than the violent method of open scandal and collusory divorce, involving the public announcement of cruelties and adulteries which have never been committed, is an open question, not admitting of a general answer. Obviously, the ideal husband and wife who give all their affection to one another, and maintain a state of cold indifference to everyone else, would be executed without benefit of clergy as a couple of heartless monopolists; for the idealist may be safely challenged to produce a single instance of a thoroughly happy marriage in which the affection which makes the marriage happy does not extend to a wide circle of friends. Just as good mothers and fathers love all lovable children, so good wives and husbands love all lovable husbands and wives. People with this gift of heart are not prevented from marrying by Don Juan's difficulty: they can be faithful to one without being unfaithful to all the rest. Unfortunately, they are no more common than the domestic terrors who are utterly incapable of living with anybody on tolerable terms. Family life may mean anything between these two extremes, from that of the southern countries where the guide-book warns the English tourist that if he asks a man after his wife's health he will probably be challenged to fight a duel, or that of the English stage, where the same evil construction is maintained on the same pretense of jealousy of private morality and the honor of womanhood, to the most cultivated sections of English and American society, where people think of our existing marriage law much as Matthew Arnold thought about Tennyson, and unfortunately keep their opinion to themselves with equal "good taste." The practical result is, superhuman pretension, extravagant hypocrisy, tolerance of every sort of misconduct provided it is clandestine, and, of course, a conspiracy of silence. On the whole I think Mr. Esmond might do worse than treat his theme over again, this time as a realist instead of a romanticist.

Even in the romantic version it strikes one as odd that it does not occur to the husband that if there is to be any poison taken, he is the man to take it. It seems to me that the natural attitude for a husband whose wife prefers another man is a purely apologetic one; though I observe that on the stage he seems to take it for granted that he is an injured person as well as an unfortunate one. No doubt my moral sense has not been properly trained on such points; so possibly I shall alter my opinion when I get married, though I confess I regard that as an additional reason for not getting married. Howbeit, taking the play, as it is, I find it continuously engaging and pleasant, showing us a humane and villainless society in which naturally sympathetic intercourse replaces the ostentatiously motived communications and revelations of the ordinary play (as if people never told their sorrows to one another spontaneously), and with parts in it that the actors can really feel and study. Miss Millard as Lois is not the somewhat romantic figure, passionate and tragic, that Mr. Esmond conceived: she has made Lois a real woman, more fascinating and interesting than any man-made woman could possibly be. Her serious, thoughtful charm, so beautifully sober and dignified, has at last found a part in which it is not disastrously wasted. The moment she enters it is evident that she has created Lois, who lives all through the play, silent or speaking, and makes it her own story. One or two of Mr. Esmond's more strained passages—notably the "Ring out the old, ring in the new," business at the end of the second act—were out of the character as she created it; but that was so much the worse for the passages. None of the others achieved anything like the same success, though Mr. Vernon would perhaps have got upon the same artistic level if his part had given him the chance. He played admirably as far as his opportunity went. For the rest, Mr. Alexander gave us a finished impersonation of Mr. George Alexander; Mr. Aynesworth was as popular as ever as Mr. Allan Aynesworth; and Mr. Waring played Mr. Herbert Waring to perfection. Mr. Vincent disguised himself to some extent as an Irish doctor, educated at Rugby, where he had acquired an accent something between that of a Ringsend coal-heaver and a Sligo drover, as an Irish gentleman naturally would at an English public school. The play is handsomely staged; and though two unfortunate gentlemen in the gallery rent the air with comfortless lamentations at being defrauded of a happy ending, the rest of the house was enthusiastic in its appreciation.

"The Misogynist," by Mr. G. W. Godfrey, precedes "The Divided Way." It is an elaborately serious background for a joke about a duke and a music-hall singer, which was so amazingly unexpected that it swept the house away. I grieve to say that Mr. Alexander, fired by the vogue of the Hero of Waterloo, dodders through the piece as an old man, croaking and piping and exhibiting his tongue so as to produce an effect of having false teeth. The sole merit of the performance is that it deceives nobody. Mr. Alexander, fortunately for himself and us, does not belong to the race of Smallweeds, who, born decrepit, can play old men at nineteen. However, we owe Mr. Alexander much; and if it pleases him once in a way to paint his face and talk like that under the impression that he is giving a lifelike illustration of one of the Seven Ages, he can depend on us all to keep our countenances and praise him to the skies. Miss Ellice Jeffries, as Kitty Denison, played with a very marked increase of sincerity and artistic courage. If she maintains that rate of improvement her position will finally justify Mr. Pinero's choice of her for a leading part in "Mrs. Ebbsmith."

TOLD YOU SO

7 December, 1895.

Mrs. Ponderbury's Past: a farcical comedy in three acts, adapted by F. C. Burnand from *Madame Mongodin.* By Ernest Blum and Raoul Toche.

A Dangerous Ruffian: a comedy in one act. By W. D. Howells. Avenue Theatre.

N O TRULY magnanimous soul ever indulges in the mean triumph of "I told you so." Exhibitions of magnanimity, however, are not the business of a critic any more than of a general in the field: for both alike the pursuit is as important as the victory, though it may be a barbarous, murderous, demoralizing cavalry business of cutting down helpless fugitives. It was Lessing, the most eminent of dramatic critics (so I am told by persons who have read him), who was reproached by Heine for not only cutting off his victims' heads but holding them up afterwards to show that there were no brains in them. The critical profession, in fact, is cruel in its nature, and demands for its efficient discharge an inhuman person like myself. Therefore nobody need be surprised if I raise an exultant and derisive laugh at the clouds of defeat, disappointment, failure, perhaps ruin, which overhang the theatre at present. Where is your Manxman now, with his hired baby and his real water? Has the desperate expedient of fitting "Her Advocate" with a new act and a new hero saved it from destruction? What of the adipose humors of "Poor Mr. Potton"?—do its authors still believe that the cheaper the article the wider the consumption; or are they mourning with Mr. Jerome K. Jerome and Mr. Willard over the ingratitude of an imaginary public of idiots to whose level they have condescended in vain? I am not, I hope, an exacting critic: I have been reproached from my own side for approving of "Miss Brown" and disapproving of "Mrs. Ebbsmith"; and although I should have advised, and been right in advising Mr. Lewis Waller to produce Ibsen's hitherto unacted and impossible "Emperor or Galilean" rather than "The Manxman," since it would have secured him at least a fortnight's business, not to mention a lifetime of artistic credit, yet something as enjoyable as "The Passport" or "The Prude's Progress" would have quite satisfied me. I graciously tolerated these plays; and they flourished: I frowned on the others; and they withered from the stage. In this I acted as most sages do, making an easy guess at what was going to happen, and taking care to prophesy it. "Dick Hallward," "Her Advocate," and "The Manxman" were nothing but lame attempts to compete with the conventicle by exploiting the rooted love of the public for moralizing and homiletics. Nobody, I hope, will at this time of day raise a senseless braying against preaching in the theatre. The work of insisting that the church is the house of God and the theatre the house of Satan may be left to those poor North Sea islanders who have been brought up to believe that it is wrong to enter a playhouse. The theatre is really the week-day church; and a good play is essentially identical with a church service as a combination of artistic ritual, profession of faith, and sermon. Wherever the theatre is alive, there the church is alive also: Italy, with its huge, magnificent, empty churches, and slovenly, insin-

cere services, has also its huge, magnificent, empty theatres, with slovenly, insincere plays. The countries which
we call Scandinavian (to the exasperation of all true
Norwegians, somehow) produce saints and preachers,
dramatists and actors, who influence all Europe. The
fundamental unity of Church and Theatre—a necessary
corollary of the orthodox doctrine of omnipresence—is
actually celebrated on the stage in such dramas as
"Brand," and in the "Parsifal" performance at Bayreuth,
which is nothing less than the Communion presented in
theatrical instead of ecclesiastical form. Indeed, the
matter comes out in a simpler way. Some time ago I
had occasion to deliver a public address on the Problems
of Poverty in Bristol. Following the custom of those
who understand such problems, I put up at the most
expensive hotel in the town, where I arrived the night
before that appointed for my own performance. After
dinner I went into the hall of the hotel to study the theatrical announcements exhibited for the convenience of
playgoing visitors. There, among bills of pantomimes
and melodramas, I found, in carved wooden frames of
"ecclesiastical" gothic design, and with capital letters
suggestive of the ten commandments, the announcements
of the churches, with the hours of service, and details
of the musical arrangements, as to which "special attention" was guaranteed. Leaving all theological and sec-
tarian considerations out of account, I have no doubt
whatever that the Bristol churchgoer has a better time
of it, in point of comfort, decency, cheapness, music, interest, edification, rest and recreation than the Bristol
playgoer. I sometimes believe that our playgoers in
London are simply stupid people who have not found
out those great "draws," the services in St. Paul's and

Westminster Abbey. Certainly, when I recall some of the evening services I have attended in cathedrals, and compare them with the dull drudgery of sitting out the Manxman, even in a complimentary stall (what must it be in the shilling gallery?) I begin to understand why it is that only the weaklings, the sentimentalists, the un-businesslike people go to the theatre, whilst the solid, acquisitive, industrious, safely selfish Englishman who *will* have the best value for his money, sticks to the church.

In the face of these facts it cannot be pretended that either our late experiments in melodrama or any other enterprises of the kind in England have ever failed through preaching and sermonizing. The British public likes a sermon, and resents an exhibition of human nature. If you bring on the stage the Englishman who lives in a single-room tenement, as many Englishmen do, and who beats his wife, as all Englishmen do under such circumstances except when their wives beat them, you will be denounced as the author of a "problem play." If you substitute an actor-preacher who declares that "the man who would lift his hand to a woman save in the way of kindness, etc.," it will be admitted on all hands that your feelings do you credit. Your popular Adelphi actor may lack every qualification save one—pious unc-tion. And his most popular act is contrite confession, just as the most popular "evangelist" is the converted collier or prizefighter, who can delight his hearers with the atrocities he committed before his second birth, whilst sanctifying the wicked story with penitent tears and sighs of gratitude for his redemption. I have followed the revivalist preacher through many an incarnation; and now he cannot elude my recognition by merely taking refuge in a theatre. In vain does he mount the stage in a barrister's wig and gown and call his familiar emotional display acting. I am not to be deceived: in his struggles with his mock passion for the leading lady I recognize the old wrestle with the devil: in his muddy joy and relief at having won a verdict of acquittal for her I detect the rapture of the sinner saved. I see him at a glance in Dick Hallward, in Pete Quilliam, in Governor Christian. Mr. Cartwright, well schooled at the Adelphi, has his trick to the life; Mr. Willard spoils him by trying to act; Mr. Lewis Waller utterly destroys him by treating him in the High Church manner; but, spoiled or unspoiled, there he is, all over the stage; and there, too, in the auditorium, is the hysterical groan and sniff which passes with simple souls as evidence of grace abounding. Why, then, has he been so unsuccessful of late? The answer is easy: he has failed to carry conviction. The congregation has said to itself, "This is not Spurgeon, it is Stiggins; and his lying lips are an abomination. The whole thing is put on to make money out of us. Does he take us for fools, with his babies and cradles, his policemen and criminal trials, his bottles of poison and slow music?" That attitude is fatal. Any gospel or anti-gospel will succeed as long as the author and the audience are making for the same end, whether by affirmation and praise, or by satire and negation. But when an author is openly insulting his patrons in the gallery by flattering their conscious hypocrisy, and complimenting them on what he conceives to be their weaknesses and superstitions, and what they themselves equally conceive to be their weaknesses and superstitions, he is predestined to damnation. To be publicly and obviously played down to is more than human nature can bear.

"The New Boy" and "The Strange Adventures of Miss Brown," on the other hand, are genuine appeals to our sense of fun. The authors frankly do their best to tickle us; and we are under no obligation to laugh if they fail, as we are to say Amen to the hypocrisies of the melodramatist. When they do not fail, they prove that they possess some humorous faculty, however schoolboyish it may be; and they seldom pretend to anything more. The danger of the "Miss Brown" business is that it leads actor-managers—Mr. Kerr, for instance, if I may judge from a report of his speech at the Playgoers' Club—into the wild error that people want to be amused and pleased, and go to the theatre with that object. As a matter of fact, they want nothing of the sort. They want to be excited, and upset, and made miserable, to have their flesh set creeping, to gloat and quake over scenes of misfortune, injustice, violence, and cruelty, with the discomfiture and punishment of somebody to make the ending "happy." The only sort of horror they dislike is the horror that they cannot fasten on some individual whom they can hate, dread, and finally torture after revelling in his crimes. For instance, if Ibsen were to rewrite "Ghosts," and make Mrs. Alving murder her husband, flog Regina, burn down the orphanage purposely, and be killed with a hatchet by Engstrand just a moment too late to save Oswald from filially taking her guilt on himself and then, after drinking poison to escape the scaffold, dying to slow music in the act of being united to Regina by Pastor Manders, the play would have an immense vogue, and be declared full of power and pity. Ibsen, being apparently of opinion that there is quite enough horror in the ordinary routine of respectable life without piling Pelion on Ossa, sends away his audience with their thirst for blood and revenge unsatisfied and their self-complacency deeply wounded. Hence their murmurs against him. What is the secret of the overwhelming reputation of Edmund Kean among the English actors of this century? Hazlitt reveals it thus: "Mr. Kean's imagination appears not to have the principles of joy or hope or love in it. He seems chiefly sensible to pain or to the passions that spring from it, and to the terrible energies of mind or body which are necessary to grapple with it." I know that some of our theatrical experts believe that the truly popular trait for a stage hero nowadays is the sort of maudlin goodnature that is an essential part of the worthlessness of the average Strand bar-loafer. But I have never seen much evidence in favor of this idea; and my faith in it is not increased by the entire concurrence of the public in my view of Dick Hallward and the barrister in "Her Advocate." What the public likes is a villain to torment and persecute the heroine, and a hero to thrash and baffle the villain. Not that it matters much, since what the public likes is entirely beside the question of what it can get. When the popular tribune demands "good words" from Coriolanus, he replies, "He that will give good words to thee will flatter beneath abhorring"; and no great play can ever be written by a man who will allow the public to dictate to him. Even if the public really knew what it likes and what it dislikes—a consummation of wisdom which it is as far from as any child— the true master-dramatist would still give it, not what it likes, but what is good for it.

This brings me to the announcement of the last nights of "The Benefit of the Doubt." A run of two months, though not brilliant in comparison with that of "Charley's Aunt," is not bad for an entirely serious work of art, especially when it is considered that some of the most important parts are so badly acted that I had to point out after the first night that they might possibly lead to the failure of the piece. The sympathetic part of the play is original and unconventional, so that the sympathy does not flow in the old ready-made channels. Now it is only by a poignant beauty of execution that new channels can be cut in the obdurate rock of the public's hardened heart; and the best stage execution that Mr. Pinero could command was for the most part ugly and clumsy. We shall presently have him sharing the fate of Ibsen, and having his plays shirked with wise shakes of the head by actor-managers who have neither the talent to act them nor the brains to understand them. Why was I born into such a generation of duffers!

By the way, I have discovered, quite by accident, an amusing farcical comedy. Somebody told me that there was a farce by Mr. W. D. Howells at the Avenue Theatre. I looked in the daily paper, but could find no mention of the name of Mr. Howells. However, it was evidently quite possible that the management had never heard of Mr. Howells, just as they had apparently never heard of me. So I went, and duly found the name "Howels" on the programme. The little piece showed, as might have been expected, that with three weeks practice the American novelist could write the heads off the poor bunglers to whom our managers generally appeal when they want a small bit of work to amuse the people who come at eight. But no doubt it is pleasanter to be a novelist, to have an intelligent circle of readers comfortably seated by their firesides or swinging sunnily in hammocks in their gardens, to be pleasantly diffuse, to play with your work, to be independent of time and space, than to conform to the stern conditions of the stage and fight with stupidity before and behind the curtain. Mr. Howell's piece was followed by a harmlessly naughty and highly entertaining adaptation by Mr. Burnand of a certain French play unknown to me, entitled "Madame Mongodin," by Ernest Blum and Raoul Toche. In it Mr. Charles Hawtrey is irresistibly droll; and Miss Lottie Venne does some clever and funny acting in addition to her old repertory of laughtraps and the inevitable though obsolescent comic song. A Miss Oliff, whom I do not remember to have seen before, comes very near making an artistic success in the title part, only missing it by a few unhappy lapses into clowning at the crucial passages, according to the tradition of the English stage, where people are always so carefully taught by the stage-manager to force the fun and spoil it. If Miss Oliff would only try the effect of playing the part with absolute sincerity throughout, and, without slackening her grip, absolutely refuse to give away her handsome style at any moment for the sake of raising a silly heehaw by a grimace or an ugly sound or gesture, she would distinguish herself considerably. Miss Ada Mallon and Mr. W. F. Hawtrey help the performance materially; and the rest, though they act very indifferently, do not hinder it.

THE OLD ACTING AND THE NEW

The Comedy of Errors. Performance by the Elizabethan Stage Society in Gray's Inn Hall, 7 December,
1895.

FOR a delightful, as distinguished from a commercially promising first night, the palm must be given
this season to the Elizabethan Stage Society's performance of "The Comedy of Errors" in Gray's Inn Hall
this day week. Usually I enjoy a first night as a surgeon
enjoys an operation: this time I enjoyed it as a playgoer
enjoys a pleasant performance. I have never, I hope,
underrated the importance of the amateur; but I am now
beginning to cling to him as the savior of theatrical art.
He alone among the younger generation seems to have
any experience of acting. Nothing is more appalling to
the dramatic author than the discovery that professional
actors of ten years standing have acquired nothing but
a habit of brazening out their own incompetence. What
is an actor nowadays, or an actress? In nine cases out
of ten, simply a person who has been "on tour" with
half-a-dozen "London successes," playing parts that involve nothing but a little business thoughtlessly copied
from the performances of their London "creators," with
long intervals spent between each tour in the ranks of
the unemployed. At the end of a lifetime so spent, the
"actor" will no doubt be a genuine expert at railway
travelling, at taking lodgings, and at cajoling and bully-
ing landladies; but a decent amateur of two years standing, and of the true irrepressible sort, will beat him hopelessly at his art. What a fate is that of these unhappy

young professionals, sick to desperation of a provincial routine compared to which that of a commercial traveller is a dream of romance, longing for a chance which they have not skill enough to turn to account even if some accident thrust it upon them, and becoming less interesting and attractive year by year at a profession in which the steady increase of personal fascination should have no limit but positive senility and decrepitude! I remember, years ago, when the Playgoers' Club was in its infancy, hearing Mr. Pinero, in the course of an address to that body, break into an enthusiastic eulogium on the actor of the past, produced by the old stock-company system, versatile, a singer, a dancer, a fencer, an elocutionist, ready to play any part at a day's notice, and equally expert in comedy, drama, melodrama, Christmas pantomime, and "the legitimate." There is some German novel in which a crowd of mediæval warriors, fired by the eloquence of Peter the Hermit, burns with a Christian longing to rush to the Holy Land and charge in serried ranks on the Paynim hosts—all except one man, who is obviously not impressed. Indignant at his coldness, they demand what he means by it. "I've been there," is his sufficient explanation. That is how I felt when I was listening to Mr. Pinero. Having been brought up on the old stock-company actor, I knew that he was the least versatile of beings—that he was nailed helplessly to his own line of heavy or light, young or old, and played all the parts that fell to him as the representative of that line in exactly the same way. I knew that his power of hastily "swallowing" the words of a part and disgorging them at short notice more or less inaccurately and quite unimprovably (three months rehearsal would have left him more at sea than three hours) was incompatible with his ever knowing his part in any serious sense at all. I remembered his one absurd "combat" that passed for fencing, the paltry stepdance between the verses of his song in the pantomime that constituted him a dancer, the obnoxiousness of utterance which he called elocution and would impart to pupils for a consideration, the universal readiness which only meant that in his incorrigible remoteness from nature and art it mattered nothing what he did. Mr. Pinero madly cited Sir Henry Irving as an example of the product of the stock-company training; but the fact is, when Sir Henry first attempted classical acting at the Lyceum, he did not know the A B C of it, and only succeeded by his original and sympathetic notions of the X Y Z. Nobody who is familiar with the best technical work of the Irving of to-day, its finish, dignity, and grace, and the exactitude of its expression of his thought and feeling, can (unless he remembers) form any idea of what our chief actor had to teach himself before he could carry veteran playgoers with him in his breach with the tradition of superhuman acting of which Barry Sullivan was, as far as I know, the last English exponent (need I say that the great Irish actor was born in Birmingham?). Barry Sullivan was a splendidly monstrous performer in his prime: there was hardly any part sufficiently heroic for him to be natural in it. He had deficiencies in his nature, or rather blanks, but no weaknesses, because he had what people call no heart. Being a fine man, as proud as Lucifer, and gifted with an intense energy which had enabled him to cultivate himself physically to a superb degree, he was the very incarnation of the old individualistic, tyrannical conception of a great actor. By magnifying that conception to sublimity, he reduced it to absurdity. There were just two serious parts which he could play—Hamlet and Richelieu—the two loveless parts in the grand repertory. I know that some people do not like to think of Hamlet as loveless, and that the Irving Hamlet has his heart in the right place, and almost breaks it in the scene with Ophelia; but this I take to be the actor's rebuke to Shakespeare rather than an attempt to fulfil his intentions. Sir Henry Irving has never thought much of the immortal William, and has given him more than one notable lesson—for instance, in "The Merchant of Venice," where he gave us, not "the Jew that Shakespeare drew," but the one he ought to have drawn if he had been up to the Lyceum-mark. Barry Sullivan, with his gift of lovelessness, *was* Hamlet, and consequently used to put his Ophelias out of countenance more than it is easy to describe. In Hamlet, as in Richelieu, it was right to create a figure whose utter aloofness from his fellows gave him an almost supernatural distinction, and cut him off from all such trifling intimacy with them as love implies. And it was his success in producing this very curious and very imposing effect that made for Barry Sullivan, in his best days (I am not now speaking of the period after 1870 or thereabout), a unique provincial and Australian reputation which carried him over parts he could not play at all, such as Othello, through which he walked as if the only line in the play that conveyed any idea to him was the description of Othello as "perplexed in the extreme," or Macbeth, who was simply Cibber's Richard (a favorite part of his) in mutton-chop whiskers. No doubt his temperament, with its exceptional combination of imaginative energy with coldness and proud timidity of the sympathetic passions, accentuated the superhuman pretension in the style of acting which he practised; but his predecessor,

Macready (if I may judge from that extremely depressing document, his diary) must have been much more like him than like Sir Henry Irving. At all events, both Macready and Sullivan had abominable tempers, and relied for their stage climaxes on effects of violence and impetuosity, and for their ordinary impressiveness on grandiose assumption of style. Once, when my father mentioned to me that he had seen Macready play Coriolanus, and I asked him what it was like, he replied that it was like a mad bull. I do not offer this as evidence that my critical faculty is an inherited one—clearly there must have been some artistic method in the bull's madness to have gained such a reputation—but I feel quite sure that when Sir Henry Irving fulfils his promise to appear as Coriolanus, no father will describe him to his son as my father described Macready to me. Barry Sullivan, then, represented the grandiose and the violent on its last legs, and could do nothing for the young Irving but mislead him. Irving's mission was to re-establish on the stage the touching, appealing nobility of sentiment and affection—the dignity which only asserts itself when it is wounded; and his early attempts to express these by the traditional methods of the old domineering, self-assertive, ambitious, thundering, superb school led him for a time into a grotesque confusion of style. In playing villains, too, his vein of callous, humorous impishness, with its occasional glimpses of a latent bestial dangerousness, utterly defied the methods of expression proper to the heaven-defying, man-quelling tyrant, usurper, and murderer, who was the typical villain of the old school, and whose flavorless quintessence will be found by the curious distilled into that instructive Shakespearean forgery, Ireland's "Vortigern." In short, Irving had to find the right expression for a perfectly new dignity and a perfectly new indignity; and it was not until he had done this that he really accomplished his destiny, broke the old tradition, and left Barry Sullivan and Macready half-a-century behind. I will not say that he also left Shakespeare behind: there is too much of the "not for an age but for all time" about our bard for that; but it is a pity that the new acting was not applied to a new author. For though Sir Henry Irving's acting is no longer a falsification of the old style, his acting versions are falsifications of the old plays. His Hamlet, his Shylock, his Lear, though interesting in their own way, are spurious as representations of Shakespeare. His Othello I have never seen: his Macbeth I thought fine and genuine, indicating that his business is with Shakespeare's later plays and not with his earlier ones. But he owes it to literature to connect his name with some greater modern dramatist than the late Wills, or Tennyson, who was not really a dramatist at all. There is a nice bishop's part in Ibsen's—— but I digress.

My point is that Sir Henry Irving's so-called training under the old stock-company system not only did not give him the individuality of his style—for to that it did not pretend—but that it failed to give him even those generalities of stage deportment which are common to all styles. The stock actor, when the first travelling companies came along, vanished before them, unwept, unhonored, and unsung, because the only sentiment he had inspired in the public was an intense desire for some means of doing without him. He was such an unpresentable impostor that the smart London person, well dressed and well spoken, figuring in plays ingeniously contrived so as to dispense with any greater powers of acting than every adroit man of the world picks up, came as an inexpressible relief. Dare I now confess that I am beginning to have moments of regret for him. The smart nullity of the London person is becoming intolerably tedious; and the exhaustion of the novelty of the plays constructed for him has stripped them of their illusion and left their jingling, rickety mechanism patent to a disgusted public. The latest generation of "leading ladies" and their heroes simply terrify me: Mr. Bourchier, who had the good fortune to learn his business as an amateur, towers above them as an actor. And the latest crop of plays has been for the most part deliberately selected for production because of the very abjectness and venality which withered them, harvestless, almost as soon as they were above ground.

And yet there is more talent now than ever—more skill now than ever—more artistic culture—better taste, better acting, better theatres, better dramatic literature. Mr. Tree, Mr. Alexander, Mr. Hare, have made honorable experiments; Mr. Forbes Robertson's enterprise at the Lyceum is not a sordid one; Mr. Henry Arthur Jones and Mr. Pinero are doing better work than ever before, and doing it without any craven concession to the follies of "the British public." But it is still necessary, if you want to feel quite reassured, to turn your back on the ordinary commercial West End theatre, with its ignoble gambling for "a catch-on," and its eagerly envious whisperings of how much Mr. Penley has made by "Charlie's Aunt," to watch the forlorn hopes that are led from time to time by artists and amateurs driven into action by the starvation of their artistic instincts. The latest of these is the Elizabethan Stage Society; and I am delighted to be able to taunt those who missed the performance in Gray's Inn Hall with being most pitiably out of the movement. The Lyceum itself could not have drawn a more distinguished audience; and the pleasant effect of the play, as performed on the floor of the hall without proscenium or fittings of any kind, and played straight through in less than an hour and a half without any division into acts, cannot be as much as imagined by any frequenter of our ordinary theatres. The illusion, which generally lapses during performances in our style whenever the principal performers are off the stage, was maintained throughout: neither the torchbearers on the stage nor the very effective oddity of the Dromio costumes interfering with it in the least. Only, the modern dresses of the audience, the gasaliers, and the portrait of Manisty next that of Bacon, were anachronisms which one had to ignore. The stage management was good as regards the exits, entrances, and groupings—not so good in the business of the speeches, which might have been made more helpful to the actors, especially to Adriana, whose best speeches were underdone. On the whole the acting was fair—much better than it would have been at an average professional performance. Egeon, one of the Dromios, and the courtezan distinguished themselves most. The evening wound up with a Dolmetsch concert of lute and viol, virginal and voice, a delectable entertainment which defies all description by the pen.

MR. JOHN HARE

John Hare, Comedian: a biography by T. Edgar
Pemberton. London and New York: George Rout-
ledge & Sons. 1895.

I N VIEW of the fact that Mr. Hare is one of the best
actors of my time, nothing has surprised me more in
reading this book than the number of impersonations
of his which I have seen and totally forgotten. A real
part well acted is to me more easily and perfectly memorable than most things; so, considering how well I remember the good parts I have seen Mr. Hare play, and
that all his parts may safely be taken to have been well
acted, I cannot help feeling that every part I forget raises
a question as to whether it was a real part or not. Further, I am reminded that Mr. Hare made a great success
as a manager—that the mounting and acting, the elaborate rehearsing and thoughtfully minute preparation of
plays at his theatre were the admiration of the critics to
whom Robertson was as much the pioneer of a new order
as Ibsen is to the present generation. In the days of Mr.
Hare's reign at the old Court Theatre, and of the St.
James's under the Hare-Kendal management, I quite
agreed in this opinion. But the Garrick period is another
affair. There was no carelessness, no slackening at the
new house; and yet it seemed to me that Mr. Forbes
Robertson and Miss Kate Rorke acted worse and worse
throughout their long engagement there; whilst as for
the stage management, a climax of something like unsympathetic imeptitude was reached in "Mrs. Lessing-

ham." No mortal playgoer, however credulous, could have believed in the third act of that play as it was put on the Garrick stage. Poor Mrs. Lessingham, fainting with the shock of catching her husband embracing another lady on the summit of an eminence visible from seven counties, or dying by her own hand, after a prolonged scene of deepening despair, in a room like Maple's shop window, had no more chance than "A Scrap of Paper" would have had if mounted in the style of "Pelléas et Mélisande." The fact is, that in the seventies and eighties, the art of stage management meant the art of making the stage look like a real room in a richly and handsomely furnished London house; and this Mr. Hare did to perfection, with every nicety of discrimination between Russell Square and Park Lane. A well-kept gentleman's garden in Surrey, or even a pretty old vicarage, he could turn out also. There was another thing that he understood. Mr. Pemberton quotes Mr. Clement Scott on Mr. Bancroft in the early Robertson days. "Think what it was to see a bright, cheery, pleasant young fellow playing the lover to a pretty girl at the time when stage lovers were nearly all sixty, and dressed like waiters at a penny-ice shop." Now these cheery, pleasant fellows, so smartly tailored and exactly true to nature in the young male as we see him at suburban garden parties or in the first-class carriage of the city train, would have made wings, flats, canvas doors and carpetless boards as ridiculous as pasteboard fowls, or white chairs with red damask seats and a strip of gold tinsel down the leg. They needed Mr. Hare's interiors to move in. And they were indeed delightful when they got them. Young persons who saw the revival of "Caste" at the Garrick in 1894 may imagine that they enjoyed it as their fathers enjoyed it. They are wrong. They can never know what it was to see on the stage a gentleman who looked like a gentleman walking into a drawing-room that looked like a drawing-room after a lifetime spent in contemplating performances compared to which an average representation of "La Traviata" at Covent Garden might pass as photographically realistic. It was Mr. Hare who carried this art to its summit; and since the youngest generation of London playgoers, taking such staging as a matter of course, may be unable to conceive the pleasure it gave when it was new, it is only fair to tell them how much they owe him for a reform which was of high artistic importance in bringing the stage into closer connection with contemporary life. I do not say that the stage drawing-rooms of the old Court and the St. James's were better than "four boards and a passion"; but they were worlds above flats, wings, sky borders and no passion, which was the practical alternative.

Now in art, as in politics, there is no such thing as gratitude. It is one thing to banish vulgarity and monstrosity from the stage and replace them by conventional refinement and scrupulous verisimilitude. It is quite another to surround a real drama with its appropriate atmosphere, and provide a poetic background or an ironically prosaic setting for a tragic scene. There are some rooms in which no reasonable person could possibly commit suicide; and when Mr. Hare provided just such a one for Mrs. Lessingham, he showed that he was not a stage manager in the same sense as Sir Henry Irving, for instance. Even in the matter of refinement he is no longer in the front rank. When Mr. Henry Arthur Jones produced "The Crusaders" at the Avenue Theatre under his own management, as a sort of polite hint to whomsoever it might concern that an author could do without an actor-manager better than an actor-manager could do without an author, he, being a disciple of Ruskin, repudiated the once admired gentlemanly apartment, and went off to Mr. William Morris in search of a beautiful room. The scene in that play called "The Parsley Garland," was the first piece of artistic as distinguished from commercial decoration I remember to have seen on the stage as a representation of a modern room. There must be some young people in the world whose first visit to a theatre was to "The Crusaders," and who afterwards went to see "Slaves of the Ring" at the Garrick. I am afraid, after the Parsley Garland, they will open their eyes very wide indeed at the suggestion implied in Mr. Pemberton's book that the ugly plutocratic interior in the first act of Mr. Grundy's play, and the appalling conservatory in the last act, where Miss Kate Rorke jumped through the fir-tree, may be taken as samples of the taste of the acknowledged chief of stage managers in that class of work. It is but fair to explain to them that the work of making the stage clean, handsome, fashionable, correct, costly, and thoroughly gentlemanly, was an indispensable preliminary to any movement towards beauty, individuality, and imaginative setting.

If Mr. Hare's scenic foundations are by this time built upon and hidden, what shall be said of the "bright, cheery, pleasant young fellows" who belonged to them? For thirty years we have sat at the play feeding our romantic imaginations on the "good form" of young stockbrokers and civil servants. Mr. Hare was always an excellent host; and when he invited us to meet those nice people the Kendals, we knew that we could count upon amusement, instruction in manners, dress, and furnishing, and the contemplation of an edifying example of stainless domestic virtue. Still, so unregenerate is human nature, that the main part of the attraction was the amusement; and the amusement depended on the circumstance that Mrs. Kendal could act and so could Mr. Hare. Even Mr. Kendal was a bit of a comedian, and was always agreeable and sincere. They represented a generation of actors who had toned their acting down and their dress and manners up to stockbroker-civil-servant pitch. This was all very well whilst it lasted; but unfortunately the drawing-room drama, being artistically a sterile hybrid, could not renew the generation of actors; and now the Kendals are replaced by couples equal to them in dress, manners, good looks, and domestic morality, but subject to the disadvantage of not possessing in their two united persons as much power of acting as there was in the tip of Mrs. Kendal's little finger-nail. Besides, there has come along the terrible Ibsen. The stockbrokerly young gentleman, standing on the stage with his manners carefully turned to the audience like the painted side of an old stage banner, has suddenly been taken by the scruff of the neck by the grim Norwegian giant, and, with one ruthless twist, whisked round with his seamy side to the footlights, to stare in helpless bewilderment at the atmosphere of poetry, imagination, tragedy, irony, pity, terror, and all the rest of it, suddenly rising in the theatre from which they had been swept, he had hoped, for ever, along with the "stage lovers nearly all sixty and dressed like waiters at a penny-ice shop." And now he may shriek, with Judge Brack, that "people don't do such things"; he may plunge back to Whitechapel Road melodrama or forward to the best imitation "problem plays"; but he will struggle in vain against the fact that the surest way

of boring yourself to death of an evening now is to go to the theatre. The drawing-room comedy of furniture and manners, with a tastefully conducted intrigue as a pretext, is as dead as Donizetti and deader. The novelty of the change from the penny-ice shopman to the gentleman is exhausted; and now the people want a change from the gentleman to the actor.

Certain fine actors of the Robertsonian epoch can still attract us with the art of that period, and are even taken as models with success by younger artists, just as Patti keeps "Una Voce" and "Bel raggio" alive, and is followed to some extent by Melba, in spite of Wagner and Calve. Mr. Hare is just such a survival. As an actor he has had to work in a drama so superficial that his fame rests largely upon that most unreal of all stage pretences, a young man pretending to be a very old one. Mr. Hare, in these parts, used to make himself up cleverly; and he is the sort of man whose voice, figure, and manner, vary comparatively little from twenty-five to seventy. But that any playgoer who had ever seen Chippendale could have mistaken Mr. Hare's business for the real thing is beyond my belief. As a matter of fact we did not make any such mistake: the fun of Mr. Hare's old men was the cleverness of the imitation, which was amusing even when his part was utterly uninteresting in itself. Now that he is between fifty and sixty, his acting of elderly parts is no longer a pretence; consequently we no longer chuckle at it: we are touched—which is much better—if the part is a touching one. Fortunately for me, the first part I ever saw Mr. Hare play (my first ten years experience as a playgoer was not gained in London) was that of the boy Archie in "A Scrap of Paper." I remember Archie perfectly—should know him if I met him to-morrow. But

Mr. Hare's made-up old men I forget as individuals, though I can recall certain stage moments in which they figured. For example, I can see him in "The Queen's Shilling" gripping Mr. Kendal's wounded arm; and the picture recalls the make-up, uniform, and general aspect of the Colonel; but this recollection of a painful scene, which would be equally vivid had the officer been the young man and the soldier the old one, is quite a different affair from recollection of a character. Again, I recollect his Jack Pontifex in "Mamma" (Duval in "Les Surprises de Divorce") as his masterpiece in farcical comedy; and Jack Pontifex was younger, not older, than Mr. Hare. His Baron Croodle in "The Money Spinner" was a genuine impersonation: I shall never forget that old blackguard. His unvenerable years, however, were the merest accident. Jack Pontifex was especially interesting to the critic because Mr. Hare has very seldom played what may be called a standard part: that is, one in which his performance can be compared with that of other eminent performers in his line. Luckily, "Les Surprises de Divorce" had been made famous by Coquelin, the greatest comedian known to us. Mr. Hare had by no means the worst of the comparison in point of execution. In the great scene in the second act, where the wretched musician, having escaped by divorce from an unbearable mother-in-law, and settled down on his remarriage into tranquil domestic felicity, sees the terrible old woman re-enter, imposed on him again in the old relation by a fresh turn of the matrimonial courts, Mr. Hare surpassed Coquelin. Coquelin clowned it, even to the length of bounding into the air and throwing forward his arms and legs as if to frighten off some dangerous animal. But he did not produce the electric effect of Mr. Hare's white, tense face and appalled stare, conveying somehow a mad speed of emotion and a frightful suspense of action never to be forgotten by any playgoer with the true dramatic memory. Coquelin's compensation in the comparison lay in the greater fulness of his contributions to the drama. He played between the lines, and quadrupled the value of the part: Mr. Hare, with his swift, crisp method, and his habit of picking up a cue as if it were a cricket-ball to be smartly fielded, only made the most of the play as it was. No doubt Mr. Hare's method is the right method for a man who forms his conclusions rapidly and gives them instantaneous and incisive expression; but Duval, in "Les Surprises," was certainly not that sort of man. Nothing could have been truer or more entertaining than Coquelin's play in the first act, where he shows out the gentleman and his daughter who have come to look at the rooms he wished to let. It was not from anything that Duval said that you saw that the daughter had made an impression on him. As he slowly came back with preoccupied gait from the door, you could read a whole chapter of unconscious autobiography in the changes of his face; and when at last, after a long but most eloquent and interesting silence, the words "Elle est charmante!" slipped from him, he had in effect left the technical cue for that speech half-a-dozen well-filled pages behind. Mr. Hare's method is too impatient, and his imagination too dry and sane for this; consequently he adds little or nothing to the written part, whereas with Coquelin the written part is always the merest skeleton of his creation. What Mr. Hare does do he does as well, and here and there better than the French comedian. It is unreasonable to say to an artist who has done so much so finely that he might have done more; and I only say it myself to encourage the others. In so rapidly progressive a business as fine art now is in England, no mortal man can lead more than one generation. No doubt Mr. Hare ought to have done for Ibsen what he did for Robertson: for example, he might have created old Ekdal in "The Wild Duck," instead of leaving that immortalizing chance to an amateur. But in his early days the standard classic was "London Assurance"; and throughout his management at the old Court and the St. James's, the plays he produced were, after all, the best to be had. Some, like "The Hobby Horse," were too good for the public; and many were excellent plays of their kind, superexcellently done. All one can say is that the poetry of the Ellen Terry days, of "New Men and Old Acres" (a piffling play, only I can still see and hear Lilian Vavasour crying like mad in it) and of "Olivia," stands the test of time better than the clever prose of the Kendal period. Miss Terry had at that time hidden somewhere about her a certain perverse devil, since exorcised by the elevating influence of the Lyceum Theatre and that actress-devouring ogre William Shakespeare, which gave the most curious naughty-child charm to Lilian and Olivia. Nowadays you can only admire or adore: then she gave you something to forgive and coaxed you to forgive it. The coaxing was a surprisingly pleasant process; and as I was one of those who experienced it, I should advise the public not to pay too much attention to my criticisms of Miss Terry, as they are sure to be grossly partial. And that partiality I owe among other things to Mr. Hare.

I leave the subject only half exhausted for lack of space. I can only add that the book ends with a testimonial to Mr. Hare's professional competency, and a recommendation of him to the encouraging notice of the

American nation from the Siddonian hand of Mary Anderson de Navarro. How proud Mr. Hare must feel! It is just like our Mary's—I mean it does credit to Madame de Navarro's feelings.

ONE OF THE WORST

One of the Best: a drama in four acts. By Seymour Hicks and George Edwardes. Adelphi Theatre, 21 December, 1895.

THE new entertainment at the Adelphi has for its object the reproduction on the stage of the dramatic effect of the military ceremony of degradation undergone not long ago in France by Captain Dreyfus. The idea is not a bad one from the Adelphi point of view; but the work of setting it into a dramatic frame has fallen into the wrong hands, the two authors' familiarity with the stage and its requirements only giving an absurdly cheerful and confident air to their feeble and slippery grip of a subject much too big for them.

The Dreyfus affair was interesting in many ways. It was French—French in the most unEnglish way, because it was not only theatrical, but theatrical at the expense of common sense and public policy. At the Adelphi Mr. Terriss is able to exclaim at the end of the piece that no English officer has ever betrayed his country; and this understanding, the value of which we are all sensible enough to appreciate, we keep up by breaking and getting rid of our Dreyfuses in the quietest possible manner, instead of advertising them by regimental *coups de théâtre* which, in addition to being as demoralizing as public executions, would shatter that national confidence in the absolute integrity of our public services and institutions which we all keep up with such admirable *esprit de corps,* not that any of us believes in it, but because each of us thinks that it is good for all the rest to believe in it. Our plan is to govern by humbug, and to let everybody into the secret. The French govern by melodrama, and give everybody a part in the piece. The superiority of our system lies in the fact that nobody dislikes his share in it, whereas the French are badly hampered because you cannot have broadly popular melodrama without a villain, and nobody wants to be cast for the villain's part. Consequently a delinquent like Dreyfus is a perfect godsend to the French authorities, and instantly has all the national limelights flashed on him, whereas here he would be quietly extinguished in support of the theory that such conduct as his could not possibly occur in the British army.

There is another weakness in the French method. Even when you have got your villain, how are you going to make him do his best for the effect of the sensation scene? At the Adelphi it is easy enough, since the villain, though he might often make a whole play ridiculous by a single disloyal intonation, can be depended on to omit no stroke of art that will intensify the loathing or louden the execrations of the gallery. It is his point of honor as an artist to blacken himself : he is paid to do it, proud to do it, and depends on doing it for his livelihood. But Dreyfus was not in this position. He had every possible motive to "queer the pitch" of the military melodrama of which he was the villain and victim ; and he did it most effectually. He declined to be impressed by the ceremony or to pretend that the parade of degradation was worse than death to him as a French soldier. He displayed a sardonic consciousness of the infinite tomfoolery of the whole proceeding, and succeeded in leaving all Europe able to think of nothing in connection with it except the ludicrous fact that the uniform which had been stripped and defaced had been carefully prepared for that stage trick the night before by having its facings and buttons ripped off in private and basted on again with light cotton. When the farce was over, he took the stage, shouted "Vive la République," and marched off, having made the hit of the piece, and leaving the Republic and its army looking like the merest crowd of "extras." This was perhaps a mistake; for the shout of "Vive la République" was, at least to English ways of thinking, out of the wronged and innocent character which Dreyfus was assuming: at least, it is certain that an English officer, if innocent, would under such circumstances either keep his feelings to himself, or else, if unable to contain them, roundly and heartily damn his country, his colonel, the court-martial, the army, the sergeant, and everybody else on whom he could with any sort of relevance bring his tongue and temper to bear.

A Dreyfus case is the less likely to arise here because we are not only free from the fear of invasion from armed neighbors which makes Continental nations so sensitive on the subject of spies, but also less childishly addicted to keeping secrets that are no secrets. Campaigns depend on strategy, fighting, and money, not on patents; and a nation which had no better idea of preparation for war than hiding a secret explosive or a new weapon or an undisclosed plan of fortification up its sleeve—an idea which appears particularly plausible to the civilian imagination—would richly deserve what it would probably get in the field. We have many ways of making idiots of ourselves; but the Continental way of arresting artists on sketching tours, and confiscating drawings which give no information that cannot be obtained at any stationer's shop where they sell maps, photographs, and railway timetables, is one which we have so far spared ourselves.

These observations are not very recondite; but they appear to have completely escaped the perspicacity of the authors of "One of the Best." In the second act an impossible K.C.B., A.D.C., declaims against the folly of England in allowing strangers to roam the land with kodaks, photographing her forts and worming out the secrets of the Tower of London, Woolwich Arsenal, Dover Castle, and other strongholds of our national independence, instead of imitating the heroic example of the foreigner by turning out the garrison and searching the pretended tourist, artist, and holiday-maker for concealed copies of the Monroe Doctrine. A gratuitously asinine opinion, I thought, which was received by the gallery with obediently asinine applause. The degradation scene showed an equal want of grasp of military life and English character. The one sentence that was taken from life as exemplified by Dreyfus was just the one sentence that stamped that gentleman as probably guilty. Lieutenant Dudley Keppel is made to finish his ordeal by shouting "God save the Queen" (the equivalent of "Vive la République"), which at such a time can only mean either that the creature is tamed by discipline to the point of being an absolute spaniel, or else that he is a genuine criminal, asserting his highmindedness in a fine stock phrase, as all rascals do whenever they get a chance. On the points of Dreyfus's bearing which seem worthy of imitation by officers in trouble, Dudley Keppel was resolutely original. He did his utmost to make the barbarous and silly spectacle a success by displaying frightful emotion. Before parting with his claymore he kissed it and then broke it across his knee, a proceeding which even the greenest country cousin in the pit must have known to be quite acutely the reverse of anything that a British officer could be conceived as doing upon any provocation or in any extremity. And yet the scene, properly rewritten, could be made highly entertaining with Mr. Fred Kerr instead of Mr. Terriss in the principal part.

It is interesting to observe that Messrs. Hicks and Edwardes seem as incapable of realizing the reality and humanity of a woman as of a soldier. I am not now alluding to the maiden of Keppel's heart. Like most such maidens she is a nonenity; and the unlucky lieutenant is driven to the most abject expedients to work up the sentiment in his love scene with her, shaking blossoms from a tree over her, and helplessly repeating a catalogue of the most affecting objects and circumstances of the scene (provided on purpose), as, for instance, "The old Abbey, the organ, the setting sun," and so on. But there is another young and beauteous female in the piece, a Miss Esther Coventry, who in the most pathetically sentimental way commits a series of crimes which Jonathan Wild himself would hardly have gone through without moments of compunction. Political treachery, theft, burglary, perjury, all involving the most cruel consequences to her father and his amiable young lieutenant, are perpetrated by her without hesitation or apology to get money for a man with whom she is carrying on an intrigue out of pure love of deceit, there being no mortal reason why he should not woo her in honorable form. Throughout all her nefarious proceedings I failed to detect any sign of its having occurred to the authors that any moral responsibility attached to this young woman. In fulfilment of their design she went about with an interesting air of having sinned and suffered, cheating, lying, stealing, burgling, and bearing false witness exactly as if she were the heroine of the play, until, in the last scene in the barrack square, the rehabilitated Keppel suddenly said, "Allow me," and gallantly ordered his general to take that wounded dove to his manly bosom and be more a father to her than ever. As in real life the young lady could not, even by the most violent stretch of judicial leniency, have got off with less than ten years penal servitude, it was difficult, in spite of the magnificent air with which Mr. Terriss proclaimed the amnesty, to quite believe that the civil authorities would submit to be set aside in this manner; but apparently they did: at all events she was still in the peace of complete absolution when the curtain descended.

On the whole, the play, even judged by melodramatic standards, is a bad one. The degradation scene is effective in a way; but what that way is may best be shown by pointing out that if a military flogging had been substituted, the effect would have been still greater, though the tax on Mr. Terriss's fortitude would no doubt have been unreasonable. The court-martial is also effective, but not more so than any trial scene must necessarily be. A trial is the last resource of a barren melodramatist: it is so safe an expedient that improvised amateur attempts at it amused even the doomed aristocrats in the Paris prisons during the Terror. The scene of the attempt to rob the safe produces a certain curiosity as to how the authors will bring about the foregone conclusion of fixing the guilt on the innocent Keppel; but the clumsiness of the solution soon melts this curiosity into a sensation like that of watching a bad chess-player. Then there is the scene in which the villain is thrown like a welsher on a racecourse to a savage crowd, who delight the audience by making as plausible a pretence of tearing him to pieces as is consistent with the integrity of Mr. Abingdon's person. The comic scenes may be divided into three parts: first, puerile jokes about the deficiencies in a Highlander's uniform and the situation of the "pistol pocket" in the bicycling suit worn by Miss Vane Featherstone; second, speeches not in the least funny which are nevertheless funnily delivered by Mr. Harry Nicholls; and third, a certain quantity of tolerable fun mixed with a few puns and personalities, evidently the invention of that gifted comedian. The rest hardly rises sufficiently above nothingness to be as much as dull; and I see no reason to anticipate an exceptionally prosperous career for the play. Mr. George Edwardes was immensely congratulated on his appearance as an author, the audience seeming to regard it as an irresistible joke, and I am rather inclined to take that lenient view myself. If I am to take it seriously I can only say that however successful Mr. Edwardes may be as a manager, he must work a good deal harder if he wishes to succeed in a really difficult profession like that of dramatic authorship.

The acting is, of course, consistently outrageous, though by no means unskilfully so. Mr. Terriss contrives to retain his fascination even in tartan trousers; and he rises fully to such heights as there are in the trial scene and the degradation scene. It is always a pleasure to hear his voice now that we have on the stage so many made-up voices which ring with monotonous sonority in the speakers' noses. With the single exception of Mr. Bernard Gould, Mr. Terriss appears to be the only serious actor in his line from whom we hear a cultivated natural voice instead of an acquired artificial one. Of Miss Millward's capacity I have no idea beyond the fact that she has clearly more than sufficient for such parts as are to be had at the Adelphi. Mr. Nicholls is an excellent actor: it is a thousand pities that his talent is only employed to put us into good humor with bad plays.

NEW YEAR DRAMAS

A Woman's Reason. By Charles H. E. Brookfield and F. C. Philips. Shaftesbury Theatre, 27 December, 1895.

IT WAS such a pleasure to see Mr. Lewis Waller and his company divested of the trappings of Manx-manity and in their right minds again, that we all received "A Woman's Reason" with more gaiety and enthusiasm than can easily be justified in cold blood. The play has been produced, as far as I can guess, by the following process. One of the authors, whom I take to be Mr. Philips, wrote a commonplace Froufrou play, in a style so conscientiously and intolerably literary that the persons of the drama do not hesitate to remark familiarly to their nearest and dearest that "Convention speaks one thing, whilst some sweeter voice whispers another." The sweeter voice in the composing of the play, I assume, was Mr. Brookfield's. Mr. Brookfield is an assiduous collector of conversational *jeux d'esprit,* and is witty enough to be able to contribute occasionally to the museum himself. Such a collection, from its very miscellaneousness, is better for ordinary theatrical purposes than a complete philosophy reduced to aphorisms; and by sticking its plums into Mr. Philip's literary dough with reckless profusion, Mr. Brookfield has produced a sufficiently toothsome pudding.

The worst of it is that the Brookfieldian plums digest and are forgotten, whilst the Philipian suet remains heavy on soul and stomach. I cannot now remember a single one of Mr. Brookfield's sallies, not even the one in which I recognized a long-lost child of my own. On the other hand, I do recollect, with a growing sense of injury, the assumption that the relation between a British officer and a cultivated Jewish gentleman who makes a trifle of seventy thousand a year or so in the City is the relation between Ivanhoe and Isaac of York, with its offensiveness somewhat accentuated by modern snobbery. When Captain Crozier proceeded to explain haughtily to Mr. Stephen D'Acosta that it was useless for two persons in their respective conditions to discuss a question of honor, as they could not possibly understand one another, I seemed to hear a voice from my boyhood —the voice of Howard Paul—singing:—

> I'm Captain Jinks of the Horse Marines;
>   And I feed my horse on kidney beans:
> Of course it far exceeds the means
>   Of a captain in the army.

It is to this rustic conception of "a captain in the army" that we owe Crozier. And yet—would you believe it?—the performance at the Shaftesbury leaves one with a stronger sense of the reality of Captain Crozier than of any other person in the drama. This is largely due, no doubt, to Mr. Coghlan, who, having given himself complete rest from acting during his assumption of the part of Mercutio at the Lyceum, now resumes it at the Shaftesbury with all the vigor of a man who has had a thorough holiday. I do not say that Mr. Coghlan's effects are made with the utmost economy of time and weight; but then it is perfectly in the character of the part and in the interest of the drama that Captain Crozier should be a comparatively slow, heavy person, in contrast to the keen, alert Jew. The presentation of a British officer as an over-eating, under-thinking person, professionally the merest routineer, one who by dint of sincere aspiration and conscientious plodding has learnt to play cards and billiards, to shoot, to bet, to do the correct thing in social emergencies, and in an irreproachably gentlemanly way to make women aware of his readiness to accept any degree of intimacy they may care to admit him to, is fair criticism of life; for wherever the social soil is manured by "independent incomes," it still produces large crops of such men (very pleasant fellows, many of them), though certainly the army has of late years become a much less eligible career for them than it was in the days of Captain Rawdon Crawley. The difficulty of giving the authors of "A Woman's Reason" credit for a clever study of an officer of his type lies in the fact that, as I have already hinted, his speeches to D'Acosta show a quite romantic ignorance of the healthy promiscuity by which English society protects itself against all permanent Faubourg-St. Germain formations. Thanks to the truly blessed institution of primogeniture constantly thrusting down the great bulk of our aristocratic stock into the ranks of the commoners, we are the most republican country in the world; and the ideas expressed by Captain Crozier at the Shaftesbury, though they might pass as part of the established currency on the Continent, and even in America, are here only the affectations of dukes' housekeepers and Hampton Court pensioners. Nor can we, when the Captain foolishly hides in the lady's bedroom from her husband, believe much more in him than in the domestic architecture which cuts that sacred apartment off from all ingress and egress save through the drawing-room. In fact, the bedroom incident elicited one of those jeers from the audience which will soon force even the most conservative West End manager to abjure through terror of the gallery that insane faith in worn-out stage tricks which seems proof against the printed persuasion of the stalls. There is much else in Captain Crozier's part which is differentiated from the conventional seducer and villain business of melodrama rather by Mr. Coghlan's acting than by the words put into his mouth; but the final touch, where he "does the right thing" by telling the usual divorce-court lie as to the lady's spotlessness, and offering to marry her when he perceives that he runs no risk of being accepted in view of her imminent reconciliation with her husband, is a genuine stroke of comedy and character.

Mr. Coghlan created the part, like a true actor, by the simple but very unusual method of playing it from its own point of view. The tradition of the stage is a tradition of villains and heroes. Shakespeare was a devout believer in the existence of the true villain—the man whose terrible secret is that his fundamental moral impulses are by some freak of nature inverted, so that not only are love, pity, and honor loathsome to him, and the affectation of them which society imposes on him a con-

stant source of disgust, but cruelty, destruction, and per-
fidy are his most luxurious passions. This is a totally
different phenomenon from the survivals of the ape and
tiger in a normal man. The average normal man is cov-
etous, lazy, selfish; but he is not malevolent, nor capable
of saying to himself, "Evil: be thou my good." He only
does wrong as a means to an end, which he always represents to himself as a right end. The case is exactly
reversed with a villain; and it is my melancholy duty to
add that we sometimes find it hard to avoid a cynical suspicion that the balance of social advantage is on the side
of gifted villainy, since we see the able villain, Mephis-
topheles-like, doing a huge amount of good in order to
win the power to do a little darling evil, out of which he
is as likely as not to be cheated in the end; whilst your
normal respectable man will countenance, connive at, and
grovel his way through all sorts of meanness, baseness,
servility, and cruel indifference to suffering in order to
enjoy a miserable two-pennorth of social position, piety,
comfort, and domestic affection, of which he, too, is often
ironically defrauded by Fate. I could point to a philan-
thropist or two—even to their statues—whom Posterity,
should it ever turn from admiring the way they spent
their money to considering the way they got it, will probably compare very unfavorably with Guy Fawkes.

However, these reflections are beside the present purpose, which is only to show how our actors have been
placed at cross-purposes with our authors by the traditional stage villain being a monster, or perversion of
nature, like Iago; whilst the gentleman who serves as a
foil to the hero in a modern West End play is not a villain
at all, but at worst a comparatively selfish, worthless fellow. As far as he is taken from life at all, he is suspi-

ciously like the average man of the world as portrayed
by Thackeray. Indeed, in the best modern plays, and
even in the best modern melodramas (for example, "Held
by the Enemy"), there is no wicked person at all. Ever
since Milton struck the popular fancy by changing the
devil into a romantic gentleman who was nobody's enemy
but his own, and thereby practically abolished the real
devil, or god of villains, as a necessary figure in the world
drama, playgoers have been learning to know themselves
well enough to recognize that quite mischief enough for
the plot of any ordinary play can be made by average
ladies and gentlemen like themselves. Captain Crozier
is not the least bit of a villain. He shows abject weakness
in allowing Mrs. D'Acosta to ruin him and make him
ridiculous by dragging him out of a seventy-thousand-a-
year mansion in which he is most comfortably installed
as tame cat, with the certainty that she will throw him
over without scruple as a moral outcast the moment she
is tired of him; but one feels that, after all, it does not
greatly matter, since the elopement is only a stage convention—one of those events which you let pass in the
theatre because they lead to interesting scenes, on the
understanding that nobody is to be held morally responsible for them. (Otherwise, it may be remarked, Mrs.
D'Acosta's treatment of Captain Crozier must be condemned as severely as her treatment of her husband.)
Crozier, in all the points at which he can reasonably be
regarded as exercising free will, behaves like a gentleman
according to his lights; and when I say that Mr. Coghlan's
success was due to his taking the character from its own
point of view, I mean that he so played it as to make clear,
when Crozier finally walked out, that he was filled with
the most complete sense of having done everything that

the most exacting social critic could have expected of him, and done it handsomely and adroitly. And the effect left upon us was that of having made the acquaintance of Captain Crozier, instead of merely seeing Mr. Coghlan with a new suit of clothes on.

The part of Stephen D'Acosta fitted Mr. Lewis Waller so closely that it was not necessary for him to make any great impersonative effort; and the same may be said of Miss Florence West, who happily obliterated all memory of her struggles with the Manxwoman. The pleasant personal qualities with which we are familiar carried Mr. Waller through sympathetically; and though there was one speech in which the authors evidently intended him to play much more forcibly—that in which Stephen D'Acosta gives his father-in-law a piece of his mind—I hardly blame him for refusing to exert himself violently for its sake, since it was hardly equal to, say, the exhortation which Molière puts into the mouth of Don Juan's father on the subject of the true gentleman. Still, the underplaying was a little hard on Mr. Brookfield, whose elaborate exit, as of a man utterly crumpled up, would have been more effective had Mr. Waller done the crumpling with due energy. Mrs. Beerbohm Tree, to whom some malignant fairy godmother must have denied the gifts of empty-headed sentimentality and hysterical incontinence which are essential to success in our drama, substituting for them the fatal disqualifications of brains, individuality, and positiveness of character, gave an amazingly ingenious imitation of the conventional Froufrou. Only once, through the genius of another member of the company, was she carried into a sincere bit of acting. This talented colleague was a Mr. Stewart Dawson, an actor not yet in his teens, but with a pleasant voice, a blarneying smile, a simplicity of manner all irresistible. The house took to him as if he were its own son; and so apparently did Mrs. Tree. I can only say that if Mr. Dawson's fascination increases with his years, it is a grave question whether he ought to be allowed to grow up. Mrs. Tree, by the way, was announced as appearing "by arrangement," as if all the rest had dropped in by accident. What has had to be arranged is evidently either Mrs. Tree's objection to appear "by kind permission of Mr. Tree," or Mr. Tree's objection to give the kind permission. This observation is, of course, not serious; but I make it for the sake of calling attention to the absurdity, and indeed the indelicacy, of the "kind permission" formula by which managers insist on publicly asserting proprietary rights in artists who are under engagement to them. Imagine one of the Reviews announcing an article on the theatre by Mr. Clement Scott as "by kind permission of the Editor of the 'Daily Telegraph'"! Why should the manager of the theatre have worse manners than an editor?

Of the other characters, Lord Bletchley, half convention, half burlesque, is cleverly played by Mr. Brookfield. He should be warned, however, that his tricky diction occasionally prevents his sentences from being quite clearly caught. The Rev. Cosmo Pretious, all burlesque, and unenlightened burlesque at that, is very well played by Mr. Henry Kemble, whose sense of character and artistic feeling have been too much wasted on plays with no characters in them. Agatha Pretious, also a burlesque figure, is a part quite unworthy of Miss Maude Millett. She has evidently been cast for it merely to drag another popular name into the bill.

I have forgotten to mention, by the way, that "A

Woman's Reason" is a play with a purpose—the same purpose as that of "Daniel Deronda." All the Jews in it are heroes and heroines, and all the Christians the meanest and feeblest wretches conceivable. Serve them right!

PLAYS OF THE WEEK

The Prisoner of Zenda: a romantic play in a prologue and four acts. Adapted from Anthony Hope's story by Edward Rose. St. James's Theatre, 7 January, 1896.

The Sign of the Cross: in four acts. By Wilson Barrett. Lyric Theatre, 4 January, 1896.

MR. ANTHONY HOPE's "Prisoner of Zenda" was an amusing attempt to get a Scott-Dumas romance out of modern life. To take the nineteenth-century hero, give him a sword and a horse, a forest to gallop through and a castle to besiege, enemies to pursue him, persons with wrists of steel to fence with, princesses to love and rescue, and all the other luxuries of a D'Artagnan, was a laudable enterprise, in pursuit of which Mr. Hope went to the shores of the Baltic, and carved an imaginary State of Ruritania out of Mecklenburg. He was so far successful that the book made pleasant reading up to within a few chapters of the end. Then the reader's heavily taxed powers of make-believe gave out. At least, that was my experience. At about the point where Rassendyl began his swimming exploits in the moat, I found it impossible any longer to forget that the whole book was a great piece of nonsense. Mere incident in a romance is not interesting unless you believe in the reality of the people to whom the incidents occur. Scott and Dumas could create real men and women for you: their merest supernumeraries, from the innkeepers whom the Musketeers cheat to Higg the son of Snell, are more solid acquaintances than Mr. Hope's heroes. Rassendyl is really nothing but a pasteboard pattern of manly attitudes to be struck in the act of doing one's duty under difficult circumstances, a figure motived by conventionalities, without individual will, and therefore without reality or humanity. If it were not for Mr. Hope's light touch and sense of fun, the whole book would be as dull and mechanical a rigmarole of adventure as its last chapters. As it is, all the attempts to indicate the serious worth and rarity of the qualities which Rassendyl carries so lightly, bore and jar us by threatening to awake our common sense, which, if aroused, must immediately put a summary stop to the somewhat silly Ruritanian gambols of our imagination.

This weakness of characterization is perpetuated in the play with some added disadvantages. The liveliest character in the book is Captain Hentzau, because, though he is not a very possible scoundrel, at least his conduct is wilful, and not obviously made to order for the British Wholesale Association for the Supply of Moral Fiction. On the stage he acquires possibility, but loses fascination. The flimsiness of Rassendyl is terribly exposed by the footlights. The notion that in England every futile, harum-scarum, good-naturedly selfish Johnny is a hero who only needs opportunity to display the noblest qualities, and have his hand kissed by veterans and high-souled ladies, is as popular, because as widely flattering, as that other idea that our yachts constitute a reserve

fleet, and our shopmen a reserve army which in case of
invasion would rush from behind the counter to hurl the
foe back in confusion from the soil of England. It is,
of course, pleasant to think that valuable qualities are
dirt cheap in our own country; but I, unluckily, am con-
stitutionally sceptical as to the heroism of people who
never do anything heroic. However disgusting this cynicism of mine may appear, I noticed that Rassendyl
pleased the audience at the St. James's in all the passages
where he appears as a reckless young gentleman impersonating the King of Ruritania for a lark, and rubbed it
the wrong way in all his attempts to pose as a king of
men. The only qualities needed for his exploit are im-
pudence and the not very uncommon sort of dare-devilry
that induces young men to risk breaking their necks at
bodily exercises for the mere excitement of the thing.
The real author and hero of it is Colonel Sapt, who risks
his life as much as Rassendyl, besides taking his chance
of the English stranger breaking down or backing out.
All the anxiety is his, as well as all the serious purpose
and contrivance. When he addresses the sham king as
"You damned young fool!" for exposing himself idly to
an unnecessary risk of discovery, the audience is sympathetic and satisfied. When he kneels down and kisses
Rassendyl's hand in homage to the innate princeliness
which that gentleman has in no wise displayed, it is impossible not to feel revolted. And there you have the
false note of the play.

Perhaps the most serious consequence of this mistake
is the Prologue. Mr. Rose knows far too much about the
theatre to suppose that the resemblance of Rassendyl to
the King of Ruritania needed any explanation. An audience will always accept a resemblance with eagerness

as a freak of nature. What Mr. Rose wanted to do was to place Rassendyl under a moral obligation to risk his life for the red Elphberg because the red Elphberg's grandfather sacrificed his life for Rassendyl's grandmother. Now, I submit not only that the motive appeals to that bogus-kingly side of Rassendyl's character which had better have been left out, but that even so its compulsion is ridiculously unconvincing. If a gentleman were to ask me to lend him half-a-crown on the strength of a relationship based on the following circumstances: to wit, that his grandfather had seduced my grandmother; fought a duel with my grandmother's husband, in the course of which he had been run through during a moment of inattention caused by the entry of the lady; declared with his last breath that he had died for her; and finally walked out of the house in his bloodstained shirt in apparently robust health, I should refer that gentleman to the Charity Organization Society.

Besides, Mr. Rose has written the Prologue in the spirit of the nineteenth-century fancier of the eighteenth century rather than in that of the eighteenth century itself. It is a pomandering sort of Prologue, thrown in, not by dramatic necessity, but for the sake of hoops and patches, snuff-boxes and silk coats—above all, a duel by candlelight, without which no eighteenth-century drama would be complete. Mr. Rose has often written pleasantly about these and other more remote and lavendery antiquities; but in giving way to them on the stage he has been beset by the temptation to lay the scene out not only for obsolete dresses and incidents, but for obsolete acting, and even obsolete drama. I should not be surprised to learn that he had pleaded hard with Mr. Alexander to have a door knocked through the proscenium in order that Miss Mabel

Hackney might enter through it with two black pages carrying her train, as the stage custom was in those days. The Prologue, in short, exhibits Mr. Rose as the man of sentimental fancies and antiquarian learning rather than as the playwright. It will be useful as a curtain-raiser; but it is not essential to the comprehension or enjoyment of the play.

The play itself, as far as the novel will let it, brings into action Mr. Rose's best qualities as a dramatist: his humor, his intelligence in the more generous issues of human feeling, and his insight, which is engagingly disabled—especially in the case of his feminine characters— by a certain shy anxiety to apologize to the lady for the intrusion, and present her with a favorable construction for what he has discovered. It is a thousand pities that the novel contained no figures sufficiently rounded and solid to make the drama really live. Still, unsubstantial as they are, they are superficially natural; and the play hops genially and adventurously along to the final speeches of Flavia and Rassendyl, which make a very pretty ending. A strong ending could only have been achieved by throwing the novel over, and changing the drunken imbecile of a king into an able but unlovable man, as whose consort Flavia might reasonably feel that her high destiny (rather a sentimental fancy, by the way, that high destiny!) would be better fulfilled than with the lovable but feather-brained Rassendyl.

The performance is a curiously haphazard one, considering its costliness and elaboration. Through the prevalent style of play is in the usual quiet St. James key, some of the characters rush on the stage supercharged with dramatic excitement, and momentarily upset all congruity of style. Mr. Cautley or Mr. Alexander will certainly either kill or be killed some night, unless the sabre fight at the end is more carefully preconcerted than it was on the first night. What is called the coronation scene—meaning the scene in which Rassendyl goes off the stage to be crowned and comes back when the ceremony is over—seems a very quiet little drawing-room-party business to a musical critic nursed on "Le Prophète" and the Wagnerian music drama; but it is enjoyable in its unsensational way. The dresses are recklessly expensive and not unhandsome. If I had never been taught to use my eyes as a critic of pictures, I might, perhaps, have been satisfied with the sunset scene in the forest of Zenda: as it was, the hopeless absurdity of the foreground light where Mr. Alexander lay at the foot of the tree, set me speculating as to when some serious attempt will be made to produce any of the subtler effects of open air on the stage. The acting was mostly very easy. Mr. Vernon, as Colonel Sapt, had the best part—indeed, in a sense the only part—and he left all the rest far behind in it. Mr. Alexander was capital in the comedy passages, and delivered his speeches in the last scene finely, but was bad in the drunken episode, which he played like a seasoned teetotaller. The rest of his part, or rather parts, was the wrong side of Rassendyl, which nothing could make really effective. Mr. Waring did what was possible to give an air of substance to the nullity called Duke Michael; and Mr. Lawrence Cautley had not the material in his lines for producing the dashingly diabolical effect of the Hentzau of the novel. The truth is that half the company are doing nothing but "supering," although they are of course neither lineless nor nameless. Miss Millard has apparently taken the most heroic measures to transform herself into a true red Elphberg. She played with a touch of passion in the later scenes; but she was a little flat in the second act through her deficiency in comedy, her sense of humor resolutely refusing to express itself artistically. Miss Olga Brandon had nothing to do but embody the description of the Mayor's wife as a pretty woman; but though the part is nothing, Miss Brandon certainly got the last inch out of it, and something over, making more of her curtsey than a good many actresses make of a speech. Miss Lily Hanbury was fairly successful in grappling with Antoinette de Mauban; and Miss Mabel Hackney, not as yet a very finished executant, conceived her part in the Prologue excellently.

Mr. Wilson Barrett has given me such unbounded delight by his feat of persuading the London critics that several of the most characteristic passages in his "Sign of the Cross" are quotations from the Bible that I have nothing but praise for him. Sterne's "tempering the wind to the shorn lamb" need never again be quoted as the champion instance of scripturization. It is true that Mr. Wilson Barrett, following the universal law of art development, has founded his Sermon on the Mount to some extent on the original one; but I can assure the public that the text of "The Sign of the Cross" is essentially original; and if Mr. Wilson Barrett writes to the papers to assure us, in the usual terms, that so far from his having taken his play from the Bible, he has never even read that volume, I am quite prepared to believe him. His literary style is altogether different. The play is a monument of sacred and profane history. The influence of Ibsen is apparent throughout, the Norwegian keynote being struck by Mr. Barrett himself in the words:—"How many crimes are committed under the cloak of duty!" With scathing, searching irony, and with resolute courage in the face of the prejudiced British public, he has drawn a terrible contrast between the Romans ("Pagans, I regret to say," as Mr. Pecksniff remarked of the sirens), with their straightforward sensuality, and the strange, perverted voluptuousness of the Christians, with their shuddering exaltations of longing for the whip, the rack, the stake, and the lions. The whole drama lies in the spectacle of the hardy Roman prefect, a robust soldier and able general, gradually falling under the spell of a pale Christian girl, white and worn with spiritual ecstasy, and beautiful as Mary Anderson. As she gradually throws upon him the fascination of suffering and martyrdom, he loses his taste for wine; the courtesans at his orgies disgust him; heavenly visions obsess him; undreamt-of raptures of sacrifice, agony, and escape from the world to indescribable holiness and bliss tempt him; and finally he is seen, calm and noble, but stark mad, following the girl to her frightfully voluptuous death. It is a tremendous moral lesson; and though I am pagan enough to most intensely dislike the flogging and racking and screaming on the stage (I really am such a bloodless creature that I take no delight in torture), yet no doubt it helps to drive the irony of the theme home.

On the intellectual side, Christianity hardly receives justice from Mr. Wilson Barrett. "Christianity is not in itself a crime," says Marcus to Nero. "Marcus argues strongly, Cæsar," is Poppea's comment. I must say I think Poppea is rather too easily satisfied. But, after all, we do not want to hear the case argued at this time of day. What we enjoy is being so familiarly in Rome that it sounds quite natural when such directions to wayfarers as "Fourth on the right from the statue of Hercules" are given by the lictors. We come into the presence of Nero, and hear him ordering a set of living torches for that evening, and boasting of what an artist he is. We see the Roman ladies at home sticking pins into their slaves, and the Roman diner-out exhausted by his second vomit. We hear the thunder of the chariot race, and see the gladiator enter the arena. And we have, as aforesaid, whips and racks, chains and dungeons, uplifted crosses and Christian martyrs, not to mention plenty of music well handled by Mr. Edward Jones, with hymns for the Christians, waltzes for the Romans, and Sullivan's "Thou'rt passing hence, my brother," and Gounod's "Nazareth" on the cornet and sackbut between the acts.

The mounting is handsome, and the stage management good and unselfish, all the parts being played with quite extraordinary spirit, and in no way sacrificed to the actor-manager's. I have never seen better work got out of a company. Mr. Wilson Barrett has honestly sunk the actor in the author, and done his best for the play, instead of for himself personally. Indeed, the one conspicuous and laughable oversight is in Mr. Barrett's own make-up. Instead of wearing the proper cropped Roman wig, he wears his own hair in his old familiar feminine fashion, with the result that when he first steps on the stage he presents such an amazing resemblance to Miss Victor that, instead of applauding him, I stared with a shocked conviction that I had that lady before me in the costume of a Roman warrior. The effect is amusing; but it spoils an otherwise manly picture.

MICHAEL AND HIS LOST ANGEL

Michael and his Lost Angel: a new and original
play of modern English life. In five acts. By Henry
Arthur Jones. Lyceum Theatre, 15 January, 1896.

O NE of the great comforts of criticizing the work
of Mr. Henry Arthur Jones is that the critic can
go straight to the subject-matter without troubling about the dramatic construction. In the born writer
the style is the man; and with the born dramatist the
play is the subject. Mr. Jones's plays grow: they are not
cut out of bits of paper and stuck together. Mr. Grundy
or Sardou, at their respective worsts, perform such feats
of carpentry in constructing show-cases for some trumpery little situation, that the critics exhaust all their space
in raptures over the mechanical skill displayed. But Mr.
Jones's technical skill is taken as a matter of course. Nobody ever dreams of complimenting him about it: we
proceed direct to abusing his ideas without delay. This
is quite right and natural. If you invent a mechanical
rabbit, wind it up, and set it running round the room for
me, I shall be hugely entertained, no matter how monstrously unsuccessful it may be as a representation of
nature; but if you produce a real rabbit which begins
running about without being wound up at all, I simply
say "Why shouldn't it?" and take down my gun. Similarly, on Mr. Jones producing a live play, which starts
into perfectly natural action on the rising of the curtain
without being wound up during an act or two of exposition, I say "Why shouldn't it?" and, as aforesaid, take
down my gun.

Dramatic Opinions and Essays

When I respond to the appeal of Mr. Jones's art by throwing myself sympathetically into his characteristic attitude of mind, I am conscious of no shortcoming in "Michael and his Lost Angel." It then seems to me to be a genuinely sincere and moving play, feelingly imagined, written with knowledge as to the man and insight as to the woman by an author equipped not only with the experience of an adept playwright, and a kindly and humorous observer's sense of contemporary manners, but with that knowledge of spiritual history in which Mr. Jones's nearest competitors seem so stupendously deficient. Its art is in vital contact with the most passionate religious movement of its century, as fully quickened art always has been. On comparing it in this relation with the ordinary personal sentiment of Mr. Grundy, and with those grotesque flounderings after some sort of respectably pious foothold which have led Mr. Pinero to his rescue of the burning Bible from Mrs. Ebbsmith's stove, and his redemption of Mrs. Fraser by the social patronage of the Bishop's wife, I unhesitatingly class Mr. Jones as first, and eminently first, among the surviving fittest of his own generation of playwrights.

But when, instead of throwing myself sympathetically into Mr. Jones's attitude, I remain obstinately in my own, I find myself altogether unable to offer to "Michael" that final degree of complete sympathy and approval which is implied in the conviction that I would have written the play that way myself if I could. As to the first two acts, I ask nothing better; but at the beginning of the third comes the parting of our ways; and I can point out the exact place where the roads fork. In the first act Michael, a clergyman, compels a girl who has committed what he believes to be a deadly sin to confess it publicly in church.

In the second act he commits that sin himself. At the beginning of the third he meets the lady who has been his accomplice; and the following words pass between them:—

Audrie.—You're sorry?
Michael.—No. And you?
Audrie.—No.

Now, after this, what does the clergyman do? Without giving another thought to that all-significant fact that he is not sorry—that at the very point where, if his code and creed were valid, his conscience would be aching with remorse, he is not only impenitent, but positively glad, he proceeds to act as if he really were penitent, and not only puts on a hair shirt, but actually makes a confession to his congregation in the false character of a contrite sinner, and goes out from among them with bowed head to exile and disgrace, only waiting in the neighborhood until the church is empty to steal back and privily contradict his pious imposture by picking up and hiding a flower which the woman has thrown on the steps of the altar. This is perfectly true to nature: men do every day, with a frightful fatalism, abjectly accept for themselves as well as others all the consequences of theories as to what they ought to feel and ought to believe, although they not only do not so feel or believe, but often feel and believe the very reverse, and find themselves forced to act on their real feeling and belief in supreme moments which they are willing with a tragically ridiculous self-abnegation to expiate afterwards even with their lives.

Here you have the disqualification of "Michael and his Lost Angel" for full tragic honors. It is a play without a hero. Let me rewrite the last three acts, and you shall

have your Reverend Michael embracing the answer of
his own soul, thundering it from the steps of his altar,
and marching out through his shocked and shamed pa-
rishioners, with colors flying and head erect and unashamed, to the freedom of faith in his own real conscience. Whether he is right or wrong is nothing to me
as a dramatist: he must follow his star, right or wrong,
if he is to be a hero. In "Hamlet" one cannot approve
unreservedly of the views of Fortinbras; but, generations
of foolish actor-managers to the contrary notwithstand-
ing, what true Shakespearean ever thinks of "Hamlet"
without seeing Fortinbras, in his winged helmet, swoop
down at the end, and take, by the divine right of a born
"captain of his soul," the crown that slips through the
dead fingers of the philosopher who went, at the bidding
of his father's ghost, in search of a revenge which he did
not feel and a throne which he did not want? Fortinbras
can, of course, never be anything more than an Adelphi
hero, because his bellicose instincts and imperial ambitions are comfortably vulgar; but both the Adelphi hero
and the tragic hero have fundamentally the same heroic
qualification—fearless pursuit of their own ends and
championship of their own faiths *contra mundum*.

Michael fails to satisfy this condition in an emergency
where a heroic self-realization alone could save him from
destruction; and if this failure were the subject of Mr.
Jones's last three acts, then the play without a hero might
be as tragic as "Rosmersholm." But Mr. Jones does not
set Michael's situation in that light: he shares his fatalism,
accepting his remorse, confession, and disgrace as inevitable, with a monastery for the man and death for the
woman as the only possible stage ending—surely not so
much an ending as a slopping up of the remains of the

two poor creatures. The last act is only saved from being a sorry business by the man's plucking a sort of courage out of abandonment, and by a humorous piteousness in the dying woman, who, whilst submitting, out of sheer feebleness of character, to Michael's attitude, is apologetically conscious of having no sincere conviction of sin. When the priest offers his services, she replies, "No, thanks, I've been dreadfully wicked—doesn't much matter, eh? Can't help it now. Haven't strength to feel sorry. So sorry I can't feel sorry." This gives a pleasant quaintness to the hackneyed pathos of a stage death; but it does not obliterate the fact that Audrie is dying of nothing but the need for making the audience cry, and that she is a deplorable disappointment considering her promise of force and originality in the first two acts. A play without a hero may still be heroic if it has a heroine; and had Mr. Jones so laid out his play as to pose the question, "What will this woman do when she discovers that the saint of Cleveheddon is nothing but a hysterical coward, whose religion is a morbid perversion of his sympathetic instincts instead of the noblest development of them?" the answer of a capable woman to such a question might have given the last three acts the attraction of strength and hope, instead of their present appeal *ad misericordiam* of sentimental despair and irrelevant bodily disease. But Audrie, though she has a certain salt of wit in her, is as incapable of taking her fate into her own hands as Michael; and the two, hypnotized by public opinion, let themselves be driven abjectly, she to the shambles and he to the dustbin, without a redeeming struggle.

It is clear, I think, that if the public were of my way of thinking, the play, good as it is of its kind, would fail;

for the public is not sympathetic enough to throw itself into Mr. Jones's attitude, and enjoy the play from his point of view, unless it can do so without going out of its own way. And I cannot help thinking that the public dislike a man of Michael's stamp. After all, stupid as we are, we are not Asiatics. The most pig-headed Englishman has a much stronger objection to be crushed or killed by institutions and conventions, however sacred or even respectable, than a Russian peasant or a Chinaman. If he commits a sin, he either tells a lie and sticks to it, or else demands "a broadening of thought" which will bring his sin within the limits of the allowable. To expiation, if it can possibly be avoided, he has a wholesome and energetic objection. He is an individualist, not a fatalist: with all his apparent conventionality there is no getting over the fact that institutions—moral, political, artistic, and ecclesiastical—which in more Eastern lands have paralysed whole races, making each century a mere stereotype of the one before, are mere footballs for the centuries in England. It is an instinct with me personally to attack every idea which has been full grown for ten years, especially if it claims to be the foundation of all human society. I am prepared to back human society against any idea, positive or negative, that can be brought into the field against it. In this—except as to my definite intellectual consciousness of it—I am, I believe, a much more typical and popular person in England than the conventional man; and I believe that when we begin to produce a genuine national drama, this apparently anarchic force, the mother of higher law and humaner order, will underlie it, and that the public will lose all patience with the conventional collapses which serve for last acts to the serious dramas of to-day. Depend upon it, the miserable

doctrine that life is a mess, and that there is no way out
of it, will never nerve any man to write a truly heroic
play west of the Caucasus. I do not for a moment suspect Mr. Jones of really holding that doctrine himself.
He has written "Michael" as a realist on the unheroic
plane, simply taking his contemporaries as he finds them
on that plane.

Perhaps it is unfair to Mr. Jones to substitute to this
extent a discussion of the philosophy of his play for a
criticism of its merits on its own ground. But the performance at the Lyceum has taken all the heart out of my
hopes of gaining general assent to my high estimate of
"Michael and his Lost Angel." The public sees the play
as it is acted, not as it ought to be acted. The sooner
Mr. Jones publishes it the better for its reputation. There
never was a play more skilfully designed to fit the chief
actors than this was for Mr. Forbes Robertson and Mrs.
Patrick Campbell. But though Mr. Jones was able to
write for Mrs. Campbell such a part as she is not likely
to get the refusal of soon again, he had to depend on
Mrs. Campbell's own artistic judgment to enable her to
perceive the value of the chance. The judgment was apparently not forthcoming: at all events, Mrs. Patrick
Campbell vanished from the bills as the day of battle
drew nigh. In such an emergency your London manager
has only one idea—send for Miss Marion Terry. Miss
Marion Terry was accordingly sent for—sent for to play
the bad angel; to be perverse, subtly malign, infernally
beautiful; to sell her soul and her lover's to the Devil,
and bite her arm through as a seal to the bargain; to do
everything that is neither in her nature, nor within the
scope of her utmost skill in dissimulation. The result
was a touching little sham, very charming in the first act,

where her entry rescued the play just as it was staggering under the weight of some very bad acting in the opening scene; and very affecting at the end, where she died considerately and prettily, as only an inveterately amiable woman could. But not for the most infinitesimal fraction of a second was she Audrie Lesden; and five acts of "Michael and his Lost Angel" without Audrie Lesden were not what the author intended. As to Mr. Forbes Robertson, Mr. Jones had undertaken to make the actor's outside effective if he in return would look after the inside of the Reverend Michael. Mr. Jones kept to his bargain: Mr. Forbes Robertson was unable to fulfil his. He made the mistake—common in an irreligious age—of conceiving a religious man as a lugubrious one. All the sympathy in the first act depended on his making it clear that the force that swept Rose Gibbard to the altar to confess was the priest's rapturous faith in the gladness of an open and contrite heart, natural to a man made over-sanguine by spiritual joy. Mr. Forbes Robertson threw away all this sympathy, and set the audience against him and against the play from the outset by adopting the solemn, joyless, professional manner and the preachy utterance of the Low-Church apostle of mortification and wrath. It is quite impossible to exaggerate the disastrous effect of this initial mistake on the performance. The more saintly Mr. Robertson looked, the slower, gloomier, more depressingly monotonous he became, until at last, in spite of Miss Terry's spoonfuls of sweet syrup, I half expected to see the infuriated author rush on the stage and treat us to a realistic tableau of the stoning of St. Stephen. What is the use of the dramatist harmonizing the old Scarlet-Letter theme in the new Puseyite mode if the actor is to transpose it back again into the old Calvinistic minor key?

As to the rest, their woodenness is not to be described, though woodenness is hardly the right word for Mr. Mackintosh, in whose performance, however, I could discover neither grace nor verisimilitude. Miss Brooke need not be included in this wholesale condemnation; but her part was too small to make any difference to the general effect. The melancholy truth of the matter is that the English stage got a good play, and was completely and ignominiously beaten by it. Mr. Jones has got beyond the penny novelette conventions which are actable in our theatre. I fear there is no future for him except as a dramatic critic.

The play is well mounted, though the church scene is an appalling example of the worst sort of German "restoration." And it has the inevitable defect of all stage churches: the voices will not echo nor the footsteps ring through its canvas nave and aisles. Mr. Forbes Robertson has been specially generous in the matter of the band. Mr. Armbruster was able to give between the acts a genuine orchestral performance of the slow movement from Raff's "Im Walde" Symphony, and as much of the andante of Mendelssohn's Italian Symphony as there was time for.

CHURCH AND STAGE

25 January, 1896.

A LITTLE squall of controversy has been raised by the church scene in "Michael and his Lost Angel" at the Lyceum. It is contended by gentlemen who get their living by going to the theatre and reporting or criticizing performances there, that Church ritual, and indeed anything of a sacred character, is out of place on the stage, and its dramatic representation a breach of good taste and an offence against public decency. Let us see exactly what this means.

Of all the vile places on earth that are not absolutely contrary to law, the vilest is a convict prison. The vilest thing in the prison is the gallows; and the vilest thing done there is an execution. Yet the prison has its chaplain; and his prayers are an indispensable part of the disgusting business of hanging a man. The most heathenish and wasteful, not to say bestial civic celebration now tolerated is a City dinner. Men go there with the intention of eating too much and drinking too much; and many of them exceed their intention. But the proceedings always commence with the ritual called "grace before meat." For wrath and violence, terror and ferocity, on a scale of the most frightful magnitude, nothing can compare with a battle, especially when the victims are poor men tempted by a shilling a day to fight for the glorification of bloodthirsty fools and cowards who sit at home at ease and gloat over sensational "special correspondence." Yet no victory is complete without the "Te Deum" by which Christian combatants assume that

their God is an accomplice in their crime, and praise Him
for it. But, if you please, there is one lawful place worse
than the gallows and the battlefields, one tolerated pursuit
more filthy than gluttony and damnable than wholesale
murder. That place is the theatre; that pursuit, playgoing. We may drag the symbols of our religion through
seas of blood, waste, riot and rapine, if only we spare it
the final outrage of mentioning it on the stage of the
Lyceum. If I am to accept this as good sense—if actors
are infamous wretches prostituting themselves to the desire of the audience to indulge a detestable vice, then pray
what am I, the critic, who sell myself to advertise such
abomination by writing seductive descriptions and eulogies of the plays with which I am especially pleased?
And what are those still more abandoned colleagues of
mine who lard the managers with flatteries which even
Mr. Wilson Barrett's Nero might find a trifle hyper-
bolical? Clearly we are baser than Molière, to whom
Christian burial was refused in France, baser than the
ballet dancer to whom the Bishop of London refused the
Sacrament (though this certainly occurred a few years
before the knighting of Sir Henry Irving) by as much
as the pandar is baser than his employer.

Let us look at the case from another point of view.
It is said that "some things" are too sacred to be represented on the stage. The phrase "some things" is highly
characteristic: it recalls the intelligent member of Par-
liament who supported the attempt to exclude the late
Charles Bradlaugh from the House of Commons on the
ground that "a man ought to believe in something or
another." But since it is just as well not to be frivo-
lously vague in speaking of sacred things, let us replace
"some things" by the mysteries of religion, which is what

the objectors would mean if, on this subject, they were earnest enough to mean anything at all. Pray, what are the mysteries of religion? Are they faith, hope, love, heroism, life, creation; or are they pews and pulpits, prayer-books and Sunday bonnets, copes and stoles and dalmatics? Even that large section of the population of these islands whose religion is the merest idolatry of material symbols will not deny that the former are the realities of religion. Then I ask the gentlemen who think that the pews and prayer-books are too sacred to be represented on the stage, why it is that they have never protested against the fact that all our dramas deal with faith, hope, love, and the rest of the essentials? The most sacred feelings and the holiest names are never long out of the mouths of our stage heroes and heroines. In the last Adelphi melodrama but two the heroine recited the service for the dead on the stage, whilst her father danced round her in a frenzy, trying to make up his mind to shoot her before the Indians took the place by storm. The critics who are protesting against the procession in the fourth act of "Michael and his Lost Angel" did not protest against that. Of course it is possible that they did not recognize it because Miss Millward did not wear a surplice during the passage, just as they mistook a homily of Mr. Wilson Barrett's the other day for the Sermon on the Mount because the actor stood on a hill in a long gown, and gave it out like a clergyman reading the lessons. But I could easily find instances for which that unpresentable excuse cannot be alleged. The real objection to Mr. Jones's play is the objection to Michael's treatment of religion as co-extensive with life: that is, as genuinely catholic. To the man who regards it as only a watertight Sunday compartment of social observance, such a view is not only inconvenient but positively terrifying. I am sorry for him; but I can assure him that the British drama is annexing steadily the territory on which he feels so uncomfortable. And whoever tries to obstruct that advance will be inevitably ground into the mud. When I want to exhibit the might of criticism, I may throw an express train off the line; but you do not catch me trying to stop the imperceptibly slow march of a glacier.

Yet another point of view. It is argued that a stage representation is only a pretence, a mockery, a sham, a thing made to simulate something that it is not by tricks of light and paint and feats of mimicry. Granted; but what, then, is to be said of the pictures in the National Gallery, in which canvas and colored clay are made to simulate, not only churches and priests, but the very persons of the Trinity themselves? Is a crucifix an offence against the sacredness of what it represents? Are religious fictions, such as "Barabbas" and "The Sorrows of Satan" at one extreme, and Goethe's "Faust" at the other, to be suppressed? The Cromwellian Puritans would have said "Yes" to all this. Those of them who believed, like the Reverend Michael, that life and religion are co-extensive, were for destroying, not only theatres, but images, pictures, statues, symbols, and simulations of all kinds. Those who held the more convenient watertight-compartment theory, thus dividing life into the sacred and profane, encouraged and rejoiced in profane art, but would not have sacred art on any terms. They would have family portraits, but no pictures of saints and virgins: they were musicians, but would not have music in church. They would have sacked the National Gallery, and burnt its most precious treasures in Trafalgar Square; and they actually did enter cathedrals, smash everything they could get at that was in the nature of statuary, pulled the organs to pieces, and tore up the music-books. In short, though they were too fond of art to want to exterminate it, they excommunicated it. Are our watertight-compartment critics willing to take the same line? Are they prepared to excommunicate art altogether, or do they wish to excommunicate the theatre only, leaving the cathedral, the picture gallery, the library, untouched? If so, this also involves them in the conclusion that some quite peculiar infamy and disgrace attaches to the theatre; and I am again compelled to submit that, since they have voluntarily chosen theatre-going as a means of livelihood, they fall under their own condemnation as infamous and disgraceful persons, unworthy as such to lead public opinion on this or any other matter. Having no such unfriendly opinion of them, I had rather coax them to retreat from their position than see them impale themselves on either horn of so inhuman a dilemma. For what alternative is left to them, except, perhaps, to follow the example of Sheridan Knowles by abandoning their profession and spending the rest of their lives in warning others against it?

The public, consisting as it does of many who do not go to the theatre, is in no way bound, as a critic is, to be loyal to it or else leave it. But the playgoing, art-supporting public may reasonably be called on to make up its mind whether religion is to be denied the services of art or not. Something may be learnt from past follies on this subject. Music, for instance, has always been highly privileged in the popular imagination. No other art has ever been conceived as practised in Heaven. Prophets may have been inspired to write books on earth; and St. Luke is supposed to have painted a portrait of the Virgin; but who ever dreamt of easels and ink-bottles, or typewriters, in Heaven? Yet what would Heaven be without its harps, and trumpets, and choir of angels? It was owing to this association of ideas that Handel met with no opposition when he popularized the oratorio. He gave us, in the concert-room, Samson and Dalila, and Manoah, and the rest of the persons in the Bible story; and no one was scandalized. But when Salvini came over here, a hundred and thirty years later, he found that Samson was out of the question in a theatre. The play-going public was perfectly willing—and, indeed, highly curious—to see him walk off with the gates of Gaza, throw his father across his shoulder with one hand and carry him away, and finally perish between the pillars under a shower of dummy Philistines. But the people who never go to the theatre might have been offended; and so Samson had to be reserved for a much more Puritan country—America. Even music itself has had to make absurd concessions to pietistic prudery. Beethoven composed an oratorio called "The Mount of Olives"; and immediately the question arose whether the Handelian privilege extended to the New Testament. After about thirty years consideration we made up our minds the wrong way, and turned "The Mount of Olives" into "Engedi," with David for the principal figure. Thirty years more, and the original work was performed at the Leeds Festival, with such complete impunity that it was evident the Engedification had been an act of gratuitous folly. We were kept for a long time out of one of the world's great possessions, Bach's St. Matthew Passion, on the same grounds. If it had been an acre of blue dirt, with a few handfuls of trumpery diamonds in it, we should have gone to war about it. Let nobody suppose that our ultimate emancipation from these silly restrictions was the result of any growth or change in public opinion on the matter. There was no such growth and no such change. On the contrary, the sort of people who were supposed to object to "The Mount of Olives" when it was first performed as a Lenten oratorio at Drury Lane in 1814 are much more numerous at present than they were then. And they are just as free to stay away from performances they disapprove of as they were then. The restrictions are always the work of half a dozen busybodies, actuated less by cowardice than by a desire to make an officious display of the undesirable quality they call "good taste."

Goethe's taste being even worse than that displayed by Mr. Henry Arthur Jones in the fourth act of "Michael and his Lost Angel," he placed the scene of the prologue to his best known drama, not in Cleveheddon church, but in Heaven itself, with the Almighty conversing with Satan on easy terms, as in the Book of Job. Some of our dramatic critics (especially those who are not suspected of reading Goethe, and who see no difference between the literary styles of St. Matthew and Mr. Wilson Barrett) will be shocked at this, and will exult in the fact that no attempt was made, or could have been made, to introduce the prologue on the English stage when the Lyceum "Faust" provided the opportunity. But I, having graduated as a musical critic, can assure my colleagues that I have seen this prologue repeatedly on no less English a stage than that of Covent Garden, under no less respectable a manager than Sir Augustus Harris. And nothing could have been more English than the manner in which the scene was represented. There was a front cloth with clouds painted on it. In the right-hand top corner (from the spectator's point of view) there was a large hole irradiated with white light, and in the left-hand bottom corner a similar hole, glowing with red light. Satan appeared bodily in the red hole and sang his speeches. Nothing but the white glory could be seen through the higher rift in the clouds; and the speeches were sung by the chorus, as in the case of the words, "Saul, why persecutest thou me?" in Mendelssohn's oratorio. This has occurred as often as Boïto's "Mefistofele" has been performed; and I have not heard up to the present that any grave social consequences have ensued, or that any person has been shocked, hurt, injured, demoralized, or other than edified and delighted—except, perhaps, when the chorus sang flat, as choruses behind the scenes are apt to do.

When there is anything artistic to be done in England, all that is necessary is to do it as a matter of course without saying anything about it. If you raise the question whether it is permissible, there will be an outcry against it as impossibly scandalous, especially if it is something that has been done over and over again for hundreds of years. If the proprietors of the French Gallery had asked the leave of the British press and public before they exhibited Van Uhde's picture of Christ sitting in a room speaking to people in tall hats and frock coats, a horror-stricken prohibition would have been voiced by writers who would have tried their utmost to get a private peep at the picture. The proprietors of the French Gallery wisely said nothing. They exhibited the picture; and all the genuinely religious visitors were greatly touched and pleased by it. If any sculptor were to ask public permission to exhibit a figure of a lady or gentleman with nothing on at Burlington House, that permission would be sternly refused. But the thing is done every year without permission, and nobody is any the worse. The man who submits a moral syllabus of a work of art to the public is a fool. Submit the work of art itself, and then the public can judge. Of course, if they dislike it they will beat it with any stick they can lay hold of. If the drama of "Michael" had pleased the critics who imagined they were scandalized by the fourth act, Mr. Jones might have introduced not only a consecration, but a baptism, a confirmation, a marriage, and a communion, as safely as the Adelphi authors introduced the service for the dead.

I do not lay down the law on this subject according to any canon of taste or theory of permissibility. I take things as I find them. I have seen not only "Michael and his Lost Angel," but "Parsifal" at Bayreuth, and the Passion Play at Ober-Ammergau. I found them good, and should be glad to see them brought within the reach of English playgoers. I have also seen "Gentleman Joe"; and I have no doubt that some of my colleagues whom Mr. Jones has shocked would be glad to see that piece brought within the reach of Bavarian playgoers. And with this reminder that you cannot attack the freedom of the plays you do not like without equally endangering the freedom of those you like, and that it is better to tolerate the catholicly religious people who are claiming for the theatre its share in the common spiritual heritage than to put a weapon into the hands of the sectarianly religious people who would make an end of the theatre altogether if they could, I leave the subject until the next week in which there happens to be nothing else to write about.

DEAR HARP OF MY COUNTRY!

The Colleen Bawn; or, the Brides of Garryowen.
Dion Boucicault's Great Drama (*sic*), in three acts.
Princess's Theatre, 25 January, 1896.

I HAVE lived to see "The Colleen Bawn" with real water in it; and perhaps I shall live to see it some day with real Irishmen in it, though I doubt if that will heighten its popularity much. The real water lacks the translucent cleanliness of the original article, and destroys the illusion of Eily's drowning and Myles na Coppaleen's header to a quite amazing degree; but the spectacle of the two performers taking a call before the curtain, sopping wet, and bowing with a miserable enjoyment of the applause, is one which I shall remember with a chuckle whilst life remains.

When I imply, as above, that the Irishmen in "The Colleen Bawn" are not real Irishmen, I do not mean for a moment to challenge the authenticity of Mr. Richard Purdon, who succeeds Dion Boucicault as Myles. Nor do I even accuse him of demonstrating the undeniable fact that the worst stage Irishmen are often real Irishmen. What I mean is that Dion Boucicault, when he invented Myles, was not holding the mirror up to nature, but blarneying the British public precisely as the Irish car-driver, when he is "'cute" enough, blarneys the English tourist. To an Irishman who has any sort of social conscience, the conception of Ireland as a romantic picture, in which the background is formed by the Lakes of Killarney by moonlight, and a round tower or so, whilst every male figure is "a broth of a bhoy," and every female one a colleen in a crimson Connemara cloak, is as exasperating as the conception of Italy as a huge garden and art museum, inhabited by picturesque artists' models, is to a sensible Italian. The Kerry peasant is no more a Myles na Coppaleen (his real name is Smith, or, at most, Ryan) than the real Wiltshire peasant is a Mark Tapley; and as for Eily, Dolly Varden as a typical English tradesman's daughter is a masterpiece of realism in comparison. The occupation of the Irish peasant is mainly agricultural; and I advise the reader to make it a fixed rule never to allow himself to believe in the alleged Arcadian virtues of the half-starved drudges who are sacrificed to the degrading, brutalizing, and, as far as I can ascertain, entirely unnecessary pursuit of unscientific farming. The virtues of the Irish peasant are the intense melancholy, the surliness of manner, the incapacity for happiness and self-respect that are the tokens of his natural unfitness for a life of wretchedness. His vices are the arts by which he accommodates himself to his slavery—the flattery on his lips which hides the curse in his heart; his pleasant readiness to settle disputes by "leaving it all to your honor," in order to make something out of your generosity in addition to exacting the utmost of his legal due from you; his instinctive perception that by pleasing you he can make you serve him; his mendacity and mendicity; his love of a stolen advantage; the superstitious fear of his priest and his Church which does not prevent him from trying to cheat both in the temporal transactions between them; and the parasitism which makes him, in domestic service, that occasionally convenient but on the whole demoralizing human barnacle, the irremovable old retainer of the family. Of all the tricks which the Irish nation have played on the slow-witted Saxon, the most outrageous is the palming off on him of the imaginary Irishman of romance. The worst of it is, that when a spurious type gets into literature, it strikes the imaginations of boys and girls. They form themselves by playing up to it; and thus the unsubstantial fancies of the novelists and music-hall song-writers of one generation are apt to become the unpleasant and mischievous realities of the next. The obsoletely patriotic Englishman of to-day is a most pestilent invention of this sort; and ever since the formation of the German Empire, the German has been dramatized with such success that even the Emperor spends most of his time in working up the character. Ireland, always foremost in the drama, may claim the credit of having invented the Irishman out of nothing—invented him without the stimulus of empire, national independence, knowledge of her own history, united population, common religion, or two penn'orth of prestige of any sort, her very rebellions having only attained eminence by giving the national genius for treachery an opportunity of surpassing all recorded achievements in that important department of revolutionary politics. Fortunately the same talent that enabled Ireland to lead the way in inventing and dramatizing national types now keeps her to the front in the more salutary work of picking them to pieces, a process which appeals to her barbarous humor on the one hand, and on the other to her keen common sense and intelligent appreciation of reality. Of course it sacrifices the advantages which the imposture secured, as I have good reason to feel; for nobody can be better aware than I am of the convenience to an Irishman in England of being able, by an occasional cunning flourish of his nationality, to secure all the privileges of a harmless lunatic without forfeiting the position of a responsible member of society. But there is a point at which shams become so deadly tiresome that they produce ungovernable nausea, and are rejected at all risks. There are signs that Ireland, never very tolerant of the stage Irishman within her own coasts, is disaffected to him even in the literature by which her scribes habitually impose on England and America. Quite lately a London publisher, Mr. Arnold, sent me a novel with the suggestive title of "Misther O'Ryan," who turned out to be the traditional blend of Myles na Coppaleen, Robert Emmett, Daniel O'Connell, Thomas Moore, Fin McCoul, and Brian Boru, as compounded and impersonated by a vulgar rascal—an Irish Silas Wegg—whose blackguardism and irremediable worthlessness the writer, evidently that very rare literary bird, an Irish author living in Ireland, had sketched with a venegful zest that was highly refreshing and, I should say, very wholesome just at present. Take any of the pictures Balzac or Maupassant have painted for us of the spiritual squalor of the routine of poor middle-class life, in which the education, the income, the culture of the family are three-quarters abject pretence; and you will not find it more depressing and even appalling than those which break through the usually imaginative atmosphere of Mr. T. P. O'Connor's reviews when the book in hand happens to touch Irish life. I showed my own appreciation of my native land in the usual Irish way by getting out of it as soon as I possibly could; and I cannot say that I have the smallest intention of settling there again as long as the superior attractions of St. Helena (not to mention London) are equally available; but since I cannot disguise from myself the helpless dependence of the British Empire on us for vital elements of talent and character (without us the English race would simply die of respectability within two generations), I am quite ready to help the saving work of reducing the sham Ireland of romance to a heap of unsightly ruins. When this is done, my countrymen can consider the relative merits of building something real in the old country, or taking a hint from that other clever people, the Jews, and abandoning their Palestine to put on all the rest of the world as a shepherd putteth on his garment, beginning with English journalism and American politics as a convenient intermediary stage to soften the transition from their present habits.

These considerations, though they bear more or less on the performance at the Princess's, are not absolutely indispensable to a reasonable enjoyment of it. I have always had a special respect for Mr. Richard Purdon because his father was Lord Mayor of Dublin when I was an impressionable boy; and I am, therefore, probably apt to overrate his talent as a comedian. Still, I can see that his Myles is not the inimitable Myles of Dion Boucicault. It is a case of the words of Mercury being harsh after the songs of Apollo. Boucicault had a charming brogue: not even the speech of the eminent journalist and M.P. named in a former paragraph of this article is more musical in sound or irresistible in insinuation— "sloothering" would be the right word, were it current here—than his. But Mr. Purdon unhappily did not learn to speak in Galway or Kerry. He bewrays the respectable Dublin citizen, whose knowledge of the brogue is derived from domestic servants drawn chiefly from the neighboring counties, and corrupted by the tongue of Dublin itself, which, like all crowded capitals, somehow evolves a peculiarly villainous accent of its own. With such opportunities Mr. Purdon, having a strong sense of fun, and being a born mimic, has no difficulty in producing a brogue; but it is not a pretty one. Further, his voice, a little coarsened, perhaps, by many years' vigorous exploitation in the interests of the aforesaid sense of fun, which seems unchastened by any very vigilant sense of beauty, is rougher than that of the late author. He has to omit the song in which Boucicault effortlessly persuaded us to accept the statement that "old Ireland was his country, and his name it was Molloy," as a complete and satisfying *apologia pro sua vita*. And the attempt to humbug Father Tom is an obvious and blundering evasion instead of what it used to be—an artless outpouring of the innocence of a poor lad who had not the wit to understand what the priest was asking, much less tell a lie to his reverence. Boucicault was a coaxing, bland-andhering sort of liar, to whom you could listen without impatience long enough to allow the carpenters time to set the most elaborate water-scene behind the front cloth. Mr. Purdon is just half a trifle too grating and boisterous, though of course the generation which does not recollect Boucicault hardly feels this. On the other hand, Miss Beaumont Collins is a much better Eily than Mrs. Boucicault, who now plays Mrs. Cregan, used to be. Mrs. Boucicault was always hopelessly ladylike, and usually made Hardress Cregan's complaints of her rusticity ridiculous by being more refined than he. Miss Collins speaks the part, which is really an engaging and almost poetic one, very prettily, and is always right about the feeling of it. Mr. Cockburn does nothing with Father Tom; but as the character happens to suit his personality, his performance passes, and is even highly praised. Mr. Tom Terriss does capitally for Hardress, besides being in earnest about his work, and so sustaining the reputation of his name. Miss Agnes Hewitt does all that can be done with the part of Anne Chute, an Irish edition of Lady Gay Spanker, and therefore one of the dreariest of Boucicault's pet vulgarities. Miss Clifton as Shelah, and Messrs. Kenney and Rochelle as Corrigan and Danny Mann, were fully equal to the occasion, though Danny did not show any of Charles II.'s sense of the tediousness of a prolonged death agony. Mrs. Boucicault's competence in the stagey work to which Mrs. Cregan is condemned goes without saying. The play, as a whole, in spite of an obsolete passage or two, and of the stupid mutilations imposed by the censorship of its day, is so far superior to the average modern melodrama, that I shall not be surprised if it repays the management handsomely for reviving it.

I regret to say that the patrons of the gallery at the Princess's, being admitted at half the usual West End price, devote the saving to the purchase of sausages to throw at the critics. I appeal to the gentleman or lady who successfully aimed one at me to throw a cabbage next time, as I am a vegetarian, and sausages are wasted on me.

THE TAILOR AND THE STAGE

15 February, 1896.

A MONG the announcements for the forthcoming season I find one concerning an entertainment of Living Pictures to be given at St. George's Hall in the first weeks of May. Mr. Coote and his supporters need not be alarmed: far from being an exhibition of nudities, these pictures, it is promised, will be an exhibition of dress, including the dress of the future as well as that of the present and of the past. Indeed, the pictures of the eighteenth century, of mediaeval Italy, of ancient Greece, and so on, are evidently only to lead up to the real point of the enterprise—the pictures of the twentieth century. The artists will be Mr. Walter Crane, Mr. Henry Holiday, Mrs. Louise Jopling, Mr. Lasenby Liberty, and Mr. G. A. Storey, R.A., who come forward to justify the ways of the Healthy and Artistic Dress Union. The aims of this Society I infer from its title, having no further acquaintance with it than an occasional glimpse of its illustrated fashion journal of twentieth-century modes, called "Aglaia."

I need not say what wild hopes such an enterprise raises in an unfortunate dramatic critic at a period when actors and actresses are little more than walking fashion-plates. The actor, in particular, with his carefully ironed new trousers, and his boots conscientiously blacked on the sole underneath the arch of the foot, is a curiously uncomfortable spectacle. The interest and fascination of dramatic storytelling are so intense that the most nonsensical stage arrangements, provided they are customary, or even the entire absence of scenery and historic costume, can be overcome by ever so little real drama and real acting. But in our theatres at present there is so seldom either drama or acting that I find myself compelled to study the adjuncts of the drama in order to prevent myself publicly and scandalously going to sleep at my post. I have gradually come to regard the leading man in a play as a set of applied tailor's measurements; so that, if any one were to get up an exhibition of clothes worn by popular actors, I would undertake, without consulting the catalogue, to point out at sight which suits were Mr. Lewis Waller's, which Mr. George Alexander's, which Mr. Coghlan's, and so on; whereas if I were to meet these gentlemen themselves in a swimming-bath, I should probably not recognize them. This does not mean that the clothes are characteristic of the men: it means that the clothes have usurped the men's place. In moments of passion the men rebel: Mr. Waller, for instance, who never escapes from the tyranny of the Maddox Street tailor (at least I have never seen him in a costume-play), always shows strong feeling on the stage by biting his lips and making a determined attempt to escape from his cloth prison at the wrists and ankles. I remember once, when he was astonishing the audience by a moment of almost passionate intensity of feeling, hearing a lady in the stall behind mine exclaim, "How wonderfully Waller is coming out!" She was perfectly right: he was coming out almost to the elbows; and the action conveyed to me irresistibly the actor's sense that if he could only come out of his tailor's tubes altogether, he could show the audience what a real man was like—which is the essence of acting. Take another example—Mr. Alexander in "The Prisoner of Zenda." In the first act (not the prologue) he appears in fashionable tourist costume, with a soft hat, thus enjoying the utmost concessions the West-End tailor makes to humanity even in holiday-time. But the suit effaces the man literally at every turn. The man has knees and elbows (the fact is proved in the other acts) ; but the suit says, "I have no knees and no elbows; and the man who gets inside me and sits down near the fire with his arms bent murders me." The trousers consent to repress the fickle flexibility of the human leg every evening for a couple of hours only on condition of reforming themselves on the stretcher during the other twenty-two, it being understood, of course, that the wearer will always be gentleman enough to recognize the necessity of lacing his boots first and putting on his trousers afterwards. Mr. Alexander has been hardened into iron by these rigorous terms. He has carried to an extraordinary degree the art of doing without his knees and elbows; and I have no doubt that the comparative coldness of his style is due to his keeping carefully away from the fire. Hence his pre-eminence among leading gentlemen. But wait for the third act of "The Prisoner of Zenda," where Rassendyl appears in an undress tunic. The suit of clothes is changed into a man; the name of Alexander springs into meaning and denotes force and personality; the actor looks alive all over as well as at the fingers and lips (an indecency which it is the great object of modern stage training to avert) ; he drops ten years of his apparent age; his spirits rise; he gambols about; he enjoys his part; and when the curtain falls and he returns to his dressing-room, he flatly refuses to resume his chains, and plays the last act boldly in his shirt-sleeves.

The more a human being is an artist by temperament,

the more intolerable to him is the hampered movement and sartorial preoccupation of the modern gentleman. My main reason for adopting literature as a profession was, that as the author is never seen by his clients, he need not dress respectably. As a stockbroker, a doctor, or a man of business, I should have had to wear starched linen and a tall hat, and to give up the use of my knees and elbows. Literature is the only genteel profession that has no livery—for even your painter meets his sitters face to face—and so I chose literature. You, friendly reader, though you buy my articles, have no idea of what I look like in the street—if you did, you would probably take in some other paper. Now if the tyranny of fashion is intolerable to the author, whose art is not one of personal display, what must it be to the actor, whose art is all personal display? As I have said, the more he is a born artist, the less he is at home in modern fashionable attire, and the more effective he is in a rational and artistic dress. Let me again illustrate from our stage. Mr. Forbes Robertson is a painter as well as an actor. Mr. Bernard Gould is that eminent black-and-white draughtsman, Mr. J. B. Partridge; and for all I know, he may be an eminent sculptor, architect, and goldsmith under three other names. Now Mr. Forbes Robertson as a modern gentleman is a deplorable spectacle; but as Romeo, in a dress designed by himself, he is handsome; and as Lancelot, in a fifteenth-century Italian costume designed by Burne Jones, he is a St. George: you hear the women in the theatre gasp with pure admiration when he appears. As to Mr. Gould, I invite those who have seen him as Biron in "Love's Labour's Lost," as Pierrot in De Banville's "Le Baiser," as Ulrik Brendel in "Rosmersholm" (a mere matter of a riding-coat and top-boots), or even in the indifferent Bulgarian uniform of Sergius Saranoff in "Arms and the Man," to go to the Criterion Theatre, and contemplate him as the fashionable seducer in Mr. Carton's adaptation of "L'Ami des Femmes." His whole aspect seems to say, "How can you expect me to seduce anybody in this confounded frock coat and this idiotic collar and scarf? They don't give a man a chance."

I might easily multiply instances. Try to conceive what our notion of Sir Henry Irving as an actor would be if we had never seen him dressed otherwise than as a fashionable doctor. Consider why the most commonplace harlequin in a provincial pantomime is so much more lively and expressive in his action than a West-End actor-manager in a modern play. No matter where you pick your illustration, you will be driven to the same conclusion: namely, that the art of acting is half strangled by the fashionable tailor. Obviously this is not the tailor's fault. He will make you a tunic and a pair of knee-breeches or knickerbockers just as willingly as a coat and trousers, if you give him the order. Why do you not give him the order? The answer must take the shape of a profound disquisition on morals and civilization.

Now that we are nearly done with the nineteenth century, it can hurt no one's feelings to remark that it has been one in which the leading faculty has been the business faculty, and the leading ambition the attainment of unprecedented riches. Functional adaptation has worked towards capitalism rather than towards art or religion. We have kept up an air of supporting the arts by substituting respectability for the beauty of life, regularity of arrangement for the beauty of form, laundry work for beauty of color, historical interest for beauty of theme, and so on. If you take a man in whom this substitution has been completely effected by deliberate precept and social environment (as far as such dehumanization is possible), and present to him a fabric which drapes in graceful folds and is beautiful in color, he will immediately pronounce it eminently unsuitable for use as a dress material. The folds are irregular, and therefore disreputable; the color is sensuous, and therefore immoral; the general effect appeals to the individual, idiosyncratic preference, and is, therefore, eccentric and in bad taste. Only, if the color be a very bright primary one—say bright scarlet or yellow—which will show the least speck of dust or weatherstain, and will not, like the tertiary colors, soften and actually take on a new beauty as it wears, he will admit its suitability for uniforms to be worn on State occasions. But for everyday wear absolute perfection means to him shiny black and shiny white—the absence of color with the maximum of surface polish, the minimum of drapery, and the most conclusive evidence of newness and washedness. At first his great difficulty was with his shirt, because folds and even outrageous crumplings were unavoidable if it was to be worn at all. But, at all events, a part of the shirt could be stiff, like a cuirass. So he took a piece of linen large enough to cover his chest, and at first, not realizing that it only needed originality and courage to immediately attain his ideal of no folds at all, arranged the folds in perfectly rectangular parallel rows, by means of his great invention of box-plaiting. Down the middle, as a last concession to the traditions of the chemise, he affixed a frill, like a row of textile parsley. Thus he produced the British Islander's shirt-front. In his delight with it, he attached sleeves and a body; starched it within an inch of its life; put it on, with a complete clergyman's suit over it; and, restless with joy, walked about, sat down, got up, and even stooped. On removing the suit, he of course discovered that the shirt was all crumpled except the front. He therefore cut a large window out of his waistcoat, through which the uncrumpled part of his masterpiece could be viewed, and cut the coat away so as not to obstruct the window. And then he was in evening dress. Later on he discarded the row of parsley; the box-plaits were next; the button-holes were reduced from three to one by the more logical spirits; variegated studs gave way to the colorless diamond or even the vapid mother-of-pearl; and finally the shirt was buttoned behind, leaving the front so unbrokenly perfect that poets and artists could not behold it without longing to write a sonnet or draw a caricature on it.

Meanwhile, the hatter and the tailor had been at work. They had observed that the human body presents two aspects—the flat and the cylindrical. They accordingly applied planes and cylinders of shiny black to it; and lo! the frock-coat, the trousers, and the tall-hat, correctly named "Cylinderhut" by the Germans. The bootmaker was baffled by Nature in applying this formula; so he adapted the human toes to the simple and regular form of a bishop's mitre, and so produced, with the help of Day & Martin, the fashionable boot.

There are persons who affirm that the cylinder hat and trousers are the most comfortable, convenient, useful, and natural coverings for the legs and head, and that on this ground they can never be displaced by the fads of dress reformers. Some of these persons know no better: others, I regret to say, are hardened and intentional liars, as you may see by their sporting suits the moment they escape from the scrutiny of London to the license of holiday life in the country. Respectability in dress is happily breaking down at a fairly rapid pace now. First the shirt-front was reduced to absurdity by its own act in asserting an independent existence as a dickey. Then it went into paper, and in that vulgar material outshone its original whiteness and shininess. Then it condescended to celluloid, so that the wearer might keep it up to the mark with his nailbrush whenever he washed his hands. Then certain women took to wearing it; and instantly the dormant sense of beauty in man woke up and saw that it was horribly ugly. Then science began to hint, as far as it could do so without compromising its social position, that starch and blacking are not material forms of cleanliness—that, if you come to that, they are material forms of dirt, destructive to the dead leather of our boots, and unhealthy for the live leather on our chests. Dr. Jaeger made the ungentlemanly but irrefragable remark that the verdict of the nose was against the black and white ideal of purity; and on that shrewd hit he established the cult of all-wool. White bread and black boots were challenged by brown bread and brown boots. A subsartorial revolution went on in underclothing; and the bolder spirits are now beginning to discard what they formerly only dodged. The bicycle "caught on"; and the man of forty discovered that it was possible to pass for thirty in knickerbockers. And so, to make a long story short, we have come to the right moment for Living Pictures from the year 1925 (say) by the Healthy and Artistic Dress Union. I respectfully recommend them to the attention of our "leading gentlemen" of the stage as a possible chance for them to persuade the public that the prevalent notion that they cannot act is but an illusion produced by their tailors.

TWO PLAYS

Jedbury Junior: a light comedy in three acts. By Madeleine Lucette Ryley. Terry's Theatre, 14 February, 1896.

On 'Change: a comedy in three acts. Adapted by Eweretta Lawrence from the German of Von Moser. (A Revival.) Strand Theatre, 15 February, 1896.

I WISH some manager would nerve me to my weekly task by producing either a very good play or a very bad one. The plays that unman me as a critic are those which are entertaining without being absorbing, and pleasant without being valuable—which keep me amused during an idle hour without engaging my deeper sympathies or taxing my attention—which, in short, would be excellent value for half a crown in a summer theatre in the Park, if only that agreeable German institution would make haste to advance with us beyond the Olympian and Wild West stage of development. It is in dealing with such plays that the critic is apt to forget the immense difference between his economic relation to the theatre and that of the playgoer. A critic not only gets a seat in the best part of the house for nothing, but is actually paid for sitting in it. The effect of this on him is highly complex. Whether the net result is to make him more exacting than the ordinary playgoer, or less, seems a simple question; but the answer varies from play to play, and from stalls to gallery. It varies even with the age of the play and of the critic; for an experienced critic is often as sulky over a new development of the drama as a skilled workman over a new machine or process; whilst a freshman is equally apt to form wild

hopes of the new thing merely because it is new: both
sides investing it with imaginary faults and qualities by
pure association of ideas, without the smallest reference
to the ~~unfortunate author's text.~~ In most cases I shou' '
say that the critic, whatever he may say in print for th
sake of a quiet life, is less easily pleased than the rest oı
the public. But with reference to the particular sort of
play now in question, I am not so sure. His verdict, if
based on the fact that *he* finds the piece worth seeing,
may differ very materially from a verdict based on the
experience of the man who has to turn out from a comfortable house in the suburbs, and make his way to the
Strand with his wife, and perhaps his daughters, at a
cost of half a guinea a head, plus travelling expenses, or
else to wait on a cold and wet night at the doors to secure
a not very advantageous or luxurious seat in the cheaper
parts of the house. It seems to me that a play must have
a very strong element of interest in it, or a performance
a very strong element of fascination, to induce a rational
person to spend the evening so expensively or uncomfortably as it must be spent at a theatre; and I have seen
play after play which would have been accepted cheer-
fully as excellent pastime on moderate terms, shunned by
the public because the terms were not moderate. The
last time I paid half a guinea for a stall was to see Duse
play Magda. I paid it without hesitation, though I had
already seen the performance (for nothing) in my professional capacity. But if you ask me whether I would
pay half a guinea to see an average London play with an
average London cast, I shall have the greatest difficulty
in conveying a negative sufficiently emphatic to do justice
to my feelings without the use of language inconsistent
with my dignity.

These reflections have been suggested to me by the two comedies produced last week, "Jedbury Junior" and "On 'Change." Both are pleasant enough in their way; but they are not fascinating, not important: the playgoer who misses them will miss nothing but an evening's amusement. If the prices ranged from one shilling for the gallery to five shillings for the stalls, I should say that both plays were excellent value for the money. As it is, I prefer not to give my opinion from that point of view. Even if you wish to know which of the two plays is the better worth going to, I must point out to you that the prices charged are not the same, except to the stalls and gallery, which are, as usual, half a guinea (a monstrous charge) and a shilling respectively. The intermediate charges are, at Terry's, seven and sixpence, six shillings, four shillings, and two and sixpence; at the Strand, six, four, three, and two shillings. That is, the prices at Terry's are higher. You will naturally conclude that the play at Terry's is better, the cast stronger, the theatre warmer, more comfortably seated, and nearer the railway station. The facts do not bear out these inferences. On the contrary, as far as there is any difference, the play is worse, the cast weaker, the theatre colder, less comfortably seated, and further from the railway station. It is a mistake to look for logic in such things. The fact that there comes every now and then a play which makes a fortune in spite of all drawbacks, leaves every manager obsessed with the hope of chancing on that play, and convinced that nothing can materially help him if he misses it, or hinder him if he hits on it.

"Jedbury Junior" is a flimsy, almost schoolgirlish, work, redeemed by the happy notion of the Fuegian marriage, which proves fertile in funny complications, and by a great number of amusing lines, for which the author, one guesses, probably supplied the opportunity rather than the actual test. She has a strong sense of fun, and ridicules everybody over forty, and most people under it, with much vivacity. Her young man is a remarkably good-hearted and affectionate young man; and her young woman, as might have been expected, has a touch of reality; but the serious passages between the other characters are, to say the least, jejune. It is impossible to expatiate on the acting, since, save the young man and young woman aforesaid, none of the parts present any difficulties upon which one dare compliment an actor of good standing. Mr. Beauchamp, Mr. Playfair, and Mr. Farquhar are amusing, Mr. Farquhar having the best of it as a butler who bowdlerizes and translates into diplomatic language the messages which his master and mistress, not being on speaking terms, charge him with in one another's presence. Mr. Kerr is more determined than ever to be an antidote to Ibsen: he is frank, manly, wholesome, and English to an overpowering degree—so unaffected in his speech, too, that when he follows Miss Millett's vanishing form with his honest eyes, and says "She's gorn!" a tear of sympathy with this good-hearted Johnny blurs the vision and softens the heart. In fact, Mr. Kerr has got in "Jedbury Junior" what every actor-manager demands from the dramatist: that is, an outrageous caricature of himself. At no point does the part get beyond his familiar routine; and though I enjoy that routine as much as anybody, I cannot reasonably be expected to deal with it as with the creation of a new character. Miss Maude Millett is more fortunate. For years it has been her fate to provide "comic relief" in couple with Mr. Sydney Brough, or some other fellow-victim.

She, too, has a routine which I know by heart. I am always glad to see her; and she generally makes me laugh once or twice; but to say that I look forward to her entrance with either hope or fear, or leave the theatre after her exit pondering on what I have seen, and resolving to be a better man in future, would be simply to tell a breath-bereaving lie. Happily, as Dora Hedway, the most human character in this flippant, stuck-together-anyhow little play, she gets an opportunity of acting, and seizes it with complete success. Probably she will not enjoy another for ten years to come; so, before she is thrust back into comic relief, I recommend all her admirers to haste to see her in the last act of "Jedbury Junior."

"On 'Change," a revised play, was new to me, as far as a piece made up of such stale material could be new. At all events, I had not seen it before; and I was duly captivated by Mr. Felix Morris's impersonation of the Scotch professor. For an old often-repeated performance it is surprisingly delicate and unexaggerated. The working up of the quarrel at the end of the first act by Mr. Morris and so skilful an old stage hand as Mr. William Farren is an excellent piece of business, and produces the best "curtain" in the piece. I warn Mr. Morris, however, that he had better hide his gifts carefully if he wishes to keep constantly before the public. I know no surer way of avoiding engagements on the stage at present than to know your business. "On 'Change" is an exceptional play in respect of its bringing into action at least four gentlemen who can act. Besides Mr. Farren and Mr. Felix Morris, there is Mr. Yorke Stephens. He, as we all know, is capital in a part which happens to fit him like a glove—the war correspondent

345

in "Held by the Enemy," Dick Rusper in "The Crusaders," Captain Bluntschli in—I forgot the name of the play, but no matter. But Joe, in "On 'Change," does not fit him like a glove; on the contrary, it would be difficult to imagine a part more foreign to his characteristic style and personality than this translation into English of the conventional German, warm-hearted, hard-working, cheerful, simple, unfashionable clerk, a good son and affectionate wooer—a provincialized, Teutonified variant of the Kerresque Johnny, in short. Yet Mr. Yorke Stephens, through the mere effect of inevitability produced by the smartness, address, and grace of a skilled and disciplined actor, gets through his unsuitable part, not only without having his appropriateness challenged at any moment, but with every appearance of having been expressly born to play it. Finally, Mr. James Welch is in the cast, revelling in the part of the Scotch philosopher's cockney landlord with fearful thoroughness. I say finally, because Mr. E. H. Kelly's much-laughed-at performance as DeHass is not acting: it is only tomfooling, which is a different matter. The part, it must be admitted, does not allow of much else; still, it is no worse than much of the stuff allotted to the others. Miss Eweretta Lawrence gives the American version of the conventional serio-comic love scene very prettily in the third act—fortunately for the play, which is rather deficient in feminine interest. Only, that dangerous business with the matches made me nervous. The weak spot in the cast is Mrs. Burnett, who should be played by an elderly actress with a strong comic talent for henpecking. The lady who plays it at present declines to conceal the fact that she is young and pretty. She is, I take it, more anxious to avoid being cast for such parts in future than to secure the success of the play.

Dramatic Opinions and Essays

The first piece at the Strand, Mr. Louis Parker's "Man in the Street," though it is not new, should not be missed, as Mr. Welch has worked up his character-sketch of the old vagabond Jabez Gover to an extraordinary pitch of completeness and intensity. At Terry's the curtain-raiser is a very ordinary sentimentality called "An Old Garden," by Hill Davies, which is pulled through by Mr. W. J. Robertson and Miss Mona Oram with conscientious sincerity and force.

One of the most remarkable pieces of realistic acting I have seen lately has not been on the stage, but on the concert platform, by Miss Beatrice Herford. Miss Herford, with the aid of a chair, pretends to be a lady with a child in a tramcar, a shop-girl, a dressmaker hired out by the day, and a maddeningly fidgety old lady in a train. Very ordinary entertainer's business, apparently—until you see it. Miss Herford began by amusing me, and ended by appalling me. But for her occasional jokes, and her funny and clever pantomime, I should, so to speak, have changed carriages, so faithfully did she reproduce the ways of irritating people. If Miss Herford goes on the stage, we shall not be at a loss for a successor to Mrs. John Wood.

PINERO AND GRUNDY ON G. B. S.

Gossip: a play in four acts. By Clyde Fitch and Leo Dietrichstein. Comedy Theatre, 22 February, 1896.

The Romance of the Shop Walker: a new and original comedy. By Robert Buchanan and Charles Marlowe. Vaudeville Theatre, 26 February, 1896.

The Theatrical World of 1895: a reprint of Mr. William Archer's criticisms of the drama during last year. With a prefatory letter by Arthur W. Pinero. London: Walter Scott. 1896.

I MUST retire politely before "Gossip" at the Comedy. An excellent play of its kind (no doubt), it is hardly the class of work I am retained to criticize. If Mr. Comyns Carr were to re-open the Grosvenor Gallery with a collection of the chromolithographs given away with the Christmas numbers of our illustrated papers for the last twenty years, I should willingly go and study the exhibition as a conspectus of the history of popular art during that period. But if he were to engage a third-rate artist to produce a composite plagiarism of them all, and exhibit that as a new work of art, I should carefully stay away. Similarly, if he were to undertake a series of revivals of all the successes of the Hare-Kendal and Bancroft managements in the 'seventies and 'eighties, I should undoubtedly profit by an attentive study of them. But to produce a hash of them, made by a couple of playwrights of no very striking attainments, as the latest enterprise of a first-rate West-End theatre, is really a rather uninteresting thing to do. If Mrs. Langtry's force were in the least a comic force; if she had the double-edged genius of Mrs. Kendal; if she were even Miss Lottie Venne or Miss Fanny Brough, both of whom she imitates by snatches; were it possible to feel as curious to see her apart from her art as it was to see the Jersey Lily of twenty years ago, I might perhaps have found "Gossip" tolerable. None of these conditions being fulfilled, I was heavily oppressed, and should not have endured to the end but for Miss Calhoun, who played admirably as Mrs. Stanford. The dresses and diamonds were, to me, dreadful. I really enjoy looking at a woman who is characteristically dressed by herself, or affectionately and beautifully dressed by satin art; but fashionable ladies hung with the trophies of their tradesmen are among my strongest aversions; and it seemed to me that this was the effect deliberately aimed at in "Gossip." The parade of jewelry was especially disappointing after the stealing of Mrs. Langtry's jewels. I have always felt sure that the theft was the work of some dramatic critic determined to get rid of that ugly colorless glitter at all costs; but what is the use of stealing Mrs. Langtry's diamonds when she purchases or hires a fresh set next day?

The authors announce on the playbill that they "have made use of several suggestions found in a novel by Jules Claretie." I can only say that if they had made use of several suggestions to be found in these columns, they would not have written the play at all. Oh, that goody-goody Amurrican husband—a Wall Street King Arthur (Tennysonian species)! And oh, that young wife who was about to run away from him when she was reminded of her own mother and her own chee-yild! Oh, my goodness! It *was* dull.

There is one notable use to which "Gossip" may be

put. Evidence has been accumulating for a couple of years past that however dangerous it may be to go ahead with the drama, it is still more dangerous to attempt to escape by going back. The two policies are fairly exemplified in the production of "The Benefit of the Doubt," followed by the production of "Gossip" at the same theatre. I hope Mr. Comyns Carr, when the run of "Gossip" is over, will publish the returns from both plays, so that we may see whether the back track really leads to the gold-mine.

The annual reprint of Mr. William Archer's dramatic criticisms—always an interesting event, and especially so now that it deals with a year in which Bernhardt and Duse contended with one another part to part—is extraspecially interesting to me this time because of its remarkable preface by Mr. Pinero. At first I could not make out what Mr. Pinero was driving at; page after page brought forth nothing but an amusing bogus autobiography. I call it bogus on two grounds. First, because it contains not a word about Mr. Pinero himself, his personality, his views, his hopes and fears for the drama, or anything else distinctly Pinerotic. It might be the autobiography of an insurance canvasser, for all the internal evidence to the contrary. Second, the particulars, that it does contain as to Mr. Pinero's lodgings and landladies, his hotels, his luggage, and the topography of Edinburgh, are not, on strict examination, credible. On this point my judgment may err; but can the reader expect me to believe such stories as that of the boy who said to the eminent dramatist, "The governor dragged me up one dirty lane and down another, and pointed out this hovel and that, and had some tale to tell almost of the very cobbles in the streets, *until he just upon bored me to suicide"?* If a boy exists who has so completely mastered the secret of Mr. Pinero's dialogue, I say produce him, name him. There is no such boy. He is an invention; and as the man who will invent one thing will invent another, I reject the whole autobiography as the merest wantonness of fiction.

But, I shall be asked, is it to be believed that Mr. Pinero has written over twenty pages of realistic romance out of pure impishness, to enjoy a laugh in his sleeve at Mr. Archer and the public? By no means: the whole autobiography is only a dramatist's device for gathering the attention of the readers to the preface so as to enable him to impart a momentous secret to the public with the fullest dramatic effect. And what is the secret? No less than that Mr. Pinero does not read *my* criticisms.

I don't believe it.

Let me again submit the matter to the judgment of the reader. Mr. Pinero, after declaring that for a fortnight after the production of one of his plays he reads nothing but "The Mining Journal," proceeds as follows (I italicize the phrases on which my case is founded) :— "One of the flaws of my system is that it robs me of the privilege of reading *much brilliant writing*. For instance, I am compelled, by my system, wholly to abstain from studying those articles upon dramatic matters contributed to a well-known journal by your friend Mr. G***** B****** S***—*of whom I protest I am, in general, a warm admirer."* Very well then, how does he know that my writing is brilliant? How can he be a warm admirer of an author he never reads—unless his admiration is excited solely by my personal appearance? Such an affectation would not impose on a baby. Besides, look at the collateral evidence. Consider the enormous improvement which took place in his work between "The Notorious Mrs. Ebbsmith," written before my dramatic articles had been in currency long enough to produce any effect, and "The Benefit of the Doubt," written when I had been in the field for a whole year! What other cause can be assigned for this beneficent change that was not equally operative between "The Second Mrs. Tanqueray" and "The Notorious Mrs. Ebbsmith"—a period of temporary decline? None— absolutely none. And yet I am to be told that Mr. Pinero reads "The Mining Journal" instead of the "Saturday Review!" Stuff! Why, Mr. Pinero is one of the most conspicuous of the very, very few playwrights we have who are more interested in the drama than in mines.

To clinch the matter, I adduce the evidence of Mr. Sydney Grundy, who actually declares that Mr. Pinero is "marching to his doom" through immoderate indulgence in the luxury of reading criticisms. There is no mistaking the vehemence, the anguish almost, of his tone. "My dear Pinero, make no mistake. These fawning first-nighters have no following: these fulsome newspapers represent nobody's opinion outside a newspaper office. You are superior to the newspapers. Don't listen to them; but make them listen to you. *If need be, fill your ears with wax, and bind yourself to the mast; but steer your own course, not theirs.* You will lose nothing: they will soon return to your heels." This is not the language of a man accustomed to see Mr. Pinero austerely passing over the "Saturday Review," the "World," and the "Speaker," and burying himself in the columns of "The Mining Journal."

There is none of Mr. Pinero's coquetry about Mr. Grundy, whose article (in "The Theatre" for March) is

well worth reading, if only for its repeated and affectionate references to myself. Mr. Grundy quotes me as "the
crankiest of the stove-pipe fanatics." I do not precisely
catch the bearing of the stove-pipe epithet. There is evidence in the article that Mr. Grundy has studied my costume too carefully to suppose that I wear a stove-pipe
hat. Perhaps he means that instead of consuming my
own smoke in decent privacy, I fuliginously obscure the
clear atmosphere of the "well-made play" with it. So
I do; but what then? A man must live. If I like my
own plays, and Ibsen's, and Shakespeare's, and Goethe's,
and Labiche's and Molière's better than "The Late Mr.
Castello" and "Les Pattes de Mouche," why should I not
say so, considering the freedom with which gentlemen
of the opposite persuasion offer *their* opinions? All the
same, I do not approve of the heartlessness of Mr. William Archer, who has gone on the war-path against Mr.
Grundy, and tomahawked his arguments, scalped his
figures, burnt his facts alive, and insulted their ashes
with taunting demands for the production of the returns
from "Slaves of the Ring," "Mr. Castello," and so on,
in order to compare them with the returns from the later
Pinero plays. This is barbarous, and only serves super-
fluously to establish the fact that Mr. Grundy has no
case—as if any one supposed that he had. For my part,
I find Mr. Grundy's article lively reading, and quite as
sensible as most of my own. Only, I would humbly ask
Mr. Grundy whether he really finds these well-made
"mechanical rabbit" plays which he champions so very
succulent? Does he ever go to see them, for instance,
except when he writes them himself? Depend on it, he
has not been inside a theatre for ten years except on his
own business. If he had to go as often as I have, he

would lose his verdant illusions as to the ravishing superiority of "Delia Harding" to "The Wild Duck" or "As
You Like It."

I was so sternly reproved for my frivolity in rather
liking "The Strange Adventures of Miss Brown," that I
hardly dare to confess that I got on very well also with
"The Shopwalker." I am as well aware as anybody that
these Buchanan-Marlowe plays (Marlowe is a lady, by
the way) are conventional in the sense that the sympathy
they appeal to flows in channels deeply worn by use, and
that the romance of them is taken unaffectedly from the
Alnaschar dreams of the quite ordinary man. But allow
me to point out that this sort of conventionality, obvious
and simple as it seems, is not a thing that can be attained
without a measure of genius. Most of the plays produced
in the course of the year are attempts to do just this
apparently simple thing; and most of them fail, not because they aim at realizing the vulgar dream, giving expression to the vulgar feeling, and finding words for the
vulgar thought, but because, in spite of their aiming, they
miss the mark. It seems so like missing a haystack at
ten yards that many critics, unable to believe in such a
blunder, write as if the marksman had accomplished his
feat, but had bored the spectators by its commonness.
They are mistaken: what we are so tired of is the clumsy,
stale, stupid, styleless, mannerless, hackneyed devices
which we know by experience to be the sure preliminaries
to the bungler's failure. Now Mr. Buchanan does not
miss his mark. It is true that he is so colossally lazy, so
scandalously and impenitently perfunctory, that it is often
astonishing how he gets even on the corner of the target;
but he does get there because, having his measure of
genius, it is easier to him to hit somewhere than to miss

altogether. There is plenty of scamped stuff in "The Shopwalker": for example, the part of Captain Dudley is nothing short of an insult to the actor, Mr. Sydney Brough; and a good half of the dialogue could be turned out by a man of Mr. Buchanan's literary power at the rate of three or four thousand words a day. Mr. Pinero or Mr. Jones would shoot themselves rather than throw such copious, careless, unsifted workmanship to the public. But the story is sympathetically imagined; and nearly all the persons of the drama are human. One forgives even Captain Dudley and Lady Evelyn as one forgives the pictures of lovers on a valentine. Mr. Buchanan does not count on your being a snob, and assume that you are ready to sneer at the promoted shopwalker and his old mother: he makes you laugh heartily at them, but not with that hateful, malicious laughter that dishonors and degrades yourself. Consequently there is, for once, some sense in calling a popular play wholesome. All I have to say against "The Shopwalker" is that there is hardly any point on which it might not have been a better play if more trouble had been taken with it; and that a little practical experience of the dramatic side of electioneering would have enabled the authors greatly to condense and intensify the scene in the last act, where the shopwalker, as Parliamentary candidate, produces his mother. It is a mistake, both from the electioneering and poetic point of view, to make Tomkins merely splenetic at this point: he should appeal to the crowd as men, not denounce them as curs. However, Buchanan would not be Buchanan without at least one incontinence of this kind in the course of a play.

The acting is excellent, Mr. Grossmith, with all his qualities in easy action, being capitally supported by Miss

Victor, Miss Nina Boucicault, and Mr. David James. Miss Palfrey improves, though not quite as fast as she might if she gave her mind to it. Miss Annie Hill is satisfactory as Dorothy Hubbard, but has not much to do. The other parts are mere routine.

THE RETURN OF MRS. PAT

For the Crown: a romantic play in four acts, done into English by John Davidson, from François Coppée's *Pour la Couronne.* Lyceum Theatre. 27 February, 1896.

HAVE you observed, reader, how almost every critic who praises "For the Crown" thinks it necessary to apologize for the fifteenth century? Fancy sane men trying to extenuate a guarantee of beauty! However, since that appears to be the proper thing to do, let me be in the fashion. Yes, there is no denying it: Mr. Forbes Robertson wears a caftan instead of a frock coat, and an exquisite martial cap of metal and ivory instead of a masterpiece by Lincoln & Bennett. Mrs. Patrick Campbell's dresses are not made by Worth: no controversy can possibly arise over her sleeves: worst of all, she does not once appear in a hat. It is true, on my credit—four acts, and not one hat. Playgoer: be generous. Overlook this: they mean well, these people at the Lyceum. But what can you expect from an actor who is a painter, and an actress who is a musician?

For the Balcan Mountains and Bulgaria no apology is necessary. Honor to whom honor is due! I—I who pen these lines—first rooted the Balkan mountains on the

English stage in "Arms and the Man"—I first saw the immense dramatic possibilities of Bulgaria. And—let me confess it—I cannot help feeling a little sore that the work of adapting "La Couronne" was not entrusted to me on this account. I feel that I could have given that heroic tale a turn which Mr. Davidson, with all his inspiration, has missed.

Somehow, I find I cannot bring myself to pass over this ridiculous apologizing for the fifteenth century with a mere ironic laugh. What does it mean? It is not the puerile chaff which the modern revival of artistic and religious feeling provoked earlier in the century, when our journalists and comic-opera parodists were too ignorant and callous to be ashamed to jeer like street boys at the pre-Raphaelite and Wagnerian movements, until even George Eliot, though on the materialist side herself, protested indignantly against "debasing the moral currency." All that ribaldry is obsolete: nobody now dreams of sneering at Mr. Forbes Robertson as "æsthetic," or conceives that to compare him to a mediæval hero-saint, in "stained glass attitudes" or otherwise, would be anything but a high compliment to him. And yet there is the unmistakable vein of apology and deprecation, if not about the costumes and scenery, at least about the play. And here we have the secret of it. The apologetic critics are thinking, not of the golden age of the arts and crafts, but of the later horrors of historical drama in five acts and in blank verse, which no more belong to the sensuously artistic fifteenth century than to the religiously artistic fourteenth century, or the sanely, humorously artistic thirteenth, since they are in fact a characteristic product of the rhetorical, intellectual, idealistic, inquisitive, logical, scientific, commercial, essentially anti-artistic period which we count as beginning with the sixteenth century, and in which we trace not the beautiful growth and flowering of the arts, but their consummation and devastation in the giant hands of Michael Angelo and Shakespeare. Those who desire to rejoice in Shakespeare must confine themselves (as they generally do) to reading his own plays. Read those which have been written since he overwhelmed English dramatic poetry with his impossible example, and you will wish that he had never been born.

In order to write a true dramatic poem, one must possess very deep human feeling. In order to write historical drama in rhetorical blank verse, one only need possess imagination—a quite different and much cheaper article. Shakespeare had both in an extraordinary degree: consequently his rhetoric, monstrous as much of it is, is so quickened by flashes and turns of feeling that it is impossible to be bored by it; whilst his feeling expresses itself so spontaneously in rhetorical forms that at the climaxes of his plays rhetoric and poetry become one. And so, since his time, every poor wretch with an excitable imagination, a command of literary bombast, and metric faculty enough to march in step, has found himself able to turn any sort of thematic material, however woodenly prosaic, into rhetorical blank verse; whereupon, foolishly conceiving himself to be another Shakespeare, he has so oppressed the stage with yards upon yards and hours upon hours of barren imagery, that at last the announcement of a new historical play in verse at a London theatre produces an involuntary start of terror among the critics, followed by reassuring explanations that although it *is* a fifteenth-century business (more or less), it is really not so bad after all.

François Coppée, as a Frenchman, has not caught the rhetorical itch in its full Shakespearean virulence; but unfortunately the milder form in which it afflicts him is duller than the English variety by just as much as Racine and Corneille are weaker than our immortal William. Therefore Mr. Davidson, as a countryman of Shakespeare's —or, at any rate, of Macbeth's—has felt bound to prepare "La Couronne" for the English stage by intensifying the sublimity of its balderdash to an extent which no audience unaccustomed to Shakespeare would stand without amazement and laughter. Accordingly Miss Winifred Emery, having to convey to us that she is somewhat bored, is condemned to do so by shrieking for the Balkan Mountains to move, and the Day of Judgment to dawn, with nothing to sustain her in this vortex of academic nonsense except the silly popular delusion that there is something fine in it all—a delusion which I will not insult her intelligence by assuming her to share. I need say no more about this aspect of the play beyond mentioning that wherever Mr. Davidson has attempted to outdo M. Coppée in rhetorical folly, he has easily succeeded. I admit that the heightened effect proves, on the whole, that when you set out to be nonsensical, the more nonsensical you are the better. But fifty million lines of such stuff will not extract from me an admission that the writer is a dramatist, much less a poet. The utmost I will concede is that since poets so great as Shakespeare and Shelley did not escape the infection, we must forgive Mr. Davidson for it, though only, I hope, on the distinct understanding that it is not to occur again.

Unfortunately for the liveliness of the play, M. Coppée's power of imagining ready-made heroic situations and characters is not fortified by any power of developing them. Bazilide and Michael Brancomir never get beyond the point at which they are first dumped on the stage: they keep saying the same things about themselves and one another over and over again until at last the spectator feels that the play would be greatly improved if most of it were presented by accomplished pantomimists in dumb show. The second act—the Lady Macbeth act—is especially wearisome in this way. A Turkish spy forces the hand of Bazilide by the masterly argument that if Michael Brancomir does not betray his country somebody else will —probably the scullion. Bazilide passes on the argument to Michael, improving the scullion into a horseboy. But poor Michael is quite unable to get any forwarder with his conventional compunction, whilst Bazilide is equally at a loss for any idea except the horseboy, on whom she falls back again and again, the whole conversation being strung up to concert pitch of absurdity by the monstrously tall talk in which it is carried on. The pair prance as if they were bounding over the Alps; but they do not advance an inch. One has only to think for a moment of Lady Macbeth tempting Macbeth, or Iago tempting Othello, to realize how comparatively stupid the poet is, and how, of all methods of marking time, the most futile is to mark it in blank verse. Even in the striking scene of the parricide, there is hardly a human note struck, except in the preliminary chat between the sentinel and the shepherd, which is a welcome relief after Bazilide's fustian. When the catastrophe approaches, father and son do not rise for a moment into any human relation with one another. The more terribly the emergency presses, the more literary do they become, taking it by turns to deliver tearing apostrophes to heaven, hell, honor, history, hope, memory, Christianity, the fatherland, the past and the future; each waiting with great politeness until the other has finished, the audience meanwhile watching patiently for the fight and the finish. In short, except as a display of rhetoric for the sake of rhetoric— a form of entertainment which is chiefly interesting as the only known means by which an author or speaker can make the public respect him for unmercifully boring it—the play has no value apart from the force of the main situation and the charm of the pretty love scenes between Militza and Constantine.

The acting, though full of matter for the critic, is mostly but poor sport for the lay spectator. Miss Winifred Emery was not well advised to accept the part of Bazilide. The original Bazilide of Coppée is a passably credible Bernhardtian wicked woman of the stage, corseted into Alexandrines, but not bombasted and hyberbolicised out of all humanity, like the pen-and-ink monster Mr. Davidson has produced in the ferment of his imagination. Nothing but a specific artistic talent, and a most tactful virtuosity in the artificial declamation and heroic bearing of the rhetorical school, could enable an actress to get through such a part with credit. Now Miss Emery's talent is a specifically prosaic one: we have repeatedly seen that the more closely her parts touch the actual life and society of our day in the classes which she has under her own daily observation, the better she acts. In "The Benefit of the Doubt" she almost persuaded us that she was the best actress on our stage. Remove the venue even so small a distance towards the imaginative region as the plays of the late W. G. Wills, and she is comparatively colorless. Shift it completely to the Sahara of rhetorical blank verse or the heights of genuine dramatic poetry, and she holds her own merely as a pretty woman and a clever professional. For Bazilide she has not even the right sort of prettiness: she is no "docile rhythmic serpent of the East." Her habit of speech is positively subversive of the poetry of tone and measure. When she says "Nothing must tarnish the greater glory of Michael's love for me," the words "greater glory" come out with a fashionable smartness at which it is hardly possible not to smile. All that can be said for her Bazilide is that by dint of going at her business with great spirit, and with a cleverness that only stops short of perceiving that she had better not have gone at it at all, she gets safely through, thanks to her great popularity, her good looks, and a resolute application of her vigorous stage talent to a bold experiment in ranting, on the pretty safe chance of the public rising at it as Partridge rose at the King in "Hamlet." Which the public obediently does, like the silly lamb it is in its moments of pretension to fine connoisseurship.

And Mrs. Patrick Campbell, what of her? Ah, the change from that mournful first night of the slain "Michael and his Lost Angel," when we were all singing, both on the stage and off :—

> "But what are vernal joys to me?
> Where thou art not, no Spring can be."

What a ballad could have been written then with the title "Come back from Dorchester"; and what terrible heart twistings we suffered when we knew that she would not come unless we gave her Henry Arthur Jones's head on a charger! Well, we gave it to her; and on the first night of "For the Crown" we agreed, before she had been three seconds on the stage, that her return was cheap at the price: nay, we would have given her Shakespeare's head

as a makeweight if she had given the faintest pout of
dissatisfaction. You will tell me, no doubt, that Mrs.
Patrick Campbell cannot act. Who said she could?—who
wants her to act?—who cares twopence whether she pos-
sesses that or any other second-rate accomplishment?
On the highest plane one does not act, one *is*. Go and
see her move, stand, speak, look, kneel—go and breathe
the magic atmosphere that is created by the grace of all
these deeds; and then talk to me about acting, forsooth!
No, Mrs. Campbell's Militza is an embodied poem; and
if it is much more a lyric poem than a dramatic one, why,
so much the worse for dramatic poetry! This time, too,
the poetry was not without a little tenderness as well as
much beauty of movement and tone. The old vituperative
note was not heard; and there was an access of artistic
earnestness and power. Possibly the vituperative mood
had exhausted itself on the devoted author of "Michael."

Mr. Forbes Robertson was torn by a struggle between
the riotous high spirits he was evidently enjoying in his
own person, and the remorse and horror which racked
him as Constantine Brancomir. However, art is never
the worse for a happy inspiration; and though in filling
the part of Constantine he was really filling a brainless
void, he filled it like an artist. Miss Sarah Brooke played
a small part well; and Mr. Dalton, as the elder Brancomir,
outfaced the nothingness of his part with sufficient assurance to impress the Partridges almost as successfully as
Miss Emery did. It was all that he could do under the
circumstances.

The play is worth seeing for its mounting alone by
those who, like myself, care very little for the spouting of
Marlovian mighty lines. Everything, from the captured
standards of the Turks to Signor Lucchesi's equestrian

statue in the style of Verrocchio, shows the choice of the artist, not the fulfilment of an order by a tradesman. The first scene, Mr. Walter Hann's "Citadel in the Balkans," with its most unrhetorical, delicately beautiful mountains stretching to the horizon in a sea of snowy peaks, is so good that one asks with some indignation whether some means cannot be invented of doing away with the ridiculous "sky borders" which deface the firmament. The stage management in this first act, by the way, is excellent. Later on it is perhaps a trifle unimaginative; and Mr. Forbes Robertson has not yet mastered the art of arranging the Lyceum stage so as to disguise its excessive spaciousness when interiors are to be represented. For instance, in the second act, since there is neither a Court procession to enter nor a ballet to be danced, the room, in view of the biting climate and Bazilide's light draperies, might be made a trifle snugger with advantage to the illusion.

In short, then, everything—except perhaps the play—is worth seeing. The spoilt children of the public have certainly strained their privilege hard by their treatment of "Michael and his Lost Angel"; but still, since "Michael" was succeeding in spite of its having completely beaten the company, whereas all the forces concerned have their share in the success of "For the Crown"—since, above all, we can now see Mrs. Patrick Campbell every evening if we will, the change in the Lyceum bill will be forgiven. No doubt Mr. Jones has lost a thousand or two; but in every other respect he has gained; and, after all, what is the loss of a thousand pounds to a successful dramatic author? Merely a stimulant to increased production, the first fruits of which we shall presently receive at the hands of Mr. Willard. And so let us be jocund, and book our places at the Lyceum without delay.

BOILED HEROINE

True Blue: a new and original drama of the ROYAL NAVY, in five acts, by Leonard Outram and Stuart Gordon, Lieut. R.N., Olympic Theatre, 19 March, 1896.

I AM often told by people who never go to the theatre that they like melodramas, because they are so funny. Those who do go know better than that. A melodrama must either succeed as a melodrama or else fail with the uttermost ignominies of tedium. But I am fain to admit that "True Blue" is an exception to this rule. It is funnier by a good deal than "H.M.S. Pinafore" in the absurd parts, and not bad, as melodramas go, in the presentable parts. The authorship has evidently been divided among many hands. In some of the epithets which Mrs. Raleigh, as the lady matador, hurls at the villain, it is impossible not to recognize the vivid style of Mr. Raleigh. One of the unnamed authors—I do not know which—is clearly an idiot; for it is not conceivable that the unspeakable fatuities of the plot can have proceeded from the same brain as the part of Strachan, or the dialogue, a good deal of which is animated and businesslike. Probably the idiot was the original begetter of the drama. As I conjecture, he submitted his play to Mr. Leonard Outram, who, as an experienced actor, at once fell under the spell which unredeemed literary and dramatic idiocy never fails to throw over his profession. He called in Lieutenant Stuart Gordon to look after the naval realism, and supply technically correct equivalents for the Avast Heavings, and Abaft the Binnacles, and

Splicing the Main Braces which we may presume the original manuscript to have contained. The Lieutenant, not being an experienced actor, no doubt suggested that if his naval realism could be supplemented by a gleam or two of common sense, it would be all the better; and I can imagine Sir Augustus Harris, on being approached on the subject of finance, not only supporting the naval officer's view with some vehemence, but taking the dialogue in hand to a certain extent himself, with his popular collaborator, Mr. Raleigh, to lend a hand when time ran short. If this hypothesis be correct, we get four authors besides the nameless idiot; and it is no small degree remarkable that the play has succeeded because the collaborators, in a sort of inspired desperation, played up to the idiot instead of trying to reclaim him. Take for example the main situation of the piece. A British cruiser is anchored at Gibraltar. Its deck is used as a sort of dramatic exchange where villains and villainesses, heroes and heroines, stroll in, like bolts out of the blue, to hatch plots and make love. First there is the lady matador who loves the captain and hates the heroine whom the captain loves. Then there is the heroine, who also loves the captain. And there is the heroine's maid, who loves the comic sailor, who loves the bottle. Suddenly the cruiser is ordered to up anchor and sweep England's enemies from the seas. The women resolve not to desert the men they love in the hour of danger. The matadoress, a comparatively experienced and sensible woman, slips quietly into the pantry adjoining the captain's cabin. The maid gets into one of those settee music boxes which are, it appears, common objects on the decks of cruisers, and is presently carried into the captain's cabin. The heroine, taught by love to divine a surer hiding-place, gets into one of the ship's boilers. Here the hand of the idiot is apparent, striking out a situation which would never have occurred to Shakespeare. Once fairly at sea, the matadoress gives way to an inveterate habit of smoking, and is smelt out by the captain. She throws her arms boldly about him, and declares that he is hers for ever. Enter, inopportunely, the navigating officer. He is scandalized, but retires. When he thinks it safe to return, it is only to find the maid emerging from the settee to dispute possession of the captain, on behalf of the heroine, with the matadoress. Hereupon he describes the ship as the captain's harem, and is placed under arrest. Then comes the great dramatic opportunity of the matadoress. Becoming acquainted, Heaven knows how, with the hiding-place of the heroine, she takes the stage alone, and draws a thrilling picture of her rival's impending doom. She describes her in the clammy darkness and dank cold of that boiler, listening to the wild beats of her own heart. Then the sensation of wet feet, the water rising to her ankles, her knees, her waist, her neck, until only by standing on tiptoe, with frantic upturned face, can she breathe. One mercy alone seems vouchsafed to her: the water has lost its deadly chill. Nay, it is getting distinctly warm, even hot—hotter—*scalding!* Immortal Powers it is BOILING; and what a moment ago was a beautiful English girl, in the first exquisite budding of her beautiful womanhood, is now but a boilerful of soup, and in another moment will be a condenserful of low-pressure steam. I must congratulate Mrs. Raleigh on the courage with which she hurled this terrible word-picture at a house half white with its purgation by pity and terror, and half red with a voiceless, apoplectic laughter. Need I describe the following scene in the stokehold ("stokehole," it appears, is a solecism)—how the order comes to fill the boiler; how the comic sailor, in shutting the manhole thereof, catches sight of the white finger of the captain's young lady; how the matadoress in disguise comes in, and has all but turned on the boiling water when the comic sailor disables the tap by a mighty blow from a sledge-hammer; how he rushes away to tell the captain of his discovery; how in his absence the fires are lighted and the cold water turned on; and how at the last moment the captain dashes in, shouting "Draw the fires from No. 7" (the heroine is in No. 7), rushes up the ladder to the manhole, and drags out the heroine safe and sound, without a smudge on her face or a crumple in her pretty white frock, amid the delirious cheers of an audience which contemplates the descending curtain as men who have eaten of the insane root that takes the reason prisoner. Many more terrors does that melodrama contain, including the public drowning of the matadoress like a rat in a trap, but nothing quite so novel as the boiling scene. The last act degenerates into mere ordinary blood and thunder, only relieved by the touching acting of Mr. Rignold on becoming suddenly penetrated, for no mortal reason that anybody can discover, with a sense of his own unworthiness and the nobility of his donkey of a captain, who, though a sufficiently handsome and pleasant fellow, displays just ability enough to justify a steamboat company in trusting him, under the guidance of an intelligent boy, with the sale of tickets for a Thames steamer. Mr. Rignold, however, is not the man to allow himself to be bereaved of a bit of acting by the absence of any motive for it. He has the only real part in the play: and he makes the most of it to the end.

Nearly thirty actors and actresses, most of them capable

and vigorous people with more or less distinct stage talents, are provided with salaries by this melodrama. They have for the most part about as much to do as the hundreds of painted spectators in the first scene (which I forgot to mention, as it is only a bullfight). Mr. Bucklaw, as the gallant, but brainless, captain, showed that he only needs to smarten himself a little—mostly in the way of enunciating his consonants—to become popular in such parts. Miss Laura Graves was irresistible as the parboiled heroine, being powerfully aided by the fact that the authors of the dialogue have thoroughly mastered the great Shakespearean secret of always making the woman woo the man. In actual life there is no point upon which individuals vary more widely than in the effect of publicity on the demonstrativeness of their affections. Some people would rather die than offer or receive the slightest endearment with any one looking on. Others are stimulated to exceptional ardor by the presence of an audience; and it is a tragic fact that these diverse temperaments are rather apt to attract one another. The shy, conscious man whose impulsive and warmhearted wife *will* caress him before a roomful of people, and the fastidious reticent woman whose husband's attitude is openly and blubberingly amorous, are familiar figures in our civilization. But I cannot recall on the stage any *ingénue* quite so reckless under the sway of the tenderer emotions as the one played by Miss Laura Graves. On all public occasions she positively showers kisses on the objects of her attachment. One wonders what a French audience would think of her. It is only when she is alone with the captain in his cabin that she subsides into something like the customary reserve of the bright and beautiful English girls of whom she is offered as an authentic type. The maid is hardly behind her mistress in respect of her indifference to publicity; but she does not take the initiative—is, in fact, more kissed against than kissing—the effect being so much worse that nobody less clever than Miss Kate Phillips could make the part popular. As it is, I congratulate the part on Miss Phillips, without in any way congratulating Miss Phillips on the part.

One of the humors of the piece is that the three stowaway ladies never enter twice in the same costume. They change as freely as if Worth had a branch establishment on board. The fact that this gross impossibility does not interfere in the least with the illusion (such as it is) of the drama is an illustration of the fact that melodramatic stage illusion is not an illusion of real life, but an illusion of the embodiment of our romantic imaginings. If melodramatists would only grasp this fact, they would save themselves a good deal of trouble and their audiences a good deal of boredom. Half the explanations and contrivances with which they burden their pieces are superfluous attempts to persuade the audience to accept, as reasonably brought about, situations which it is perfectly ready to accept without any bringing about whatever. The second-rate dramatist always begins at the beginning of his play; the first-rate one begins in the middle; and the genius—Ibsen, for instance—begins at the end. Nothing is odder about "True Blue" than the way in which the same authors who heroically disregard the commonest physical possibilities in the matter of boilers and millinery, timidly and superstitiously waste half the first and second acts in useless explanations of the villain's designs. The thousands of fiery Spaniards waiting for the bull to appear in the ring are repeatedly supposed to sit in respectful silence for five minutes at a stretch whilst the first and second villains stroll into the arena to discuss at great length the political situation which has led to the presence of a British cruiser at Gibraltar (as if that were the most improbable place for it in the world), and which renders it desirable, from their own point of view, that the cruiser should be sunk. Even if these explanations were intelligible or plausible, they would only waste time: as it is, they are stupid.

In looking over one or two criticisms of "True Blue" I have been astonished to find the writers complaining that there is too much realism and too little melodrama in it. When a man who has just been regaled on boiled heroine asks for more, it is only good manners to congratulate him on his appetite; but it is also well to point out that he has not the public on his side. The really entertaining part of "True Blue" is Lieutenant Stuart Gordon's part. The cooking of Alice Marjoribanks is only funny as a bogus monstrosity at a fair is funny; but the weighing of the anchor is both interesting and exciting. It is true that the interest is not strictly dramatic: it is the sort of interest that makes people visit a man-of-war at Portsmouth; but then this is the very sort of interest to which "True Blue" is addressed. The fact that I did not catch half the expository dialogue in the first act did not disappoint me in the least—quite the contrary; but I deeply resented the gruff unintelligibility of the orders by which the anchor-weighing process was directed, as I really wanted to know about that. What "True Blue" wants is more of the fresh naval routine, and less of the stale melodramatic routine. Why not allow the captain to descry the Venezuelan fleet on the horizon, and give us the process of preparing for action? Why not display in the third act a more interesting section of the ship, showing us both above and between decks? Why allow the catastrophe to be brought about by an impossible valet lamely rubbing out the pencil-marks on the captain's chart with a piece of india-rubber, instead of by a torpedo, or a hundred-ton projectile from the enemy, or—if the maximum of probability is preferable—a collision with some other British cruiser? I am convinced, with all respect to the contrary opinion of some of my colleagues, that in this play Lieutenant Gordon worked on the right lines, and his melodramatist collaborators on the wrong ones. The play is emphatically not the thing at the Olympic; and that is precisely why "True Blue" is better worth seeing than most exhibitions of its class.

MARY ANDERSON

A Few Memories. By Mary Anderson (Madame de Navarro). London: Osgood, McIlvaine & Co. 1896.

THIS book is an actress's confession: consequently I should not, under ordinary circumstances, dream of believing a word of it. Nevertheless I do believe it, because I cannot find the actress in it any more than I was ever able to find her in the Mary Anderson who danced down to the Lyceum footlights like "a wave o' the sea" nearly ten years ago. What I do find is a strong-minded, clever, intelligent, self-reliant, and self-respectful girl whose hobby was Shakespeare. The statement that Mary Anderson was no actress is one which I am prepared to make, but not to defend. If I meet an American tourist who is greatly impressed with the works of Raphael, Kaulbach, Delaroche, and Barry, and I, with

372

Titian and Velasquez in my mind, tell him that not one of his four heroes was a real painter, I am no doubt putting my case absurdly; but I am not talking nonsense for all that: indeed to the adept seer of pictures I am only formulating a commonplace in an irritatingly ill-considered way. But in this world if you do not say a thing in an irritating way, you may just as well not say it at all, since nobody will trouble themselves about anything that does not trouble them. The attention given to a criticism is in direct proportion to its indigestibility; and I therefore say boldly that Mary Anderson was no actress. In no page of these Memories can you find any trace of the actress's temperament. Mary Anderson is essentially a woman of principle, which the actress essentially is not: the notion that all bravery, loyalty, and self-respect depend on a lawless and fearless following of the affectionate impulses—which is the characteristic morality of the artist, especially the woman artist of the stage—is, to her, simple immorality. The actress lives only to give herself away so that she may gain the love of the whole world: Mary Anderson, asking what it shall profit her to gain the whole world if she loses her own soul, retires or rather recoils from the stage before her apprenticeship is over, because she cannot gratify her love of Shakespeare and rhetoric without giving herself away to the public nightly to be stared at. To her this grudging of herself is a virtue —an element of strength of character: it vanquishes her stage-craze finally because she does not see that a woman with the fit genius can do nothing better for the world than make this sacrifice to it. The full justification of such a sacrifice—the power to become thereby the mother of the world's noblest sympathies and deepest feelings— cannot convince her: it is perceived by her reason as a duty, an excuse, and (when performed and done with) a consolation; but it does not glow at her heart as a passion and a fulfilment. The individualist in her triumphs in the end: the inner mandate which she finally obeys is "Individual, perfect thyself," which finally triumphs over all other mandates—over "Artist, perfect thy work," and "Woman, help thy kind." Here is her whole confession on the subject:—

"While on my way to England I could not help reviewing the eight years I had just finished. The retrospect brought as much pain as pleasure. The chief good my work had accomplished, I felt, was the assurance, verbally and by letter, from many young men and women, that the examples of such characters as Parthenia, Ion, and Evadne, in particular, had helped them in their daily lives and strengthened them in moments of despondency and temptation. Their gratitude to me, as the humble exponent of these *rôles,* was my most valued applause; for it proved that, in a measure, I had fulfilled the vocation, so long ago dreamed of, in undertaking a dramatic career. My efforts had, as a rule, been successful; but the strain of constant travel, the absence of home comforts in the ever-changing hotels, the responsibility of rehearsals, support, stage-management, and, above all, the extreme publicity of the life, had already begun to be distasteful to me. The disappointments connected with the art itself —the painting one's pictures with one's own person, in the full gaze of the public, the dependence upon inartistic people (often compelled to use the theatre as a trade) for carrying out the most cherished conceptions, and the constant crumbling of ideals—made me, young as I was, long to leave the stage for the peace and privacy of domestic life. I had a greater desire than ever to work, but away from the direct eye of the public. The life of a poet, composer, writer, or painter seemed ideal; for they could express their innermost thoughts through the impersonal mediums of canvas, music, literature, and still be protected by that privacy which is so dear to most women."

Here you have the whole position: the cold sense of duty steadily weakening instead of warming from its first record in her autobiography as the mere priggishness of a stage-struck schoolgirl to her retirement, and the conception of musicians and poets as exceptionally private persons minding their own innermost business in a vacuum, instead of strenuously throwing themselves into the most yearning and vital intercourse with humanity. Here is a passage which will drive home, as no comment of mine could, the absolute *deadness* of Mary Anderson's conception of artistic beauty:—"I remember a visit to the studio of one of the most prominent French sculptors in Paris. After seeing everything in both of the huge ateliers, Lord Lytton, a singularly able critic in all matters artistic, suggested a visit to the Morgue as a means of driving from our minds the hideous creations we had seen. We gladly assented; and, indeed, the three or four figures we saw there were far more beautiful, with the calm majesty of death upon them, than any of the representations of life we had seen in the studio."

The really compelling mandate which sent Madame de Navarro forth on her career seems to have been "Mary: be not thyself, but somebody out of Shakespeare," conditioned only by an inexorable resolution to be first or nowhere. When she was an unknown country girl of sixteen she managed to induce John McCullough to visit her family. On hearing her spout her favorite bits of Shake-

speare, he had the enormous good-nature to offer to allow her to try her hand on the stage as Lady Anne in
"Richard III." "I answered," this "humble exponent"
tells us (with a full sense of the humor of her audacity),
"that I would rather not play second fiddle, even to him."
It was magnificent; and she lived up to it and went
through with it. The position she wanted to begin with
(in her teens) was that of Mrs. Siddons. It is useless to
gasp at such presumption; for she got what she demanded. She knew that it was childish to cry for the
moon; so she simply said, with quiet dignity, "Be good
enough to take that moon down from its nail and hand it
to me." Which was accordingly done. The world which
once sent Mrs. Siddons back to the provinces as a failure
prostrated itself like a doormat to kiss the feet of Our
Mary.

It may be said that this success was nothing more than
the vogue of a very pretty woman; but Mary Anderson
was neither the only pretty woman who wanted to be
Mrs. Siddons nor the prettiest. The live statue of Galatea
was a most graceful ornament, no doubt; but it was a
statue for all that; and the public neither cares nor dares
to fall in love with statues. No: "Our Mary" was not a
beauty merely: she was an ideal. We made a type of her,
just as we made a type of Mr. Gladstone; and though the
type was the work of our imagination, and Miss Anderson
was no more our ideal Mary than Mr. Gladstone is our
ideal Grand Old Man, yet it was a certain force and integrity of character in themselves that led to their being
selected for idealization. There is plenty of other evidence of this force of character in Madame de Navarro's
book. She could work; she could endure; she had a way
and a will of her own; she could plan and execute enter-

prizes; she could make friends and hold her own among the ablest people of her day; she was sensible and respectable in business and conduct (an extraordinarily rare thing both on and off the stage); she was normal, popular, and intelligible in her methods and ambition; and, being young, she exercised her qualities without the oppressive and sometimes dangerous knowledge of their power which comes with years and with the discovery of the comparative infirmity of the rest of the world. A strong, proud, positive character of this kind, enhanced by a fine person, lends to declamation and rhetoric, but not to sympathetic acting. Its jealous reserve, its reluctance to wear its heart on its sleeve, its very superiorities to the passions and frailties, the humilities, confessions, and renunciations of the truly poetic drama, which has for its material the instictive human creature rather than the moralist and reasoner, disqualify it for the stage, except when the business in hand is rhetorical blank verse in five acts. "Seldom during my stage life," says Madame de Navarro, "have I ever been able to say of any performance, 'That is my best work.' In all my years before the public, I have only once been satisfied with my acting of Bianca, once in Ion, never in Perdita, and only once in Hermione." With this must be taken many other passages in her book, showing her strong preference of rhetorical and intellectual parts to sympathetic ones, even when both were by Shakespeare; her enthusiasm for stage antiquaries like Talfourd and Taylor; and her antipathy to the modern dramatists whose Heddas and Noras are making short work of the declamatory statue heroines. Her final criticism on herself, of course, is her retirement from the stage before she had reached the prime of life, or attained that rich and

spirited middle period of artistic development which succeeds the efforts of the ambitious apprentice. The reason
she gives is significant enough. "Many and great in-
ducements," she says, "have since been frequently offered
me to act again; but

> 'Il en coûte trop cher pour briller dans le monde.
> Combien je vais aimer ma retraite profonde!
> Pour vivre heureux, vivons cachés.' "

Note how she assumes, this girl who thinks she has
been an artist, that the object of going on the stage is
to sparkle in the world, and that the object of life is
happiness! After all, despite her character and force,
one sees that Our Mary has never grown up—that Galatea has never been awakened. I cannot help wondering
what would happen if she were. The other day, in a
discussion as to the best way of casting Ibsen's "Little
Eyolf," a question arose as to who should play the part
of Asta, failing the co-operation of some tried exponent
of Ibsen. I said, "Why not Mary Anderson?" I could
not persuade any one that I was serious. And yet, why
not? Madame de Navarro has declaimed, spouted, stat-
uesqued, Shakespeared, and all the rest of it, to the height
of her girlish ambition. She has also for seven years
"lived hidden." Why should she not now try real acting,
if only as a novelty? May not the publication of this
book be taken as a sign that the charms that sages have
seen in the face of seclusion are palling? It is true that
Madame de Navarro says—and carries conviction when
she says—"I am content to be forgotten, except by such
friends as I hope will always keep a place for me in their
hearts (a rather large exception, considering that these
friends include the playgoing public of England and

America). But it seems to me reasonable to believe that my experience may be of some service to those who have, or think they have, an aptitude for acting. I have written these pages more for young girls, who may have the same ambitions that I had, than for any one else; to show them that all that glitters is not gold; and thus to do a little towards making them realize how serious an undertaking it is to adopt a life so full of hardships, humiliations, and dangers." This explains, and very honorably explains, a great part of the book; but where do those charming portraits come in? What moral are the young girls to draw from the profile drawing by F. D. Millet, the sketch in oils by Mr. Watts, the adorable photograph of Mary at sixteen, Mr. Boughton's Pauline portrait picture, the half-length in Albanian costume, and the 1895 photograph, the most womanly and beautiful of them all? I flatly do not believe that this portrait is exhibited to warn young girls against the hardships and dangers of the stage: I believe it is there solely to make us go down on our knees and beg Our Mary to come back to us. Which I accordingly do, without reservation. I will never admit that the girl could act unless the woman makes me change my opinion.

The book contains many an interesting passage on which I have not space to expatiate. I may note hurriedly, but with much gratification, that Madame de Navarro's experience on several points supports views which I have often expressed in these columns. She precisely confirms all that I have urged against the old stationary stock companies; and she asks, as I have asked, why women do not try their hands at theatrical management. Her instructions how to baffle an actor-manager who gets you with your back to the footlights and talks down the stage at you should be studied by the whole company at the —Heavens! I all but let the name slip. The records of her very American searches after relics of Shakespeare and Dickens are quaint, and suggest, I regret to say, an almost inconceivable audacity of imposture on the part of those Britons who follow the industry of impersonating the originals of Dickens's characters and pointing out the houses mentioned in his novels. When she played Rosalind at Stratford-on-Avon, "the stage was decorated with blossoms from Shakespeare's garden; the flowers used by Rosalind and Celia, as well as the turnip gnawed by Audrey, had been plucked near Anne Hathaway's cottage; the deer carried across the stage in the hunting chorus had been shot in Charlcot Park for the occasion by one of the Lucys." Bless her innocence!

I close the book with its subject unexhausted, just as the author did. The life of the girl rhetorician is only the first volume. The second volume should be the life of a true dramatic artist. If Madame de Navarro will only live that volume, I, the critic, will gladly write it in these pages.

NIETZSCHE IN ENGLISH

Nietzsche contra Wagner, etc.: vol. 1 of the collected works of Friedrich Nietzsche. Translated by Thomas Common. London: Henry & Co. 1896.
A Mother of Three: a new and original farce in three acts. By Clo Graves. Comedy Theatre, 8 April, 1896.

I T IS with a most opportune consideration for my Easter holiday that Messrs. Henry & Co. have just issued the first volume of their translation of the works of Friedrich Nietzsche. And such a volume, too! containing everything that he wrote just before he reached the point at which Germany made up its mind that he was mad, and shut him up, both figuratively and actually. Whilst I am still at large I may as well explain that Nietzsche is a philosopher—that is to say, something unintelligible to an Englishman. To make my readers realize what a philosopher is, I can only say that *I* am a philosopher. If you ask incredulously, "How, then, are your articles so interesting?" I reply that there is nothing so interesting as philosophy, provided its materials are not spurious. For instance, take my own materials—humanity and the fine arts. Any studious, timorously ambitious book-worm can run away from the world with a few shelvesful of history, essays, descriptions, and criticisms, and, having pieced an illusory humanity and art out of the effects produced by his library on his imagination, build some silly systematization of his worthless ideas over the abyss of his own nescience. Such a philosopher is as dull and dry as you please: it is he who brings his profession into disrepute, especially when he talks much about art, and so persuades people to read him. Without having looked at more than fifty pictures in his life, or made up his mind on the smallest point about one of the fifty, he will audaciously take it upon himself to explain the development of painting from Zeuxis and Apelles to Raphael and Michael Angelo. As to the way he will go on about music, of which he always has an awe-stricken conceit, it spoils my temper to think of it, especially when one remembers that musical composition is taught (a monstrous pretension) in this country by people who *read* scores, and never by any chance listen to performances. Now, the right way to go to work—strange as it may appear—is to look at pictures until you have acquired the power of seeing them. If you look at several thousand good pictures every year, and form some sort of practical judgment about every one of them—were it only that it is not worth troubling over—then at the end of five years or so you will, if you have a wise eye, be able to see what is actually in a picture, and not what you think is in it. Similarly, if you listen critically to music every day for a number of years, you will, if you have a wise ear, acquire the power of hearing music. And so on with all the arts. When we come to humanity it is still the same: only by intercourse with men and women can we learn anything about it. This involves an active life, not a contemplative one; for unless you do something in the world, you can have no real business to transact with men; and unless you love and are loved, you can have no intimate relations with them. And you must transact business, wirepull politics, discuss religion, give and receive hate, love and friendship with all sorts of people before you can acquire the sense of humanity. If you are to acquire the sense sufficiently to be a philosopher, you must do all these things unconditionally. You must not say that you will be a gentleman and limit your intercourse to this class or that class; or that you will be a virtuous person and generalize about the affections from a single instance—unless, indeed, you have the rare happiness to stumble at first upon an all-enlightening instance. You must have no convictions, because as Nietzsche puts it, "convictions are prisons." Thus, I blush to add, you cannot be a philosopher and a good man, though you may be a philosopher and a great one. You will say, perhaps, that if this be so, there should be no philosophers; and perhaps you are right; but though I make you this handsome concession, I do not defer to you to the extent of ceasing to exist. After all, if you insist on the hangman, whose pursuits are far from elevating, you may very well tolerate the philosopher, even if philosophy involves philandering; or, to put it another way, if, in spite of your hangman, you tolerate murder within the sphere of war, it may be necessary to tolerate comparatively venial irregularities within the sphere of philosophy. It is the price of progress; and, after all, it is the philosopher, and not you, who will burn for it.

These are shocking sentiments, I know; but I assure you you will think them mere Sunday School commonplaces when you have read a little of Nietzsche. Nietzsche is worse than shocking, he is simply awful: his epigrams are written with phosphorus on brimstone. The only excuse for reading them is that before long you must be prepared either to talk about Nietzsche or else retire from society, especially from aristocratically minded society (not the same thing, by the way, as aristocratic society), since Nietzsche is the champion of privilege, of power, and of inequality. Famous as Nietzsche has become—he has had a great *succès de scandale* to advertise his penetrating wit—I never heard of him until a few years ago, when, on the occasion of my contributing to the literature of philosophy a minute treatise entitled "The Quintessence of Ibsenism," I was asked whether I had not been inspired by a book called "Out at the other side of Good and Evil," by Nietzsche. The title seemed to me promising; and in fact Nietzsche's criticism of morality and idealism is essentially that demonstrated in my books as at the bottom of Ibsen's plays. His pungency; his power of putting the merest platitudes of his position in rousing, startling paradoxes; his way of getting underneath moral precepts which are so unquestionable to us that common decency seems to compel unhesitating assent to them, and upsetting them with a scornful laugh: all this is easy to a witty man who has once well learnt Schopenhauer's lesson, that the intellect by itself is a mere dead piece of brain machinery, and our ethical and moral systems merely the pierced cards you stick into it when you want it to play a certain tune. So far I am on common ground with Nietzsche. But not for a moment will I suffer any one to compare me to him as a critic. Never was there a deafer, blinder, socially and politically inepter academician. He has fancies concerning different periods of history, idealizing the Romans and the Renaissance, and deducting from his idealization no end of excellences in their works. When have I ever been guilty of such professorial folly? I simply go and look at their works, and after that you may talk to me until you go black in the face about their being such wonderful fellows: I know by my

senses they were as bad artists, and as arrant intel-
lect-mongers, as need be. And what can you say to a
man who, after pitting his philosophy against Wagner's
with refreshing ingenuity and force, proceeds to hold
up as the masterpiece of modern dramatic music, blazing
with the merits which the Wagnerian music dramas lack
—guess what! "Don Giovanni," perhaps, or "Orfeo,"
or "Fidelio"? Not at all: "Carmen," no less. Yes, as
I live by bread, as I made that bread for many a year
by listening to music, Georges Bizet's "Carmen." After
this one is not surprised to find Nietzsche blundering over
politics, and social organization and administration in
a way that would be impossible to a man who had ever
served on a genuine working committee long enough—
say ten minutes—to find out how very little attention the
exigencies of practical action can be made to pay to our
theories when we have to get things done, one way or
another. To him modern Democracy, Pauline Christianity, Socialism, and so on are deliberate plots hatched by
malignant philosophers to frustrate the evolution of the
human race and mass the stupidity and brute force of
the many weak against the beneficial tyranny of the few
strong. This is not even a point of view: it is an absolutely fictitious hypothesis: it would not be worth reading were it not that there is almost as much evidence for
it as if it were true, and that it leads Nietzsche to produce some new and very striking and suggestive combinations of ideas. In short, his sallies, petulant and impossible as some of them are, are the work of a rare spirit
and are pregnant with its vitality. It is notable that
Nietzsche does not write in chapters or treatises: he
writes leading articles, leaderettes, occasional notes, and
epigrams. He recognizes that humanity, having tasted

the art of the journalist, will no longer suffer men to inflict books on it. And he simplifies matters, quite in the manner of the leading article writer, by ignoring things as they are, and dealing with things as it is easiest, with our prejudices and training, to think they are, except that he supplies the training and instils the prejudices himself as he goes along, instead of picking up those that lie about the street as one does in writing leaders for the daily press.

There are two reasons why I can say no more than this about Nietzsche. The first is that I am lying on a hillside in the sun, basking, not working. The second is that I must reserve some space for Miss Clo Graves's "Mother of Three" at the Comedy, which has plucked me up from that hillside by the roots.

Miss Graves has somewhat obscured my justification for introducing Nietzsche in a column devoted to the drama. That justification, of course, is that though plays have neither political constitutions nor established churches, they must all, if they are to be anything more than the merest tissue of stage effects, have a philosophy, even if it be no more than an unconscious expression of the author's temperament. Your great dramatist philosophizes quite openly: his lines become famous as aphorisms, and serve in the intercourse of philosophers as words serve in the intercourse of ordinary mortals. All the philosophers who are really alive nowadays maintain intimate relations with the fine arts: Schopenhauer and Nietzsche belong as inevitably to the critic's library as Goethe and Wagner. But I am bound to say that there is not much philosophy in Miss Clo Graves's play. However, there is plenty of fun in it, and in that fun there lurks occasionally a certain sense of the humor of indecency which drives me to conclude that Miss Clo Graves is an Irish lady. The Irish have a natural delicacy which gives them a very keen sense of indelicacy; and a good deal of the humors of "A Mother of Three" betrays the countrywoman of Sheridan and Swift rather than of Mr. Pinero. To this I can make no effective objection, since we maintain a Censor to prevent questions of sex and parentage being treated properly and seriously on the stage, and to license their improper and flippant treatment, which is at least more tolerable than no treatment of them at all. Miss Graves, struck, no doubt, by the success of "Charlie's Aunt" and "The Strange Adventures of Miss Brown," in which the main joke is the dressing up of a man as a woman, has tried the effect of dressing up a woman as a man. The effect was rather unexpected. Miss Fanny Brough, whose comic force in parts belonging to her own sex no one can deny, no sooner changed her skirt for a pair of shepherd's plaid trousers and a frock coat than she suddenly became quite genuinely tragic. I have never seen the peculiar tragic feeling of impending catastrophe more unmistakably produced than in the second act, where Miss Brough, provoking roar after roar of not very refined laughter by the delivery of lines which she drove home, apparently in spite of herself, with the deadliest cleverness, seemed to be torn by a cumulative agony of rage and shame. This had so nearly passed the limit of her endurance when the curtain fell, that when it rose again for a moment in response to the applause, she seemed to have nothing of her self-possession left, exvept a precarious remnant of the mere habit of it. I can only compare the effect to that of Salvini's closet scene in "Hamlet." That an artist capable of producing it should have been driven to do so in the wrong place by her revolt against such a heartless misuse of her powers as the thrusting of her into what can only be described, at best, as a not very decorous piece of buffoonery, is pitiful enough; but the incident will not have been altogether an unhappy one if it opens the eyes of our dramatists to the extent to which they have been wasting on mere farce a talent which evidently has a rare intensity of emotional force behind it. Perhaps I misunderstood Miss Brough, who may have been giving us a serious artistic study of Mrs. Murgatroyd's feelings, uninfluenced by any repugnance of her own to her part; but there can be no mistake as to the effect, which might even have upset the piece if the lines had been less funny.

The play has, as its chief merit, a sustained jocularity which keeps the audience laughing pretty continuously. A good deal of the stage business is frank burlesque; and the acts end, in a rather old-fashioned way, not at any period in the action, but at some climax of absurdity from which no other extrication is possible. But the play is by no means brainless; and it is astonishing how much this small mercy counts for in the theatre.

Miss Rose Leclercq, Miss Beringer, Mr. Cyril Maude, and Mr. Felix Morris are in the cast—more to its advantage than their own. The curtain-raiser is a piece called "The Guinea Stamp," by Mr. Cyril Hallward. It consists principally of cant, and is badly spoken and indifferently acted.

TWO EASTER PIECES

The Sin of St. Hulda: a new romantic drama. By
G. Stuart Ogilvie. Shaftesbury Theatre. 9 April,
1896.

Biarritz: a musical farce. By Jerome K. Jerome.
Lyrics by Adrian Ross. Music by F. Osmond Carr.
Prince of Wales Theatre. 11 April, 1896.

OUR managers owe so much to Mr. Stuart Ogilvie
that they can do no less than occasionally produce, presumably at his own expense, dramas
of his which I feel they would hardly accept from me.
But it is not altogether a misfortune that these works
are produced to please Mr. Ogilvie rather than to please
the public; since no manager, however cynical, would
attribute to Mr. Ogilvie or any other individual fellow-
creature the depravity and silliness of taste which everybody ascribes as a matter of course to all their fellow-
creatures collectively. Nevertheless Mr. Ogilvie's plays
are to some extent the worse for his culture and his
independence. They have the defect of being second-
hand: that is to say, they have the unreality, and consequently the tediousness, of the images which the imagination produces when, instead of being solidly fed on
experience, it is merely excited by the contemplation of
other works of art. Nobody can sit out "The Sin of St.
Hulda" without seeing that Mr. Ogilvie has read dramas
and romances, has looked at pictures, and listened to
operas. But it is equally clear that he has never met a
real St. Hulda in his life. He may here ask me sarcas-
tically whether *I* have ever met one—whether they grow
on every bush for dramatists to study. I reply, un-

abashed, "In London, yes." The nearest Salvation Army
barrack or London Mission will supply half a dozen
saints of infinitely greater sanctity and heroism than the
waxwork angel whom Miss Kate Rorke impersonates at
the Shaftesbury. The education movement, the hospital nursing movement, and all the movements for the
realization of religion in social reform have been largely
the work of women of heroic devotion and sometimes of
extraordinary eloquence, many of them alive and accessible to anybody who sincerely wishes to understand
themselves and their work. They present to the dramatist's study temperaments rich in the passionate qualities, and personal histories rich in the struggles and
braveries, which are the material of tragedy; whilst their
characters positively sparkle with the incongruities and
ironies and contradictions which are the life of comedy.
Among our dramatists, Mr. Henry Arthur Jones alone
seems capable of realizing the existence of these masses
of dramatic material lying ready to his hand. Mr. Pinero,
in "The Notorious Mrs. Ebbsmith," hardly got beyond
certain irresolute recollections of newspaper notices of
"platform women"; and it is clear that Mr. Ogilvie does
not even read the newspapers because they are not written in blank verse. He holds up a blurred mirror to the
librettos of Meyerbeer's "historical" operas, and would
like, one guesses, to make the stage affect the audience
as the pictures of Delaroche and Gérome have affected
him. This method—the method of bringing a reaping
machine to glean a crop from a field after the harvest—is
barren: great writers—Sir Walter Scott, for instance—
may have amused themselves with it sometimes; but its
results are counted among their exercises or follies, not
among their masterpieces. If Mr. Ogilvie finds that he

is only affected by works of art, he may at once give up
all hope of producing them; for this is the characteristic
stigma (I thank thee, Max, for teaching me that word)
of the born amateur. If, on the other hand, he is affected
by real life, then the sooner he sets about representing
it at first hand in his dramas the better. For I think
there is not much of it in "The Sin of St. Hulda." I say
I think, because to a good deal of the play I did not
listen. I cannot defend this negligence, or deny that it
was my business—my paid business—to listen to every
word; but I could by no means achieve it. The blank
verse flowed in at one ear and out at the other without
producing any sort of activity between the two. I collapsed in this way more especially when St. Hulda was
on the stage. St. Hulda is a combination of Delaroche's
"Christian Martyr" with the "Woman with a Past."
She is herself incommoded by the incongruity, and wants
to confess, but will not come to the point because she
has to save her secret up for the last act—a miserly and
evasive policy, exasperating from the dramatic point of
view. She proves, I am afraid, that Mr. Ogilvie has a
chivalrous imagination, which is the sort of imagination
that never produces a real woman. Not that the men
are much more real; but they presume less on their unreality, and are consequently less tedious. They all begin with a considerable air of becoming important presently—so considerable, in fact, that it was quite late in
the evening before I finally despaired of them. Prince
Otho in particular was a rare impostor in this way. In
spite of his rather Tappertitian beginning by making a
haughty noble who had formerly insulted him publicly
clean his boots, he kept up appearances long after I had
given up Heinrich, Knipperdolling, and Manteuffel (a

walking gentleman who entered as is he were going to eclipse Louis XI. and Richard III.) as men of straw. In this he was powerfully abetted by his impersonator, Mr. Cartwright, who seems to possess stage temperament and susceptibility to an extraordinary degree without any backing to them. He sometimes makes clever—even delicate—strokes by instinct; and his staginess is not altogether unoriginal; but he seems unable to connect any of the things he can do with any definite conception of character. Mr. Kemble almost made a part out of the Burgomaster: as it was, he certainly made a picture of him. Mr. Lewis Waller, as Heinrich, apparently shared my opinion of St. Hulda; for he was as cool a lover as ever I saw, taking the lady's death with a Christian resignation which belied the lamenting lines he had to utter. Here, as in the second act of "A Woman's Reason," he seemed quite disabled, when the moment came for a display of pitiable abandonment, by his own dignity and good sense. But in the prouder passages he played with unexpected force, and in the climax to the third act rose fully to the situation, and struck in his defiance of Otho up to the hilt. Nobody would have recognized in this bold and handsome young mediaeval knight the sentimental leading man struggling with his tailor, with whom Mr. Waller's admirers have hitherto been familiar.

Miss Kate Rorke did what all experienced and competent actresses do when they have a great many blank-verse lines to deliver, and no part. She fell back on her style. It was all very intelligent, and very musical, and very plastic; and it had a certain technical interest, just as Mme. Patti practising her scales would have had. But there was a great deal too much of it; and I have rarely experienced a more refreshing relief than when, on the company being called on the stage to receive applause at the end, Miss Rorke smiled quite naturally, and beckoned to Mr. Ogilvie to come forward. That little touch of sincerity gave away all the rest of her performance, revealing its utter formality in a flash.

The play would, I am afraid, be rather dull if it were not for a certain operatic fire which serves Mr. Ogilvie for solid Shakespearean power. Heinrich standing fascinated by the vision of St. Hulda at the end of Act I., Otho's Mephistophelean laugh at the end of Act II., St. Hulda's denial at the end of Act III., and the apotheosis at the end of Act IV. are all operatic, and all as effective in that way as they can be without music. The sword combat, in which Mr. Cartwright inadvertently nearly clove Mr. Waller in twain, and the death of the heroine, are in the same taste. The costumiers have made the most of the swaggering hats and plumes, puffs and slashes, square-toed shoes and two-handled swords, which we know from Holbein and Dürer; but the result is handsome and "historical" rather than artistic. The fact that Miss Rorke's saintly dresses are too Victorian to be interesting, and that three of the four scenes are German interiors, the open-air one being dark, crowded, and very artificially lighted for the sake of Miss Rorke's halo, produces a certain heaviness of effect. A dramatist should never forget that plays want plenty of fresh air. Half the charm of "For the Crown," the success of which has probably helped to smooth the way for "St. Hulda," lies in its liberal supply of mountain ozone.

I have rarely seen an audience so unanimous as that which crowded to witness the first representation of "Biarritz" at the Prince of Wales Theatre It was unanimous in hope at the beginning, unanimous in doubt in the middle, and unanimous in derision at the end. "Biarritz" is sure to run triumphantly for several years, since nothing but the substitution of "special features" for every five minutes of the original work, and their frequent renewal, involving the conversion of the whole into a variety entertainment, could possibly keep it in existence for a fortnight. What Mr. Jerome K. Jerome was thinking of when he wrote it is hard to imagine; but he has written to the papers promising to explain everything when the worst is over. As to Mr. Lowenfeld, he appears to have been exercising his judgment, with the usual result. The only promising idea in the piece from the Prince of Wales Theatre point of view, is the placing of the scene in a hotel. This gives openings for those sallies of schoolboyish blackguardism which are supposed to throw a spell of fascinating wickedness round the "musical farces" which serve as a setting to the jewel of Mr. Arthur Roberts's talent. Thus an old gentleman, having, like Mr. Pickwick on a celebrated occasion, lost his room and forgotten its number, wanders about in his dressing-gown asking everybody for his wife; and when he is at last taken upstairs by a chambermaid, a knowing laugh cackles up from the young gentlemen who think they know what large Continental hotels and their chambermaids are—never having been in one. When every obvious and uninteresting variation on this is exhausted, Mr. Roberts comes to the rescue with a song, in which he describes how he met in Piccadilly a woman who lived in St. John's Wood as somebody's mistress; how he accosted her; what he gave her for supper; and how he went to St. John's Wood with her. The story was much less interesting than an ordinary police case;

but when Mr. Roberts had sung it, the audience seemed proud of him, and he seemed proud of himself. He also made mirth by his manner of beginning his conversations with women by the remark, "Where have I seen you before?" which is understood to be the formula by which gentlemen in the Empire Theatre promenade get over the embarrassment of addressing ladies to whom they have not been formally introduced. I confess I found this desperately dull. Witty things can be said by witty people about prostitution, as about any other subject; but prostitution is not a merry subject in itself—rather the reverse. For the rest, Mr. Roberts gabbled, and dropped his aitches, and got from one of his favorite points to another anyhow, not thinking his audience worth the trouble of maintaining any style or taking any care. Naturally, a comedian who has no great respect for himself has none for the public who encourage him. However, I have no right to preach at Mr. Roberts: all I am entitled to say is that I am tired of his mannerisms and that his Leicester Square pleasantries bore and offend me.

If "Faith, creating what it feigned" (a Shelleyan motto prefixed by Mr. Ogilvie to "St. Hulda") broke down in the case of a favorite like Mr. Roberts, who has talent enough to fall back on acting as a means of livelihood when the public begins to tire of his present occupation, it need hardly be said that his colleagues were not more fortunate. I appreciate the brightness and determination with which Miss Kitty Loftus asserts herself as "a jolly little folly" (so Mr. Ross expresses it), with uncommon gifts as a dancer, singer, and speaker; and as soon as I am fortunate enough to find her dancing a single step, singing a single note, or speaking a single line, in a really uncommon way, I shall admit her pretensions and renounce my present heresy, which is, that Miss Kitty Loftus is a vivacious young lady who works very hard at being gay and pretty without knowing exactly how artists manage such things. Miss Phyllis Broughton dances her old dance, smiles her old smile, and sauces her old sauciness with her old success as if they and she had been invented yesterday. Miss Sadie Jerome, in attempting to repeat the success of her Lalage Potts song, only betrays the fact that she has gained nothing by her appearance in "Gentleman Joe" but a relapse into amateurishness. Miss Millie Hylton maintains a certain degree of artistic form, playing a trivial part prettily enough. Some of the other ladies on the stage have no artistic business there at all. Why are there so many mannerless girls, graceless girls, silly girls, impudent girls, and girls condemned to hopeless ugliness by having to wear trousers with jackets cut to fit waists like corset advertisements—a stupidity that would make Psyche herself unpresentable? I object to all these austerities: I am voluptuary enough to like nice girls, interesting girls, well-dressed and well-grouped girls; and I conceive the duties of a manager as including the selection and engagement of such girls and no others. Two minutes of "Biarritz" would reconcile a Trappist to his monastery for life.

The best part of the entertainment is Mr. Osmond Carr's music—mere stereo, no doubt, much of it, but smart, appropriate stereo. A few of the numbers are pretty and musically witty. And the music has been thoroughly well got up by Mr. Herbert Bunning, who handles the band excellently.

PUNCH AND JUDY AGAIN

The Rogue's Comedy: a play in three acts. By Henry Arthur Jones. Garrick Theatre. 21 April, 1896.

A SAFE rule for the dramatist is, "When in doubt, revive Punch and Judy." Mr. Henry Arthur Jones is not in doubt; but he is in dudgeon— not peevish personal dudgeon, but artistic, philosophic dudgeon, inevitable after the unnatural death of "Michael and His Lost Angel." Accordingly, he has fallen back on Punch and Judy, the eternal rogue's comedy, tempting the business dramatist by its assured popularity, and fascinating the artist dramatist by its unlimited depth, which yet involves no obligation to fully fathom it or else fail. Success is safe at any depth, from an inch downwards. At the street corner, with a deplorable Judy, an infant thrown out of the window, a dog Toby, and a few assorted types of law and order culminating in a hangman and a devil, the great issues of the comedy can be ribaldly touched to the music of pipes and drum. At the other end of the range, Mozart's "Don Giovanni," the world's masterpiece in stage art, is only Punch on a higher plane. Every brace of vagabonds can master and perform the one; the greatest artists in the world can, at their best, only bungle through the other. Between the two lies all philosophic comedy, high and low, with its Faustuses, its Robert Macaires, its Affable Hawks, its Jeremy Diddlers, its common Joeys with red-hot poker and sausages, its Pierrots, and, since last Tuesday night, its Mr. Bailey Prothero. The first question about him, then, is as to which of his ancestors in the great family of Punch's reincarnations he most resembles. Not that rare bird the Mozartian Don assuredly. It is true that Bailey drinks four glasses of champagne, and "bucks up," as he expresses it, after them; but he cannot sing a pæan to the joy of life like "Finch' han dal vino," nor need our actors so miserably fail in catching his ecstasy as to drive any one to find a new mode of utterance for its wicked rapture through the mechanism of the most brilliant of instruments, as Liszt was driven in the Don's case. Bailey does not cut a figure in the high comedy region: his place is in melodramatic farce. This suggests Robert Macaire; and there is certainly a family resemblance; but as Robert was an entire and perfect scoundrel, and we cannot nowadays bear to damn any one, Bailey has been made a good husband and father. As a rascal redeemed by sentiment, he is more like that amiable young relative of the family, the Chevalier des Grieux, only older, coarser, and without Manon Lescaut. Instead of Manon, he has a lawful wife, so far like Mrs. Jerry Cruncher in "A Tale of Two Cities," that her habit of "flopping"—that is, kneeling down in prayer—jars on her husband. I do not think much of Mrs. Prothero. Her humanity is sacrificed to write up the actor-manager's part—a sacrifice of the eternal to the temporal. In the first act we see her enjoying an income of £80 a year and dressing like Mrs. Langtry on it, her dramatic function being to act as her husband's confederate in his fortune-telling business. Not until the second act does she develop a tender conscience; and even then she makes no difficulty about shutting it up tight at her husband's urgent request, herein departing from the example of Mrs. Cruncher, who braved boots and pokers rather than refrain from praying steadfastly against the success of Mr. Cruncher's illicit pursuits as a resurrection-man. When, in the third act, Judy Prothero allows Bailey to assure their son that of his mother, at least, he need never be ashamed, it is impossible not to revolt at the recollection of her active complicity in the duperies of the first act. It is all very well for Mr. Jones to set her to catch sympathy for Mr. Willard; but the plain truth is that she is just as bad as Bailey—worse, in fact, because she sets up religious pretensions to be morally superior to him whilst living on the profits of his swindling.

The characterization of the figures which surround Bailey Prothero does not go very deep. Of course Mr. Jones, with his fertile imagination and humorous observation, could no more miss individualizing a figure here and there than Dickens could. The most entertaining result of his powers in this way is Mr. Robert Cushing, who plays Bertrand to Prothero's Macaire so faithfully that when his unfortunate habit of purloining the spoons comes into play, the scene needs nothing but a creaking snuff-box in Mr. Willard's hands to take us back to the Auberge des Adrets at once. But the characterization is capital underneath the farce, and very funny. The wretch is so feeble that even his efforts to swear do not get beyond a fat, flat, twaddle-toned "Oh my goodness gracious!" The abject folly of his perfectly sound plea of "total loss of self-respect," and the helpless way in which he succumbs to every opportunity of doing wrong, even with the certainty of ignominious detection staring him in the face, not only make highly ticklesome buffoonery, but hit off in a few strokes the leading lines of a hopelessly ricketty and rotten moral constitution. Cushing is the best character in the play; and though he is only on the stage for a few minutes, I am not sure that Mr. Standing, who plays him to a miracle, is not luckier than Mr. Willard himself in his part. Another personage who is purely comic in his dramatic function, but yet individualized as a character type, is the silly-billy Lord Dovergreen, a little burlesqued by Mr. Sydney Brough, but not spoiled. Lord Bicester is also a vivid thumbnail sketch; and there is life in Miss Proye and Lambert the footman. These people not only say funny things, but say them with a genuine character modification—not a mere trick of phrase or manner. For all that, the play is not one of Mr. Jones's best. That part of the dialogue which is mere social chatter is not nearly so witty as the small talk in "The Masqueraders"; and as to the high comedy of "Rebellious Susan," it is quite out of sight. Some of the characters are downright bad: for instance, Lord John Bucklow is the hackneyed old stage roué—the "man of pleasure become a man of pain," as Charles Reade put it—with the hackneyed manner and make-up. Mr. David James, with his simperings, and his dammes, and his whistlings of the intervals of the common chord (as if that were a possible nervous trick), certainly acts him as badly as possible; but the part invites his abuse of it. Lady Clarabut, again, is nothing but a night's work for Lady Monckton; and the two lovers decorously carry on the story without stepping forward into any sort of individuality. In short, the leading characters are not characters at all, but only supports for Bailey Prothero. In a play by Mr. Grundy, or any other votary of the "well made" or mechanical rabbit play, I should not complain of this, since everybody knows that if a mechanical rabbit is to move, it must have wheels for entrails; but one expects living members from Mr. Jones. At all events,

one pays him the compliment of noticing the appearance
of automata among his characters as a thing not altogether to be expected. As to the character for which this
sacrifice has been made. I confess I should like, before
judging it finally, to see it played by a genuine comedian
—say Mr. Wyndham or Mr. Hare. Mr. Willard is a
good actor, but not of that kind. He begins with comic
"character acting" laid on in hearty and by no means
delicate strokes; and when the vein changes, he plunges,
without the slightest gradation, head over heels into
melodrama. His grip throughout is far too strenuous to
admit of dainty handling: he grinds out his words at a
clerically low pitch with a voice that has changes but no
inflexions, wedging his face into a mask that can be instantly rearranged for mirth or melancholy, but which
has no shades, and can therefore tell of moods and shocks,
but not of processes or fluctuations. The part presents
certain well-marked main aspects—the rogue at work,
the rogue triumphant, the rogue alarmed, the rogue reckless, the father wounded, the father tender, and the husband good-natured. These being patent and unmistakable, Mr. Willard seized on them vigorously enough;
but as each one recurred he treated it exactly as he had
treated it before, with a single facial expression and a
single tone; so that his performance resolved itself into
a repetition of some half-dozen effects, and would have
become monotonous but for the activity with which the
author kept the story going. In fact, it did become
monotonous, especially in the matter of voice, wherever
the author's pace slackened. Nevertheless it kept the
audience in good humor by its geniality and sustained
vigor; and in the final scene it had pathetic strength—
the final exit, with the shake-hands with the son and the

"Buck up, old girl" to the wife, was admirable; but of the subtle, continuous, exquisitely nuanced acting, apparently infinite in variety, which becomes classical in high comedy—such work as we have seen in Duse's Mirandolina, Coquelin's Duval, Hare's Baron Croodle, Charles Mathews's Mercadet, and Jefferson's farcical heroes—there was not a trace. It is true that the play itself, as I began by saying, is melodramatic farce rather than high comedy; but all the classical examples I have cited are examples of high comedians playing in farces. I should add that the character of Bailey Prothero is completely redeemed from the falseness and crudity of melodrama by many admirable touches, notably the absence of conventional exaggeration in the fatherly emotion, which is presented for exactly what it is worth by the author with an acute nicety that is also stealthily humorous. Fortunately, this is one of the points to which Mr. Willard's performance does justice.

Miss Oliffe, who played Mrs. Prothero, was new to the critics, though I had had the luck to discover her at the Avenue during the illness of Miss Alma Stanley some time ago. She deepened the favorable impression I received on that occasion, and will, I have no doubt, soon be a familiar and indispensable figure in our London casts. The end of that will be, I suppose, that she will give up acting, and have all her parts written expressly for her. Indeed, of the play as a whole I cannot say that it altogether escaped that rawness and uneasiness of presentation from which Mr. Jones's recent plays have suffered so frightfully, the truth being that the moment our actors are taken out of the routine parts which are merely the latest dramatizations, or rather stagings, of their own personal peculiarities—the moment, in short, they are called upon to impersonate new characters instead of being presented with old characters that impersonate them—they lose their style, and even their ease and assurance; so that Mr. Jones's originality is positively made a means of worrying the audience into a longing to get back to that familiar little world in which Mr. Sydney Brough makes love to Miss Maud Millett under the parental eyes of Miss Rose Leclercq and Mr. Cyril Maude, whilst some nice leading lady and gentleman give object lessons in fashionable dressing and polite courtship and marriage to the graduates of suburban society. This is the real explanation, I believe, of the fact that for some time past every play with any sort of originality in it has provoked three or four weak-souled first-nighters in the gallery to utter piteous howls on the appearance of the author at the fall of the curtain. Mr. Jones, having, not unnaturally, no sort of taste for deliberate and premeditated incivility, declined to make the customary appearance on Tuesday night. It took twenty-five minutes to convince the audience that he was in earnest. They cheered and called and applauded until they were physically exhausted; then stopped to recover, and returned to the charge again and again; then, as their numbers dwindled, intoned a long, melancholy note like the organ giving the diapason to the orchestra before an oratorio performance; then hooted dismally; and finally sang "We won't go home till morning," the strains of which, like Haydn's Farewell Symphony, died away as the performers stole away one by one and left the theatre empty. And then I went home too.

THE IMMORTAL WILLIAM

The Shakespeare Anniversary Celebration at the Metropole Theatre, Camberwell, 23 April, 1896.

WITHIN reason, I am always prepared to do honor to Shakespeare. Annual celebrations are all very well in theory, and are almost as popular with the people who don't take any part in them, and don't intend to, as Annual Parliaments are with the people who never vote and never electioneer; but outside that large circle they are too much of a good thing. I have long ceased to celebrate my own birthday; and I do not see why I should celebrate Shakespeare's. There can be no objection in the world to Mr. Benson, or Mr. Greet, or any one else in the Shakespearean business taking the fullest advantage of an anniversary to give that business a fillip; but whoever expects me to put myself every 23 April in an attitude at all differing from my attitude on the 23 October is doomed to disappointment. I went to Camberwell on the afternoon of last Thursday week because, on the whole, I thought it my business to be there; but when the Irving Dramatic Club wanted me to resume work the moment I got back to the West End by going to "Cymbeline" at St. George's Hall, I struck. Shakespeare is for an afternoon, but not for all time. Under ordinary circumstances I should have done the other thing—that is, gone to see the amateurs in the evening instead of the professionals in the afternoon; but it happened on this occasion that the professional cast was the fresher, younger, and more interesting of the two; so I went to Camberwell. Let me not, however, exaggerate my own virtue by leaving it to be inferred that I got there in time. The hour appointed was half-past two; and though I spared neither energy nor expense in my journey, making no less than three separate embarkations in train, 'bus, and tram, at a total cost of four-pence, it was three o'clock before the Metropole was sighted. This had two grave consequences. First, Camberwell had rallied round the Bard so multitudinously that the offer of untold gold could procure me nothing better than a mere skylight of a box, from which my view of the legitimate drama was considerably foreshortened. Second, I was late for Miss Dorothy Dene's Juliet. This I greatly regretted; for I have not seen Miss Dorothy Dene since the now almost remote days when Mr. Henry Arthur Jones was making his reputation by writing melodramas for Mr. Wilson Barrett at the Princess's. Why? Here was a young lady who had, not the painted show of beauty which is so common on the stage, and so tedious, but that honest reality of it which is useful to painters. Her speech showed unusual signs of artistic cultivation; she had plastic grace; she took herself and her profession seriously; and her appearances in leading parts were not unpopular. The mystery is, what became of her? Did she fall into the abyss of opulent matrimony? Did the studio violently reclaim its adored model? Did she demand impossible terms? Or were the managers obdurate in their belief that there is only one safe sort of actress— the woman who is all susceptibility and no brains? Far be it from me to deny that every deviation from this type involves a certain risk of unpopularity—of a demand on the part of the actress, or rather the woman, that in the intercourse between her and the public the wooing and the worth shall not all be on one side. Further still be it from me to forget the fact that in cases of positive genius for the stage no question as to the dignity of the actress's occupation can arise. For instance, Duse is clearly a most laborious artist hard at work, and not a pretty woman making an exhibition of herself. But the appearance of a Duse is as rare on the stage as that of a woman who absolutely cannot act at all. Most of the routine of our leading theatrical work in London is done by ladies who are not altogether artists and not altogether exhibitions, but who eke out a little art with more or less personal attractiveness. Probably the reason our managers prefer the brainless-susceptible woman is that she is a ready-made actress as far as she can act at all; and small blame to them, since we have no apprenticeship system to secure to a manager the services of an actress whom he trains, and no system of training to replace the apprenticeship system. But I get so tired of the brainless-susceptible heroine that even an American lecturer would sometimes be a relief to the eternal sympathetic leading lady, who is called sweetly womanly because, having nothing but her sex to insist on, she insists on that continually. And yet, since women of the other sort get no engagements, it ends in her being the only one who gets sufficient stage practice to be trusted with important parts, whence it comes that the important parts never are important. We want more women of the clever, positive type on the stage (also men). We also want more objectively beautiful women on the stage; for your brainless-susceptible one is often your beautyless-susceptible: she may appeal to your sentimentality; but a sculptor or a painter would not look twice at her from his dry business point of view; and her graces of carriage and movement are of the cheapest. Her hold on the stage is largely a result of the stage's hold on her through her disadvantage of being fit for nothing else; so that economic necessity does for her what irresistible vocation does for an actress of genius—gives her, that is, the unconditional singleness of aim and pertinacity which move mountains in the long run. The clever, positive woman, on the other hand, has alternative activities: she has ability and character enough to make her living in other professions, or to discharge social and domestic duties as the wife of a Philistine citizen in a responsible, capable, respectable way. Granted that she may have only the makings of a second-rate actress in her, she would probably make second-rate acting much more important than a good deal of what passes as first-rate acting at present; and her influence on the drama would be highly beneficial owing to her demand for real parts in which to put forth her brains and skill against the rivals who rely on sex and sympathy in every kind of part. It takes all sorts to make a stage, just as it takes all sorts to make a world; and we do not get all sorts at present. We get the geniuses and the *hystériques;* but the intermediate talents, however promising, are driven back from a profession in which brains and self-respect have no chance against emotional facility and neurotic sexuality. The latter are invaluable, the former quite useless, in an empty part which is nothing but the merest cue to the imagination of the audience; but confront the facile, neurotic, empty-headed actress with a part which demands not only sympathy but intelligence and trained nervous energy; not only "womanly" softnesses and graces but plastic, picturesque, vigorous action; nay, ask her to deliver a ten-line speech—not a hysterical explosion, but a speech with thought as well as feeling in it—and you will soon find how a dramatic author is hampered at present by the limited compass of the instruments at his disposal. There are always clever, educated, ambitious young women ready to try their fortune on the stage; but how are they to get the necessary experience to make skilled artists of them? It takes years of practice to develop their power of emotional expression; for most educated women have been trained to fight against emotional expression because it is a mode of self-betrayal. Now self-betrayal, magnified to suit the optics of the theatre, is the whole art of acting; and the strong, continent woman, unless she is descended from generations of actors, is certain to be beaten at first on the stage by the hysterical, incontinent one, or even by the stupid, prosaic hereditary actress who, within certain limits, acts as a duck swims. Under present conditions this handicap is sufficient to baffle the clever recruit drawn from the newly emancipated women of the middle class in her quest for engagements, thus depriving her of the practice necessary to train her, and so defeating her attempt to gain a footing on the stage. The theatre is unable to keep and drill able-bodied and able-minded recruits; and the result is that the class of work which would in any other profession be perfectly within the competence of the rank and file, has to be entrusted to the leaders. And even the leaders are often more remarkable for what is called social charm than for any rarer artistic qualification.

On the whole, perhaps it is as well that I did not see Miss Dorothy Dene; for it is not conceivable that disuse has matured her powers, or years increased her natural suitability to the part of Juliet. Just at present I am more anxious about Miss Dorothea Baird, whom I did see, as Rosalind. Rosalind is to the actress what Hamlet is to the actor—a part in which, reasonable presentability being granted, failure is hardly possible. It is easier than Trilby up to a certain point, though it will of course hold much more acting. Miss Baird plays it intelligently and nicely; and this, to such a very pretty Ganymede, is enough to secure success. How far the niceness and intelligence of the pretty young lady will develop into the passion and intuition of the artist, or whether the prettiness will develop into the "handsome is as handsome does" fascination which holds the stage for many years against Time, remains to be seen. All that can be said at present is that Miss Baird's Rosalind is bright and pleasant, with sufficient natural charm to secure indulgence for all its shortcomings. Of these the most serious is Miss Baird's delivery of the lines. Everybody by this time knows how a modern high-schoolmistress talks—how she repudiates the precision, the stateliness, the awe-inspiring oracularity of the old-fashioned schoolmistress who knew nothing, and cloaks her mathematics with a pretty little voice, a pretty little manner, and all sorts of self-conscious calineries and unassumingnesses. "Poor little me! what do *I* know about conic sections?" is the effect she aims at. Miss Baird's Rosalind has clearly been to the high school and modelled herself upon her pet mistress if not actually taught there herself. But that dainty, pleading, narrow-lipped little torrent of gabble will not do for Shakespeare. It is so unintelligible across the footlights that even I, who know "As You Like It" almost as well as I know Beethoven's Pastoral Symphony, could not always catch what she was saying. This being so, it may safely be taken that Camberwell did not catch more than a very small conic section of it. For even an expert cannot make sense of Elizabethan blank verse at a first hearing when it is delivered at the rate of 200 words a minute and upwards. Besides, its lyrical flow, if such a tiny ladylike patter can be credited with so broad a quality, is not that of Shakespeare's verse. The effect is like a canary trying to sing Handel.

Mr. H. B. Irving is in the full flood of that Shakespearean enthusiasm which exalts the Bard so far above common sense that any prosaic suiting of the action to the word and the word to the action seems to be a degradation of his genius to what Nicholas Rowe called "a mere light of reason." Mr. Irving gave us the closet scene from "Hamlet." He entered, surcharged with Fate, and instead of Hamlet's sharp, dry, "Now, mother: what's the matter?" followed by his reply to her affected "Thou hast thy father much offended," with the purposely blunt "Mother: *you* have my father much offended," gave us a most tragic edition of the conversation, with the yous altered to thous, and an agitated slip or two to enhance the effect. When he lifted the arras and found that he had killed Polonius instead of the King, he betrayed not the smallest surprise, but said, in a superior tone, "Thou wretched, rash, intruding fool, farewell!" much as if he were dismissing a deservedly and quite intentionally flogged schoolboy. He was resolved to make an effect by seizing the Queen and throwing her down on the floor ; and the moment he selected was in the middle of the following passage :—

> "At your age
> The heyday in the blood is tame: it's humble,
> And waits upon the judgment; and what judgment
> Would step from this to this?"

The Queen was floored after the phrase "and waits upon the judgment," showing that at Mr. Irving's age the heyday in the blood does not wait upon the judgment, but has its fling (literally) regardless of reason. The only dramatic profit from this proceeding was the point given to the Ghost's "But see! amazement on thy mother sits." Nevertheless, the performance, nonsensical as it was, was not ridiculous. Mr. Irving is not altogether unsuccessful in his attempts to be tragic and to make effects; and if he could only bring his tragedy and his effects into some intelligent relation to the drama in hand, he would find himself highly complimented in the "Saturday Review." To be abstractly and irrelevantly tragic; to brandish a sword; to discourse in blank verse; to stagger and fall and hurl frail heroines away, is just as absurd in "Hamlet," if done at the wrong moment, as it would be in "Box and Cox." There are people so unfit for the stage that they could not do these things even at the right moment without making the audience laugh. That is not Mr. Irving's case. When he learns what to do and when to do it, he will not be at a loss as to how to do it. More than that it is impossible to grant him at present. The scenes from "As You Like It" included nothing of Jaques except the few scraps of dialogue between the pessimist and Orlando; and no exception can be taken to the way in which these were handled by Mr. Irving. He dressed and looked the part well.

The best bit of work was Mr. Bernard Gould's Orlando; the worst, Mr. Ben Greet's Touchstone. Mr. Greet put himself out of the question before he had been two minutes on the stage by the profound stroke of picking one of Orlando's sonnets from a tree, and reading from it the impromptu burlesque:—

> "If a hart do lack a hind,
> Let him seek out Rosalind," etc.

This was a new reading with a vengeance. He was not much more successful as executant than as Shakespearean student. He completely missed the piled up climax of the speech to William, and was, in short, as bad a Touchstone as a critic could desire to see. It is no disgrace to an actor to be unable to play Touchstone; but why, under these circumstances, and being a manager, he should cast himself for it, passes my understanding. Mr. Rawson Buckley played Oliver very well, but persisted, as usual, in dressing himself smartly, and then describing himself as "a wretched ragged man, o'ergrown with hair." Mr. Gould managed his part, especially the difficulties of the sham courtship with Ganymede, better than I can remember having seen it managed before; and some of his lines were finely spoken; but he was not Orlando. Orlando's intelligence is the intelligence of the heart: he always comes out best as an amiable, strong, manly, handsome, shrewd-enough-to-take-care-of-himself, but safely stupid and totally unobservant young man. Now, Mr. Gould plays with his head; his intelligence is always on the alert; and he is so observant that in spite of his many valuable stage qualities he almost disqualifies himself as an actor by his draughtsman's habit of watching himself and every one else so keenly and interestedly that he is more apt to forget his part than to forget himself in it. The born actor looks in: Mr. Gould looks on. He acts like a good critic, and probably represses his tendencies— if he has any—to the maudlin self-sympathy, the insane egotism, the bottomless folly, the hysterical imaginative mendacity which—with the help of alcohol—make acting easy to some men who are for all other purposes the most hopeless wastrels. However, I do not object: I recognize the fact that the ascendency of the sentimental amorphous actor means the ascendency of the sentimental amorphous drama, and that the critical actor, like Mr. Gould, is indispensable to a drama with any brains in it. Still, the critical actor need not be also a draughtsman actor. I once elaborately explained to Mr. Gould a part of which I was myself the author. He paid me the closest attention; retired to ponder my utterances; and presently returned with a perfectly accurate and highly characteristic drawing of me, which I shall probably never live down. And if I had been Shakespeare explaining Orlando, it would have been just the same.

THE FARCICAL COMEDY OUTBREAK

The New Baby: a deception in three acts. Adapted by Arthur Bourchier from "Der Rabenvater," by H. F. Fischer and J. Jarno. Royalty Theatre, 28 April, 1896.

Monsieur de Paris: a play in one act. By Alicia Ramsey and Rudolph de Cordova. Royalty Theatre.

A Night Out: a farcical comedy in three acts. By Georges Feydeau and Maurice Desvallières. English version. Vaudeville Theatre, 29 April, 1896.

ONE of the strongest objections to the institution of monogamy is the existence of its offspring, the conventional farcical comedy. The old warning, "Beware how you kiss when you do not love," ought to be paraphrased on the playbills of all our lighter theatres as "Beware how you laugh when you do not enjoy." To laugh without sympathy is a ruinous abuse of a noble function; and the degradation of any race may be measured by the degree of their addiction to it. In its subtler forms it is dying very hard: for instance, we find people who would not join in the laughter of a crowd of peasants at the village idiot, or tolerate the public flogging or pillorying of a criminal, booking seats to shout with laughter at a farcical comedy, which is, at bottom, the same thing—namely, the deliberate indulgence of that horrible, derisive joy in humiliation and suffering which is the beastliest element in human nature. I make these portentous observations not by way of breaking a butterfly on a wheel, but in order to bring out with violent emphasis the distinction between the high and the base comedy of errors—between "Pink Dominos" and "Twelfth Night"; or, to illustrate from another art, between the caricatures of Leech or Gavarni and those which mark the last intolerable stages of the degradation of Ally Sloper (who in his original Ross-Duval days was not without his merits). To produce high art in the theatre, the author must create persons whose fortunes we can follow as those of a friend or enemy: to produce base laughter, it is only necessary to turn human beings on to the stage as rats are turned into a pit, that they may be worried for the entertainment of the spectators. Such entertainment is much poorer fun than most playgoers suspect. The critic, trained to analyse all his artistic sensations, soon gets cured of the public's delusion that everything that makes it laugh amuses it You cannot impose on him by the mere galvanism of the theatre; for all its manifestations, from the brute laughter produced by an indecency or a bout of horseplay, to the tricks, familiar to old actors, by which worthless explosions of applause can be elicited with mechanical certainty at the end of a speech or on an exit, become so transparent to him that, instead of sharing the enthusiasm they excite, he measures merit by their absence. For example, one of the admirable points in Mrs. Patrick Campbell's performance in "For the Crown" is the way in which, after her recitation of the butterfly poem, she avoids the round of clapping which any third-rate actress could get for it—however execrably it might be delivered—by simply finishing it with a swagger and waiting for the audience to make a fool of itself. I have no doubt that many old stagers regard this as the ineptitude of a novice letting a sure point go "for nothing" or "without a hand." But everybody remembers the recitation; everybody is struck by it; everybody is conscious of a spell which would be broken by any vulgar attempt to "bring down the house": the commercial result being that people go to see Mrs. Campbell, whereas they stay at home when there is nothing to be enjoyed at the theatre except the galvanic tricks of the trade. If it could once be borne in upon the mental darkness of most of our public performers that the artists who draw best are not those who are fondest of making the noisy and hysterical section of the audience interrupt the play—that, in fact, applause in the middle of an act is not only discreditable on most occasions to both actor and audience but bad business as well—we should get vastly better work at the theatres.

I shall now, perhaps, be understood (if not, no matter) when I class the laughter produced by conventional farcical comedy as purely galvanic, and the inference drawn by the audience that since they are laughing they must be amused or edified or pleased, as a delusion. They are really being more or less worried and exhausted and upset by ill-natured cachinnation; and the proof is that they generally leave the theatre tired and out of humor with themselves and the world. Lest I should err here on the side of over-much righteousness, let me hasten to admit that a little galvanism may be harmless and even beneficial in its effect on the lungs and liver; but three acts of it is too much. I first learnt the weariness of it from "Pink Dominos," although that play had an excellent third act; and I have been wearied in the same way by every new version. For we have had it again and again under various titles. Act I., John Smith's home; Act II., the rowdy restaurant or casino at which John Smith, in the course of his clandestine spree, meets all the members of his household, including the schoolboy and the parlormaid; Act III., his house next morning, with the inevitable aftermath of the complications of the night before: who that has any theatrical experience does not know it all by heart? And now here it is again, with a fresh coat of paint on it, and as rotten as ever underneath.

But farcical comedy, like any other stage entertainment, may become artistically valuable, and even delightful, through fine execution. "Pink Dominos" is memorable, not for itself, but for the performances of Wyndham and Clarke. One remembers the charm of Miss Eastlake before she took up the heavy and violent work of supporting Mr. Wilson Barrett in tragic melodrama; and this generation, contemplating Sir Augustus Harris with awe, little suspects how lighthearted he was as Harry Greenlanes. Since then, Mr. Hawtrey, Mr. Penley, and Miss Lottie Venne have managed to keep up the notion that farcical comedies are intrinsically amusing with considerable success. But the moment an attempt is made to run this sort of dramatic work on its own merits, its fundamental barrenness and baseness assert themselves and become intolerable. Therefore I shall make no pretence of discussing as drama the two specimens just produced at the Royalty and Vaudeville. Suffice it that the Royalty piece, "The New Baby," is, from that point of view, so far beneath contempt that it never once rises to the point of even suggesting the disgust which its story would rouse in any one who took it seriously; whilst "A Night Out," at the Vaudeville, though a masterpiece of ingenuity and urbanity in comparison to the other, is essentially the same as previous nights out, from that in "Pink Dominos" downwards, and reproduces the stage arrangements of the second act of "Forbidden Fruit" pretty faithfully. But it is noteworthy that although "The New Baby" includes incest in its bewilderments, and one of the central incidents of "A Night Out" is the sudden retirement of a gentleman from a supper party on a pretext which Smollett might, and probably would, have employed, they are comparatively free from that detestable, furtive lubricity which was the rule twenty years ago. Farcical comedy used to have the manners of a pimp. It is now progressing upward towards the morals of Tom Jones.

The question then being one of acting, we had better start by making certain allowances: first, for the absence from the cast of those light comedians who have been specially successful in this class of entertainment, and, second, for the homeliness of our English attempts to volatilize ourselves sufficiently to breathe that fantastic atmosphere of moral irresponsibility in which alone the hero of farcical comedy, like Pierrot or Harlequin, can realize himself fully. On the understanding that these difficulties have not been surmounted, one may say that "A Night Out" is not in the main badly acted. Mr. Giddens's humor, brought into play with apparent reck-

Dramatic Opinions and Essays

lessness, but really with most skilful discretion, is irresistible. Mr. Sugden's Paillard could not be improved without overdoing the part; and Mr. Wyes has at last succeeded in presenting the peculiar monstrosity he has invented for stage purposes with something like a real artistic command of it. Mrs. Edmund Phelps's performance as Madame Pinglet (frankly pronounced Pingly) is clever; but there are two points in which it might be improved. The business of grovelling on the floor in the third act is shockingly ugly; and the grimace by which she expresses extreme discomfiture is, owing to the turning up of the corners of the mouth, in effect a smile, not unlike that of Bailey Prothero in "The Rogue's Comedy." Miss Fannie Ward is a determined young lady with plenty of assurance, and gumption enough to simulate the not very subtle emotions of her part plausibly enough; but she is hardly an artist. Miss Pattie Browne, the inevitable maid who seduces the inevitable schoolboy, is merely that impossible superstition, the stolidly bouncing English stage chambermaid. In this, and in such details as the crudity with which the second waiter keeps senselessly shouting Madame Paillard's name with an obvious consciousness of the mischief he is doing, not to mention the unnecessary noisiness of some of the scenes, one sees the chief fault of the production—puerility of stage management. Mr. Seymour Hicks has given way to his sense of fun, forgetting that a stage manager should have no sense of anything except fine art.

But if the management is immature at the Vaudeville, what is it at the Royalty? Alas! it is hardly to be described. Here is Mr. Bourchier, a born actor—the likeliest successor, so far, to Mr. Wyndham in light comedy —with a theatre of his own and an excellent company,

418

the centre of which is well knit together by private as well as artistic ties, and with a handsome capital in personal popularity and good wishes to reinforce his cash balance, positively playing with his chances like an undergraduate. I protested mildly against the way in which "The Chili Widow" was romped through. No doubt it was jolly; but it was not artistic management, and it was hardly acting. But "The New Baby" is worse. Mr. Bourchier has not only cast himself for an elderly part which he is physically unfit for—a part which might be played appropriately by James Lewis—but he treats it as a pure lark from beginning to end, rattling along anyhow as if nothing mattered so long as his good humor and high spirits infected the audience sufficiently to keep them smiling. In desperation I ask Mr. Bourchier, does he really think he is keeping himself up to his work at the Royalty? Would any other manager stand from him the happy-go-lucky playing he stands from himself with apparent complacency? Would any other author allow him to do so much less than his best at the very moment when he should be concentrating his intensest energy on the consolidation of his position? Does he expect me to pay him any higher compliment than to admit that his performance is at least good enough for the play he has selected? There are two well-acted parts in "The New Baby," and only two. Miss Alice Mansfield, a very clever actress, does for the piece what Mr. Giddens does for its rival at the Vaudeville; and Mr. W. G. Elliott plays the fiery Spaniard as conscientiously and excellently as Mr. Bourchier himself would perhaps play it if he were the actor and Mr. Elliott the manager. Mr. Blakeley almost succeeds by his well-known grimaces and attitudes in persuading the audience that he has a real part. But the play is too foolish to have much chance even of a success of folly.

The strongest part of the Royalty performance is a one-act drama, of exceptional merit as such things go, entitled "Monsieur de Paris," in which Miss Violet Vanbrugh, instead of trifling with her talent as she did in "The Chili Widow," plays a purely romantic part with striking effect. The sanguinary ending of the play is as mechanical, obvious, and unimaginative as a Chicago pig-sticking; and Miss Vanbrugh, by overrating its value, attempts—what no thoroughly expert actress would attempt—a sustained and unvaried crescendo of forcible expression which only betrays the fact that it is her imagination and not her feeling that is at work; but the performance proves a great deal as to her remarkable qualifications for more serious work on the stage. May I add without offence that in the finest diction "crime," "quick," "true," and "heaven" are not vehemently dissyllabic?

I never go to celebrations and never write about them. What is more, I never eat supper. But I went to the Hotel Cecil yesterday week to shake hands with Mr. Wyndham, and never succeeded in getting within a dozen yards of him. It was an amazing spectacle. There we were in our thousands—players and authors and critics—geniuses and beauties—lost sheep strayed from the Philistine fold of respectability—the disgraces of our own families—the delight of everybody else's families—the mighty *cabotinage* of London in all its fascination, and all its unlimited capacity for flattery, champagne, and asparagus. Nine out of every ten guests were players by profession; and fully one out of every two hundred and fifty could really act—first among these, beyond all challenge, Wyndham himself, whose health was proposed by that tragic comedian, the Lord Chief Justice. I say nothing of the peers and politicians and other interlopers: a crowd of them can be seen anywhere. I missed Sir Henry Irving and Miss Ellen Terry: they, like Mr. John Hare, were in America. I also missed Ibsen, greatly to my surprise. But it was a wonderful occasion, for all that—excellently managed and worked up, no doubt, but none the less owing the extremity of its huge success to its genuineness as a demonstration of admiration and regard for Mr. Wyndham.

HENRY IV.

Henry IV. Part I. Haymarket Theatre. 8 May, 1896.

THIS is a miserably incompetent world. The average doctor is a walking compound of natural ignorance and acquired witchcraft, who kills your favorite child, wrecks your wife's health, and orders you into habits of nervous dram-drinking before you have the courage to send him about his business, and take your chance like a gentleman. The average lawyer is a nincompoop, who contradicts your perfectly sound impressions on notorious points of law, involves you in litigation when your case is hopeless, compromises when your success is certain, and cannot even make your will without securing the utter defeat of your intentions if any one takes the trouble to dispute them. And so on, down to the bootmaker whose boots you have to make your tortured feet fit, and the tailor who clothes you as if you were a cast-iron hot-water apparatus. You imagine that these people have professions; and you find that what they have is only, in the correct old word, their "mystery"—a humbug, like all mysteries. And yet, how we help to keep up the humbug! I know men of quite exceptional intelligence—men so sceptical that they have freed their minds from all philosophic and religious dogma, who nevertheless read the "Lancet" and the "British Medical Journal" from end to end every week as devoutly as any superstitious washerwoman ever read "Zadkiel" or "Old Moore," and not only believe it all, but long tremblingly for the next symptom that will give them an excuse for calling in the medicine man to mistake typhoid fever for influenza or paint their tonsils with caustic when their kidneys are out of order. Every week they have some joyful tidings for me. Another disease has been traced to its germ; an infallible destroyer of that germ has been discovered; the disease has been annihilated. What wonderful triumphs has not science enjoyed in my time! Smallpox has been made totally impossible; hydrophobia has vanished; epilepsy has yielded to the simplest of operations; the pangs of angina pectoris have been relieved as if by magic; consumption is a dream of the past; and now there is to be no more diphtheria. Instead of vainly seeking, as of old, for a universal remedy, we are the proud discoverers of a dozen, and can change with the fashion from one to another. Mercury, salicylic acid, iodide and bromide of potassium, hashed thyroid, antipyrine, with lymphs innumerable: there they are, making us all safe and happy until we are unfortunate enough to fall down in a fit, or get bitten by a mad dog, or fall sick with an ugly rash and a bad pain in our backs when we promptly place ourselves in the hands of the very gentleman who wrote to the "Times" to pledge his honor and reputation, founded on a pyramid of vivisected rabbits, that such things could never happen again. Depend upon it, if Macbeth had killed Macduff, he would have gone back to the Witches next day to ask their advice as to the best way of dealing with Malcolm.

It is the same with all the professions. I have other friends who are law-mad—who believe that lawyers are wise, judges high-minded and impartial, juries infallible, and codes on the brink of perfection. The military-mad and the clergy-mad stalk at large throughout the kingdom. Men believe in the professions as they believe in ghosts, because they want to believe in them. Fact-blindness—the most common sort of blindness—and the resolute lying of respectable men, keep up the illusion. No mortal, however hard-headed, can feel very safe in his attempts to sift the gold of fact and efficiency out of the huge rubbish-heap of professionalism.

My own weakness is neither medicine, nor law, nor tailoring, nor any of the respectable departments of bogusdom. It is the theatre. The mystery-man who takes me in is not the doctor nor the lawyer, but the actor. In this column I have prated again and again of the mission of the theatre, the art of the actor, of his labor, his skill, his knowledge, his importance as a civilizing agent, his function as a spiritual doctor. Surely I have been in this the most ridiculous of all dupes. But before you lay me down in derision, never to read my articles again, hear my excuse. There is one sort of human accomplishment that cannot be dismissed as a figment of the spectator's imagination. The skill with which a man does that which he has done every day for twenty years is no illusion. When the operative at his mule in the cotton-mill pieces the broken yarn, when Paderewski at his Erard grand plays a sonata, he is not hypnotizing you, or inviting you to make-believe. He is actually doing things that would be miracles if done by an untrained man. Or take him who, with no eye to cotton cloth or the interpretation of Beethoven, does difficult things for the sake of their difficulty, simply as marvels: for instance, the acrobat. You cannot deny the reality of his feats. His complete physical self-possession, his ambidexterous grace, his power of making several deliberate movements in the space of a pang of terror—as when, for example, he will coolly alter the disposition of his body at a given moment, whilst he is falling headlong through the air: all these accomplishments of his really exist, and are by no means the product of the imagination of an innocent clergyman, sitting in the auditorium with his nose buried in a volume of Shakespeare, and ready to take the word of the newspapers next day for what is happening on the stage. Now, am I to be greatly blamed for having supposed that the actor was a genuinely skilled artist like the acrobat, only adding to the skilled mastery of his powers of movement a mastery of his powers of speech, with an ear for verse, a sense of character, a cultivated faculty of observation and mimicry, and such higher qualities as Nature might throw into the bargain? There were great examples to mislead me: Kean was a harlequin as well as a Hamlet; Duse's Camille is positively enthralling as an exhibition of the gymnastics of perfect suppleness and grace; and I have seen Salvini come out before the curtain to accept a trophy from an admirer in a stage box with more art and more fascination—the whole thing being carried out in strict accordance with certain rules of his art—than an ordinary skirt dancer could get into the clumsy imposture she calls dancing after two years' hard practice. Further, it has been a matter of common observation in my generation that the burlesque of the Byron-Farnie-Reece-Burnand period did not, as it turned out, prove a bad training for the people who played in it. Nobody will contend, I imagine, that the training was intellectual: the secret lay in the music, the dancing, the marching, the fantastic walks round, the boundless scope for physical agility, the premium which the very barrenness and vulgarity of the entertainment placed on personal feats and on mimicry. Even that terrible stage calamity, the stock actor of the old régime, learnt something more from the Christmas pantomime than he would have known without it.

I plead then that acting is potentially an artistic profession, and that by training and practice a person can qualify himself or herself to come to a manager or author and say, "Within the limits imposed by my age and sex, I can do all the ordinary work of the stage with perfect certainty. I know my vowels and consonants as a phonetic expert, and can speak so as to arrest the attention of the audience whenever I open my mouth, forcibly, delicately, roughly, smoothly, prettily, harshly, authoritatively, submissively, but always artistically, just as you want it. I can sit, stand, fall, get up, walk, dance, and otherwise use my body with the complete command of it that marks the physical artist." An actor might know all this, and yet, for want of the power to interpret an author's text and invent the appropriate physical expression for it, never, without coaching, get beyond Rosencrantz or Seyton. It is, therefore, only the minimum qualification of a skilled stage hand; and if an actor is not that, then he is merely a stage-struck unskilled laborer or handy man, and his "conceptions" of Ibsen or Shakespeare are mere impertinences. I naturally concluded that the minimum was in force, and acting a real profession. Alas! that only proves that my desire and hope got the better of my observation—my imagination of my experience.

However, I am cured now. It is all a delusion: there is no profession, no art, no skill about the business at all. We have no actors: we have only authors, and not many of them. When Mendelssohn composed "Son and Stranger" for an amateur performance, he found that the bass could only sing one note. So he wrote the bass part all on that one note; and when it came to the fateful night, the bass failed even at that. Our authors do as Mendelssohn did. They find that the actors have only one note, or perhaps, if they are very clever, half a dozen. So their parts are confined to these notes, often with the same result as in Mendelssohn's case. If you doubt me, go and see "Henry IV." at the Haymarket It is as good work as our stage can do; but the man who says that it is skilled work has neither eyes nor ears; the man who mistakes it for intelligent work has no brains; the man who finds it even good fun may be capable of Christy Minstrelsy but not of Shakespeare. Everything that charm of style, rich humor, and vivid and natural characterization can do for a play are badly wanted by "Henry IV.," which has neither the romantic beauty of Shakespeare's earlier plays nor the tragic greatness of the later ones. One can hardly forgive Shakespeare quite for the worldly phase in which he tried to thrust such a Jingo hero as his Harry V. down our throats. The combination of conventional propriety and brute masterfulness in his public capacity with a low-lived blackguardism in his private tastes is not a pleasant one. No doubt he is true to nature as a picture of what is by no means uncommon in English society, an able young Philistine inheriting high position and authority, which he holds on to and goes through with by keeping a tight grip on his conventional and legal advantages, but who would have been quite in his place if he had been born a gamekeeper or a farmer. We do not in the first part of "Henry IV." see Harry sending Mrs. Quickly and Doll Tearsheet to the whipping-post, or handing over Falstaff to the Lord Chief Justice with a sanctimonious lecture; but he repeatedly makes it clear that he will turn on them later on, and that his self-indulgent good-fellowship with them is consciously and deliberately treacherous. His popularity, therefore, is like that of a prizefighter: nobody feels for him as for Romeo or Hamlet. Hotspur, too, though he is stimulating as ginger cordial is stimulating, is hardly better than his horse; and King Bolingbroke, preoccupied with his crown exactly as a miser is preoccupied with his money, is equally useless as a refuge for our affections, which are thus thrown back undivided on Falstaff, the most human person in the play, but none the less a besotted and disgusting old wretch. And there is neither any subtlety nor (for Shakespeare) much poetry in the presentation of all these characters. They are labelled and described and insisted upon with the roughest directness; and their reality and their humor can alone save them from the unpopularity of their unlovableness and the tedium of their obviousness. Fortunately, they offer capital opportunities for interesting acting. Bolingbroke's long discourse to his son on the means by which he struck the imagination and enlisted the snobbery of the English people gives the actor a chance comparable to the crafty early scenes in "Richelieu." Prince Hal's humor is seasoned with sportsmanlike cruelty and the insolence of conscious mastery and contempt to the point of occasionally making one shudder. Hotspur is full of energy; and Falstaff is, of course, an unrivalled part for the right sort of comedian. Well acted, then, the play is a good one in spite of there not being a single tear in it. Ill acted—O heavens!

Of the four leading parts, the easiest—Hotspur—becomes pre-eminent at the Haymarket, not so much by Mr. Lewis Waller's superiority to the rest as by their inferiority to him. Some of the things he did were astonishing in an actor of his rank. At the end of each of his first vehement speeches, he strode right down the stage and across to the prompt side of the proscenium on the frankest barnstorming principles, repeating this absurd "cross"—a well-known convention of the booth for catching applause—three times, step for step, without a pretence of any dramatic motive. In the camp scene before the battle of Shrewsbury, he did just what I blamed Miss Violet Vanbrugh for trying to do in "Monsieur de Paris": that is, to carry through a long crescendo of excitement by main force after beginning fortissimo. Would it be too farfetched to recommend Mr. Waller to study how Mozart, in rushing an operatic movement to a spirited conclusion, knew how to make it, when apparently already at its utmost, seem to bound forward by a sudden pianissimo and lightsome change of step, the speed and force of the execution being actually reduced instead of intensified by the change? Such skilled, resourceful husbandry is the secret of all effects of this kind; and it is in the entire absence of such husbandry that Mr. Waller showed how our miserable theatre has left him still a novice for the purposes of a part which he is fully equipped by nature to play with most brilliant success, and which he did play very strikingly considering he was not in the least sure how to set about it, and hardly dared to stop blazing away at full pitch for an instant lest the part should drop flat on the boards. Mr. Mollison presented us with an assortment of effects, and tones, and poses which had no reference, as far as I could discover, to the part of Bolingbroke at any single point. I did not catch a glimpse of the character from one end of his performance to the other, and so must conclude that Shakespeare has failed to convey his intention to him. Mr. Gillmore's way of playing Hal was as bad as the traditional way of playing Sheridan. He rattled and swaggered and roystered, and followed every sentence with a forced explosion of mirthless laughter, evidently believing that, as Prince Hal was reputed to be a humorous character, it was his business to laugh at him. Like most of his colleagues, he became more tolerable in the plain sailing of the battle scene, where the parts lose their individuality in the general warlike excitement, and an energetic display of the commonest sort of emotion suffices. Mr. Tree only wants one thing to make him an excellent Falstaff, and that is to get born over again as unlike himself as possible. No doubt, in the course of a month or two, when he begins to pick up a few of the lines of the part, he will improve on his first effort; but he will never be even a moderately good Falstaff. The basket-work figure, as expressionless as that of a Jack in the Green; the face, with the pathetic wandering eye of Captain Swift belying such suggestion of character as the lifeless mask of paint and hair can give; the voice, coarsened, vulgarized, and falsified without being enriched or colored; the hopeless efforts of the romantic imaginative actor, touching only in unhappy parts, to play the comedian by dint of mechanical horse-play: all that is hopeless, irremediable. Mr. Tree might as well try to play Juliet; and if he were wise he would hand over his part and his breadbasket to Mr. Lionel Brough, whose Bardolph has the true comic force which Mr. Tree never attains for a moment.

Two ideas have been borrowed from the last London revival of "Henry V." by Mr. Coleman at the Queen's Theatre in Long Acre. One is the motionless battle tableau, which is only Mr. Coleman's Agincourt over again, and which might just as well be cut out of cardboard. The other is the casting of Miss Kate Phillips for Mrs. Quickly. As Mrs. Quickly is plainly a slovenly, greasy, Gampish old creature, and Miss Phillips is unalterably trim, smart, and bright, a worse choice could not have been made. One would like to have seen Miss Mansfield in the part. Mrs. Tree, as Lady Percy, did what I have never seen her do before: that is, played her part stupidly. The laws of nature seem to be suspended when Shakespeare is in question. A Lady Percy who is sentimentally affectionate, who recites her remonstrance with Percy in the vein of Clarence's dream in "Richard III.," and who comes on the stage to share the applause elicited by the combats in the battle of Shrewsbury, only makes me rub my eyes and wonder whether I am dreaming.

Besides Mr. Lionel Brough and Mr. Lewis Waller, there were three performers who came off with credit. Mr. Holman Clark played Glendower like a reasonable man who could read a Shakespearean play and understand it—a most exceptional achievement in his profession, as it appears. Mr. D. J. Williams, who played

William in "As You Like It" the other day at the Metropole, and played him well, was a Smike-like and effective Francis; and Miss Marion Evans was a most musical Lady Mortimer, both in her Welsh song and Welsh speech.

The chief merit of the production is that the play has been accepted from Shakespeare mainly as he wrote it. There are cuts, of course, the worst of them being the sacrifice of the nocturnal innyard scene, a mutilation which takes the reality and country midnight freshness from the Gadshill robbery, and reduces it to a vapid interlude of horseplay. But the object of these cuts is to save time: there is no alteration or hotchpotch, and consequently no suspicion of any attempt to demonstrate the superiority of the manager's taste and judgment to Shakespeare's in the Daly fashion. This ought to pass as a matter of course; but as things are at present it must be acknowledged as highly honorable to Mr. Tree. However, it is not my cue just now to pay Mr. Tree compliments. His *tours de force* in the art of make-up do not impose on me: any man can get into a wicker barrel and pretend to be Falstaff, or put on a false nose and call himself Svengali. Such tricks may very well be left to the music-halls: they are altogether unworthy of an artist of Mr. Tree's pretensions. When he returns to the serious pursuit of his art by playing a part into which he can sincerely enter without disguise or mechanical denaturalization, may I be there to see! Until then let him guard the Haymarket doors against me; for I like him best when he is most himself.

RESURRECTION PIE

Jo: a drama in three acts, adapted from Charles Dickens's "Bleak House." By J. P. Burnett. (A Revival.) Theatre Royal, Drury Lane. 14 May, 1896.

The Matchmaker: a new comedy in four acts. By Clo Graves and Gertrude Kingston. Shaftesbury Theatre. 9 May, 1896.

Rosemary: a new play in four acts. By Louis N. Parker and Murray Carson. Criterion Theatre. 16 May, 1896.

THERE is a strain of resurrectionism in all of us, I suppose. In the most eligible places we get suddenly smitten with a hankering to take another look at some dull district where we were born; or in the British Museum Library we turn from the treasures of literature and abuse the services of the staff to get out some trumpery story-book that we read in the nursery; or we suddenly lapse, between the acts of a Wagnerian performance, into a longing curiosity to hear "I Puritani" or "Don Pasquale" once more. Fortunately most of these whims cost too much to be carried very far. We can afford to make a sentimental journey, or to hunt up an old book, but not to produce an old opera or an old play. There is only one man among us who is an exception to this rule. That man is Sir Augustus Harris. And what a resurrectionist he is! When my theme was music, I used egotistically to suspect him of a fiendish fancy for tormenting me personally; for in the very middle of a phase of advanced operatic activity, with "Die Meistersinger" figuring in the repertory with a comparatively venerable air beside a group of the most modern Italian and French works, he would suddenly stretch out his imperial hand; drag some appalling tenor from I know not what limbo of street-piano padrones, penny-icemen, and broken choristers; set the wretch to bleat "Ah sì, ben mio," and roar "Di quella pira" just once; and then snatch him for ever from the ken of a coldly astonished London season, leaving no trace of his adventure except my own infuriated protests and an inscrutable smile on the countenance of the impresario. That smile may have meant sentimental memories of auld lang syne, or it may have meant such derision as a wise man allows himself when he has given a witty lesson to a foolish generation—I never could tell; but before I had recovered my temper and settled down to "Die Meistersinger" and the rest, there would come along an obsolete seventeen-stone prima donna who could sing "O mio Fernando," and get through regular old-fashioned arias with florid cabalettas at the ends of them. Immediately "La Favorita" would be dug up to rattle its skeleton for a night on the shuddering boards; and again I would go home, boiling with rage, to rack my brains for every extremity of sarcastic or indignant remonstrance. And again the impresario would smile inscrutably. Finally, having done my worst, I abandoned the criticism of music and devoted myself to the drama. Yet here again I meet the resurrectionist impresario as resurrectionist manager; and again I am unable, for the life of me, to guess whether he is a sentimentalist turning to *ses premières amours,* or a preceptor giving those of us who find fault lightly with his modern achievements a stern object lesson in the strides he has had to make to get away from a ridiculous and overrated past.

Dramatic Opinions and Essays

At some remote date which I have not precisely ascertained—somewhere between the drying of the Flood and the advent of Ibsen—"Bleak House" shared the fate of most of Dickens's novels in being "adapted to the stage." The absurdity of the process is hardly to be described, so atrociously had these masterpieces to be degraded to bring them with the competence of the theatre; but the thing was done somehow; and the Artful Dodger, Smike, Micawber, Peggotty and Jo were born again as "famous impersonations." I am less versed in these matters than some of our older critics; but it has been my fate at one time or another to witness performances founded on "Pickwick," "Oliver Twist," "Dombey and Son," and "David Copperfield." The fame of other adaptations of Dickens reached me, notably that of "Bleak House," with Miss Jennie Lee as the crossing-sweeper; but I never saw "Jo" until the other night, when Sir Augustus revived it at Drury Lane, just as he might have revived "Semiramide" at Covent Garden. The revival is under the direction of the author of the adaptation, Mr. J. P. Burnett, who has evidently conducted it with the strictest fidelity to its traditions; so that we can now see for a few nights what stage work was like in the days when Dickens, the greatest English master of pathetic and humorous character presentation our century has produced, did *not* write for the theatre. And truly the spectacle is an astonishing one, though I well remember when its most grotesque features were in the height of the melodramatic fashion. What will the stage sentimentalities on which I drop the tear of sensibility to-day seem like a quarter of a century hence, I wonder!

One facility offered to the stage by Dickens is a description of the persons of the drama so vivid and precise that no actor with the faintest sense of character could mistake the sort of figure he has to present, even without the drawings of Browne and Barnard to help him out. Yet each attempt only proves that most of our actors either have no character sense or else have never read Dickens. The Drury Lane revival has plenty of examples of this. One would suppose that Mr. Snagsby, with his nervous cough, his diffidence, his timid delicacy, and his minimizing formula of "not to put too fine a point on it," could hardly be confused with a broadly comic cheese-monger out of a harlequinade, nor the oily Chadband in any extremity of misunderstanding be presented as a loose-limbed acrobat of the Vokes-Girard type. Imagine the poor pathetically ridiculous Guster not only con-demned to mere knock-about buffoonery, but actually made to fall down in a *comic* epileptic fit on the stage! Bucket has his psychology considerably complicated by the fact that the author has rolled him up with Mr. Jarn-dyce and the Cook's Court policeman; so that there are three characters in one person, a trinitarian expedient which presents an absolutely insoluble problem to the actor. As to Mr. Guppy, he is not within a thousand miles of being himself. What Jobling-Weevle, and Small-weed, and Miss Flite, and George and the rest would have been like if they had been included in the adaptation can only be guessed with a qualm. Literary criticism was more apt to remonstrate with Dickens for caricature than to mistrust his touch as too subtle, and his outlines as too elusive, for the man in the street to appreciate. On the stage, one perceives, Dickens was impossible because he was infinitely too poetic, too profound, too serious, too natural in his presentment of things—in a word, too dra-matic for the theatre of his day. Not that I shall allow any one to persuade me that "Jo" was ever anything more than third-rate work at any period of our stage history; but it must have been much more highly esteemed when it was first perpetrated than it is now, even by an audience invited at "cheap summer prices," and so carelessly catered for, that in the scene in which Guppy explains to Esther Summerson that what she takes for smoke is a London fog, we are treated to the most brilliantly sunshiny front cloth the scene-dock of Drury Lane affords.

All that can be said for Miss Jennie Lee's "Jo" nowadays is that if the part had been left between herself and Dickens, something credible and genuinely moving might have come of it. But Mr. Burnett has carefully laid out his lines and stage business for the crudest and falsest stage pathos and stage facetiousness. Jo is one moment a cheeky street arab, and, the next, is directly expressing, to slow music, not the darkened ideas of Jo, but Mr. Burnett's version of the compassionate horror roused in the social and political consciousness of Dickens by the case of Jo and his fellow-outcasts. Dickens himself is not wholly guiltless of this: in the novel one or two of Jo's speeches are at bottom conscious social criticisms; but it is not the business of the dramatist to develop a couple of undramatic slips in a novel into a main feature of the leading part in a play. Lady Dedlock, no longer bored, but fearfully and tragically serious in her crinoline and flounces (wild anachronisms, surely, if the play is to be dated by the costumes of Tulkinghorn, Bucket and Snagsby), is quite worth seeing, especially on her visit to the graveyard, where she combines a now ludicrously old-fashioned sort of distressed heroine business with a good deal of the Ghost in Hamlet, old style. How Miss

Alma Stanley has contrived to recover the trick of a vanished stage mode so cleverly, and to keep her countenance meanwhile, I know not. But she does it with wonderful success; and I hope she will never do it again. Mrs. Rouncewell, excellently played by Miss Fanny Robertson, is called Mrs. Rouncell in the playbill; and the number of newspaper notices in which this blunder is reproduced may be taken as the number of critics who have never read "Bleak House."

Perhaps, now I come to think of it, the "Jo" enterprise is not Sir Augustus Harris's at all, but only Mr. Burnett's. Whether or no, I prefer "La Favorita."

The untimely end of "The Matchmaker" at the Shaftesbury rather weakens any interest that may attach to my opinion of it. In its combination of cynicism as to the society represented by the fashionable marriage market, and sentiment as to pet individuals, with a humorousness that is nothing if not naughty, it is thoroughly characteristic of the phase of social development represented by the two ladies—a London actress and a London journalist respectively—to whose pens we owe it. This is as much as to say that "The Matchmaker" was as sincere as its authors could make it without dropping the usual affectation of taking life farcically; and as they have some bright dramatic talent between them, the play, though tacked together anyhow, and built on the sandiest of foundations, might, in a summer theatre at reasonable prices, have done very well, though of course at the Shaftesbury in May, with all the comfortable seats costing half-a-guinea or six or seven shillings, no great success was possible. Two scenes, the pathetic one in the first act between Miss Lena Ashwell and Mr. Lewis Waller, and the comic one in the third between Mr. Waller and Miss Beatrice Ferrar, will be remembered when some more successful plays are forgotten. It was particularly interesting to see how sympathetically Mr. Waller responded to the note of genuine pathos in the first scene, although in "A Woman's Reason" and "The Sin of St. Hulda" he hardly succeeded in even pretending to respond to the conventional demands of the pretentious but unreal despair piled up for him in these works. The effect was completed by the playing of Miss Ashwell, the touching quality of whose acting, both in comedy and sentiment, is now finding the cultivated artistic expression it lacked in former seasons.

As to "Rosemary," at the Criterion, there is very little to be said; for though it is a pleasant piece of storytelling, it does not really supply a motive for the very remarkable display of acting which Mr. Wyndham imposes on it, and to which it owes its success. His performance may almost be called acting in the abstract, like those mock dialogues in which a couple of amateur comedians amuse a drawing-room by simply bandying the letters of the alphabet to and fro with varying expressions. It is quite possible to be most powerfully affected by an emotional demonstration of which the cause is hidden: indeed, I have known a case in which an actress, off the stage, gave such poignant expression to her feelings that a visitor came to the conclusion that she had lost her favorite child, whereas the actual provocation, as it turned out, was the exhibition of somebody else's name on a poster in letters an inch longer than hers. If a foreigner were to enter the Criterion half way through the third act of "Rosemary," he would be greatly struck by Mr. Wyndham's acting; but if he were asked to guess the nature of Sir Jasper Thorndyke's grief, he would certainly suggest something much more serious than the disappointment of a man of forty at being unable to marry a pretty young girl, quite a stranger to him, on whose wedding he had just stumbled. The truth is that the play has one pervading defect. It is engaging, humane, fanciful, well written, refined, humorous according to a somewhat literary conception of humor, and full of happy reminiscent touches and a pardonable Dickens worship; but it is continuously silly; and in the hands of actors who were no better than their parts it would, I suspect, act very vapidly indeed. In the last act—a nonogenarian monologue—the lines, though no doubt very nice and sympathetic, are dramatically aimless; and although I am quite aware that we shall never get the drama out of its present rut until we learn to dispense on occasion with dramatic aim in this sense, and allow feeling to flow without perpetually working up to points and situations, yet that sort of freedom must be conquered, not begged— a feat that can hardly be achieved in an openly and shamelessly old-fashioned play like "Rosemary." However, I will not pretend that I found it tedious; indeed, Mr. Wyndham entertained me better than I expected, considering that the art of senile make-up, in which Mr. Hare wasted half his career, is to me the most transparent and futile of impostures. For the rest, there are half a dozen pleasant and popular artists in half a dozen pleasant and popular—but always silly—parts; and the management is admirable, as it always is at the Criterion.

G. B. S. ON CLEMENT SCOTT

From "The Bells" to "King Arthur": a critical record
of the first-night productions at the Lyceum Theatre
from 1871 to 1895. By Clement Scott. London:
John Macqueen. 1896.

Shaw v. Shakespeare and Others: an article by W.
A. (Mr. William Archer) in the current number of
"The World.'

30 May, 1896.

M R. CLEMENT SCOTT is not the first of the great dramatic critics; but he is the first of the great
dramatic reporters. Other men may have hur-
ried from the theatre to the newspaper office to prepare,
red hot, a notice of the night's performance for the morning's paper; but nobody did it before him with the knowledge that the notice was awaited by a vast body of readers
conscious of his personality and anxious to hear his
opinion, and that the editor must respect it, and the sub-
editor reserve space for it, as the most important feature
of the paper. This strong position Mr. Scott has made
for himself. His opportunity has of course been made
by circumstances—by the growth of mammoth newspapers like the "Daily Telegraph," the multiplication of
theatres, and the spread of interest in them; but it has
not been made for Mr. Scott more than for his competitors; and the fact that he alone has seized it and made
the most of it in a metropolis where every adult is eager
to do his work for nothing but the honor and glory and
the invitations to first nights, proves, you may depend on
it, that his qualifications for the work are altogether extraordinary.

The main secret of Mr. Scott's popularity is that he is above all a sympathetic critic. His susceptibility to the direct expression of human feeling is so strong that he can write with positive passion about an exhibition of it which elicits from his colleagues only some stale, weary compliment in the last sentence of a conventional report, or, at best, some clever circumlocutory discussion of the philosophy of the piece. Whoever has been through the experience of discussing criticism with a thorough, perfect, and entire Ass, has been told that criticism should above all things be free from personal feeling. The excellence of Mr. Scott's criticisms lies in their integrity as expressions of the warmest personal feeling and nothing else. They are alive: their admiration is sincere and moving: their resentment is angry and genuine. He may be sometimes maudlin on the one hand, sometimes unjust, unreasonable, violent, and even ridiculous on the other; but he has never lost an inch of ground by that, any more than other critics have ever gained an inch by a cautious, cold, fastidious avoidance of the qualities of which such faults are the excesses. Our actors and actresses feel the thorough humanity of his relation to them; and they commonly say—except in those gusts of fury at some unfavorable notice in which they announce that they make it a rule never to read criticisms at all— that they would rather be "slated" by Mr. Scott than praised by colder hands. By colder hands they generally mean Mr. William Archer, who has made himself as eminent as Mr. Scott, and complementary and antidotal to him, at the opposite pole of contemporary dramatic criticism. The public believes in Mr. Scott because he interprets the plays by feeling *with* the actor or author— generally more, perhaps, with the actor than the author—

and giving his feeling unrestrained expression in his notices. An average young University graduate would hang himself sooner than wear his heart on his sleeve before the world as Mr. Scott does. And that is just why the average young University graduate never interests any one in his critical remarks. He has been trained to do nothing that could possibly involve error, failure, self-assertion, or ridicule; and the results of this genteelly negative policy are about as valuable as those which might be expected by a person who should enter for a swimming race with a determination to do nothing that could possibly expose to the risk of getting wet. Mr. Scott, in spite of his public school education, is happily not that sort of person. He understands the value of Lassalle's dictum that "History forgives mistakes and failures, but not want of conviction."

Now for Mr. Scott's shortcomings. The most amiable of them is a desire to give pleasure and gain affectionate goodwill. This, in the absence of any provocation to the contrary, guarantees to everybody, from Sir Henry Irving down to the most friendless novice thirsting for a little encouragement, a flattering word or two in the "Daily Telegraph." No doubt he is very often helpful with judicious encouragement; but he is occasionally shameless in his gratuitous kindliness. This might not do any harm if he could always be depended on to be annoyed by bad work; but unfortunately this is not the case. His extraordinary susceptibility is, as I advisedly described it, a susceptibility to the direct expression of human feeling, and to that alone. Interpose any medium between him and the moving, uttering, visible human creature, and he is insulated at once. It may be the medium of music; it may be painting; it may even be the reflective thought inspired by passion instead of the direct instinctive cry of the passion itself: no matter: the moment the substitution is effected Mr. Scott loses his distinction; writes like any Philistine citizen of ordinary artistic tastes; and is crowed over by every whippersnapper in his profession whose eyes and ears and powers of abstract thinking have been trained a little by practice on the outside of the arts, and by an academic course of philosophy. In this collection of his Lyceum criticisms we find him brought face to face with the remarkable development of the pictorial side of stage art effected by Mr. Comyns Carr when he succeeded in bringing the genius of Burne-Jones, the greatest decorative artist of his time, to bear on the production of "King Arthur." Mr. Scott, instead of being delighted with the result, was simply incommoded and disturbed by the change in the accustomed arrangements. He complained that King Arthur wore black armor instead of looking like Mr. Henry Neville dressed in a roasting-jack and a flaxen wig; and he was scandalized at the knights having their hair cut. "Where," he asks, "is the fair hair, where the robes, where the drapery, where the air of dignity and distinction, in this tight-fitting, black, tin armor? An actor of the highest distinction has to work desperately hard to counteract the impression for which he is not in the least responsible. It was decided—we know not for what reason—that all the principal actors in this play should wear their own hair, Bond Street cut. Never was there a play where assumed hair seemed to be more imperative."

Again, when Mr. Scott touches on the subject of music, he distinguishes between "melody" and "classical music," and is so deeply depressed by sonata form that even the slow movement from Raff's "Im Walde" symphony struck

him as an unpardonably dismal business when Herr Armbruster played it at the Lyceum on the first night of
"Michael." He also complains because Gounod's music
is not used in the Lyceum "Faust." Painting and music
seem to affect his imagination as ruins affected the imagination of Sir Walter Scott—that is, by setting him
thinking of something else. His criticism of all stage
effects, scenic or personal, which appeal to the cultivated
intelligence of the eye and ear, instead of to the heart,
is quite commonplace.

When I say that Mr. Scott is also unable to recognize
a feeling when it is presented to him in the form of a
thought—unless of course that thought has been so long
associated with it that the distinction between them has
vanished, and the utterance of the thought has become
the natural expression of the feeling—I touch the disability which has brought him into conflict with the later
developments of the drama. Like all energetic spirits, he
was a pioneer at first, fighting for the return to nature
in Robertson's plays against the stagey stuff which he
found in possession of the theatre. Since that time the
unresting march of evolution has brought us past Robertson. Our feeling has developed and put new thoughts
into our heads; and our brains have developed and inter-
preted our feelings to us more critically. Ideas which
were formerly only conceived by men of genius like Ibsen,
or intensely energetic spirits like Nietzsche, are freely
used by dramatists like Sudermann, and are beginning to
creep into quite ordinary plays, just as I can remember
the pet discords of Schumann and Wagner beginning to
creep into the music-hall after a period of fashionable
novelty in the drawing-room. When Ibsen's "Ghosts"
forced the old ideas to take up the challenge of the new,

Mr. Scott was the only critic whose attack on Ibsen was really memorable. In the ranks which he led there was plenty of elderly peevishness and envious disparagement, virtuous indignation and vicious scurrility, with the usual quantity of time-serving caution among the more considerate; but Mr. Scott alone, looking neither forward nor backward, gave utterance to his horror like a man wounded to the quick in his religion, his affections, his enthusiasms—in the deepest part of him. I greatly doubt whether to this day he has any adequate conception of the way in which he pitched into us who were on the other side during those moments when he was persuaded that we were filthy-minded traffickers in mere abomination. But he came off with the advantage of the doughty fighter who lays on with conviction: he had not only the excitement of the combat and the satisfaction of making his quarterstaff ring on the heads of his adversaries, but he sowed no harvest of malice, rather establishing on us the claim of an old opponent, always a strong claim in a free country. The incident was the more curious because I am persuaded that if the feeling that is at the bottom of "Ghosts" were presented dramatically as a simple and direct plea for the right of a man of affectionate, easy, convivial temperament to live a congenial life, instead of skulking into the kitchen after the housemaid, and stealing a morsel of pleasure in the byways of drink and disease when his conscientiously conventional wife and her spiritual adviser were not looking, Mr. Scott would be one of its most merciful critics. But Mr. Scott is not a thinker: whatever question you raise with him you must raise as a question of conduct, which is a matter of feeling, and not of creed, which is a matter of intellectual order. The notion that when conduct conflicts

with creed, the question as to which of the two is in the
wrong is an open one—that it is not alone humanity that
is constantly on its trial, but the ethical, political, and
religious systems that claim implicit obedience from
humanity—that a deliberate violation of these systems
may be, not a weakness to be pitied and pardoned, but an
assertion of human worth to be championed and carried
to victory in the teeth of all constitutions, churches, principles, and ideals whatsoever: this, which explains all that
is peculiar in the attitude of the modern movement, especially in dramatic poetry, has no meaning for Mr. Scott.
He will not, when the time comes, be an enemy of the
drama which tacitly assumes it: his sympathy will secure
him against that; but the drama which asserts and argues
it—which is polemical rather than instinctive in its poignancy—will never be tolerated by him.

I need not say that a volume of criticisms dealing with
Lyceum productions exclusively does not cover those
newly opened regions in which the steadiness of Mr.
Scott's footing is doubtful. The book is full of old drawings by Mr. Barnard, which, however, are surpassed in
delicacy, charm, and fidelity by the newer ones from the
hand of Mr. Partridge (Mr. Bernard Gould), and photographic portraits, among which I miss that of Mr. Scott
himself. Perhaps the few notes I have made above on
my fellow-critic may help to supply the deficiency. For
form's sake, I will add just this ghost of a criticism on a
passage in the book. When "Olivia'" was revived at the
Lyceum, Mr. Scott was so much touched by the point at
which the Vicar, trying to lecture Olivia for her wickedness, breaks down and clasps her in his arms (who does
not remember Miss Terry's head dropping as she took
the attitude of the reproved child?), that he records with

enthusiasm the astonishment and delight of the house, adding, "As regards acting, it was a moment of true inspiration, a masterpiece of invention." But now, in cold blood, Mr. Scott will agree with me, I think, that the invention is clearly the author's, and that the original Vicar produced the same effect. Indeed, to my mind, he produced it better than Sir Henry Irving, whose embrace I thought too loverlike. Mr. Hermann Vezin, a less passionate actor, was for that very reason a more old-fashionedly fatherly Dr. Primrose than his eminent successor.

Mr. Archer's article in the "World" is an elaborate demonstration that my opinion of "Henry IV." at the Haymarket is not a criticism, but a purely theoretic deduction from my race, my diet, my politics—in short, my nature and environment. And he argues that it is a monstrous injustice that Mr. Beerbohm Tree should be made to suffer for my nature and environment. What outrageous nonsense! Besides, Mr. Tree is infinitely obliged to me; for all London, it appears, is flocking to the Haymarket to see whether "Henry IV." is really so bad as I think it.